POWER PLAYS

POWER PLAYS

An Inside Look at the Big Business of the National Hockey League

GIL STEIN

A BIRCH LANE PRESS BOOK
Published by Carol Publishing Group

To Barbara—loving wife, honest critic, best friend

A Birch Lane Press Book
Published by Carol Publishing Group
Birch Lane Press is a registered trademark of Carol Communications, Inc.

Editorial, sales and distribution, and rights and permissions inquiries should be addressed
to Carol Publishing Group, 120 Enterprise Avenue, Secaucus, N.J. 07094

In Canada: Canadian Manda Group, One Atlantic Avenue, Suite 105, Toronto, Ontario,
M6K 3E7

Carol Publishing Group books may be purchased in bulk at special discounts for sales
promotion, fund-raising, or educational purposes. Special editions can be created to
specifications. For details, contact Special Sales Department, Carol Publishing Group, 120
Enterprise Avenue, Secaucus, N.J. 07094.

Manufactured in the United States of America
10 9 8 7 6 5 4 3 2 1

Library of Congress Cataloging-in-Publication Data

Stein, Gil.
    Power plays : an inside look at the big business of the National
Hockey League / Gil Stein.
        p.   cm.
    "A Birch Lane Press book."
    Includes index.
    ISBN 1–55972–422–6 (hc)
    1. National Hockey League—Finance.   2. Hockey—Economic aspects.
3. National Hockey League—History.   I. Title.
GV847.8.N3S84   1997
796.962′64—dc21   95–25994
                                                              CIP

Contents

Preface

Contrary to popular belief, hockey is not the ultimate spectator sport. That honor goes to the game *behind* the game of hockey, the one that is played by some of the richest and most powerful men in North America—the members of the National Hockey League board of governors. Behind closed doors, there are power plays, stickhandling, bare-knuckle fisticuffs, and shoot-outs that put to shame anything you will ever see on the ice. I was privileged to have had a front row seat, attending every NHL board of governors meeting for twenty-one years, from May 1972 through June 1993. As I share with you some of what I saw and heard, I hope you will be as intrigued as I was to witness the behind-the-scenes action that shaped the modern game of hockey in North America.

This book describes events which took place over a twenty-one-year period. The narrative is founded upon personal recollections, document review, and, in some cases, assumptions based on analysis of known facts and results. A discerning reader should have no trouble identifying which source is applicable in each case. In all instances, what is depicted is believed to be a true account of what occurred.

Acknowledgments

Just as it takes a village to bring up a child, as an author I found that it takes many villagers to write a book. I appreciate the help I was given in researching twenty-five years of NHL history, and also the many brilliant and insightful editing suggestions I received from caring friends and family members. Of course, some of the contributions were more significant than others, but all were valuable. I thank all the NHL officers and employees who helped bring me up-to-date on the league's financial picture and the rapidly changing roster of NHL governors, and provided me with other invaluable data and research assistance. They know who they are, but shall remain nameless here to protect them from possible recrimination.

I am deeply indebted to my wife, Barbara, and to our children, Andrew, Holly, and John, for their countless hours of tender care in checking every word I wrote and giving me editorial and content feedback that improved and enriched my writing. Barbara's unerring sense of right and wrong served as my conscience, and Holly's talent for straight talk kept me from blurring the focus of my stories with unwieldy words. It would be difficult to find a more dedicated Flyers fan than Andy, who retains in his photographic memory an encyclopedia of Flyers trivia despite the many demands of his life as a lawyer. And his younger brother, John, knows more about past, present, and future NHL hockey players than a lot of general managers I have known. I am certain John would have made an excellent hockey general manager had he not opted instead to become an M.D.

I thank Arthur Kaminsky for believing in me and in the book I knew I had to write. Arthur is not only an agent nonpareil, but also a gifted and talented writer on his own. I was fortunate to have had access to his rich hockey background and appreciate his many editorial contributions.

I am grateful to my friend John L. Dusseau, who knows nothing about hockey but everything about writing. John, who is now retired from his career as editor in chief of W. B. Saunders Company, passed along a number of bon mots from the vast literary vault in his memory bank, and also went on a "which" hunt—showing me when to use "that." He also taught me when to hyphenate, when not to, and that punctuation marks belong inside the quotes. John, I thank thee for casting thy pearls before Stein.

Hillel Black is my publisher's editorial director. During the course of his very professional editing of my manuscript, we had our share of differences over how the stories I wished to relate should best be presented to readers. Comparing the finished product with my earlier drafts, I am thankful that he was stubborn enough to win most of the skirmishes.

Bing Leverich, Don McSweeney, and Rosanne Rocchi were outstanding lawyers with whom I worked in the past. I thank them for providing specifics needed to authenticate some memorable tales.

I will never forget the Flyers players whom I represented in various criminal courts. With help from the acute memories of Allan McEachern (chief justice of the court of appeals of British Columbia), and former Flyers players Joe Watson and Bob Kelly, I was able to recall and recreate those colorful experiences.

I wish to thank my former NHL colleagues Ken Sawyer (former vice president of finance), Steve Ryan (former vice president of marketing), Marcel Aubut (former president and governor of the Quebec Nordiques), Jim Lites (president and alternate governor of the Dallas Stars) and Peter O'Malley (alternate governor of the Washington Capitals) for sharing their recollections and expertise with me.

I am grateful as well for the contributions of my friends Marc Howard (renowned Philadelphia TV anchor) and Jay Moyer (executive vice president and legal counsel of the National Football League).

And a final word of thanks for the staunch loyalty and love of my wife, children, children-in-law, grandchildren, sisters, brothers-in-law, and other true friends during some less-than-pleasant moments in the past. They gave me the strength to carry on and to write this book. I shall always be grateful.

Introduction

One of the first things you realize when you step into the National Hockey League is that things are not always what they appear to be from the outside. Yet so much is written about the NHL. Illusions are created by writers with vivid imaginations, but often their intelligence sources are limited and sometimes they are deliberately manipulated. As a result, there are two levels of perception—the public one shared by the legion of hockey followers who devour everything they can find that is written about the NHL, and the truth known only to insiders. This might not seem a very profound observation, for such deception goes on to a degree in every family and every walk of life. But, somehow, it seems especially applicable to hockey.

I believe the roots may be found in the nature and spirit of hockey players, who are inveterate kidders, and to whom the hoax is as much second nature as skating. Over the years I have found them to be young men who achieve fame and fortune battling ferociously on the ice, while— somehow—never losing touch with that gift of playfulness with which they, and all of us, were endowed at birth. There is nothing that a grizzled and toothless hockey veteran enjoys more than a good practical joke played on one of his teammates. A player who makes the mistake of falling asleep on the team plane can expect to wake up with one pant leg cut off, or a shoe missing, or chewing gum in his hair, or a newspaper aflame in his lap. Players have been known to return to the dressing room after practice and find their shoes nailed to the ceiling. After his locker room shower, many an unsuspecting player has been greeted with a blast of talcum powder in his face when turning on his hair dryer.

Most teams have a ritual through which a rookie must be put before he is accepted by teammates. Frequently the rite of passage is the haircut, where a rookie's tousled locks are brutishly shaved in blotches by the team's veterans. The resultant coiffure is less attractive than what is seen at Marine boot camp, and usually causes the victim to either shave his head or wear a hat in public until his hair grows out.

One of the more imaginative and classic practical jokes played on rookies is the legendary snipe hunt, a tradition of the Chicago Black-hawks that former Blackhawk defenseman Ed Van Impe brought with him to Philadelphia after being claimed by the Flyers in the 1967 expansion draft. The execution of a successful snipe hunt requires an elaborate conspiracy among team members, trainers, and local law enforcement authorities. With thanks to the now-defunct *Philadelphia Evening Bulletin*, here is the tale of Flyers rookie Bob Kelly and his snipe hunt initiation into the NHL:

> One day in early November 1970, naïve and unsuspecting twenty-year-old Flyers rookie winger Bob Kelly, fresh out of the small town of Oakville, Ontario, overheard his new teammates talking in the locker room about snipe hunting.
>
> "What the hell are snipes?" he asked.
>
> "They're sorta like pigeons," said Flyer captain Ed Van Impe.
>
> "Can you eat them?" Kelly asked.
>
> "Only the breasts," answered Van Impe. "My wife cooks them in wine sauce and are they ever delicious."
>
> His appetite whetted, Kelly asked if he could go along on the next snipe hunt.
>
> "No rookies allowed," barked Flyers forward Earl Heiskala.
>
> Kelly kept begging and finally the Flyers relented.
>
> "We're going snipe hunting on Monday night," Heiskala said. "You can come along if you want."
>
> Kelly couldn't wait and was as excited as a toddler on Christmas morning when the Flyers rendezvoused behind Howard Johnson's restaurant in Media, Pennsylvania, at 9:00 P.M. on Monday, November 16, 1970.
>
> "Bet I get the biggest one," said Kelly, who was wearing a bulky sweater, dungarees, and army boots.
>
> "Bet you don't," said goalie Doug Favell, who arrived with an enormous laundry bag slung over one shoulder.
>
> The rest of the Flyers came equipped, too. They carried long poles, white netting and flashlights. Kelly had a small, battery-powered spotlight.
>
> "Now," instructed Heiskala, "you know how we do this. We beat the bush with the poles and when the snipes begin to fly, shine a light on them. They'll become confused and fly into the netting and get all tangled up. Then, we grab them and toss them in the bag."

Led by Dave Bowman, the Flyers videotape machine operator, everyone piled into three station wagons and headed for the hunt scene in the small Pennsylvania town of Nether Providence. Once there, the cars were parked alongside the highway and everyone moved up a dirt road into the woods.

"Here's where we split up," said Bowman. "Bob [Kelly], you and Earl [Heiskala] head further up the road. I'll take some of the other guys around this way."

While Kelly was up the road stringing the netting between trees, Favell "spotted" the first snipe and the rest of the team headed back to the station wagons.

"There goes one, Snoopy [Flyers forward Garry Peters]," Favell yelled. "Get it!"

"How come we haven't seen any?" Kelly asked Heiskala.

"Because you aren't calling them," answered Heiskala.

With that, Kelly began emitting strange sounds and became so engrossed he never noticed a car pulling up the dirt road.

"Uh-oh," said Heiskala as the car came to a halt, "the cops."

"Hold it right there," said one of two burly policemen. "What are you guys doing?"

"Hunting," said Heiskala.

"Hunting what?" asked the officer.

"Snipes," said Kelly.

When Kelly could produce no identification or hunting license, the officers ordered him into their patrol wagon. Heiskala, meanwhile, made a break for it.

"Halt!" screamed one of the policemen, who then fired a shot.

"You winged him," said the other. "We'll take this guy in, then come back and look for him."

Once at a nearby police station, Kelly—who later admitted being scared to death—was photographed, fingerprinted, and thrown into a dingy cell.

"When they found out I was a citizen of Canada, they started talking about deporting me and everything," Kelly later related.

Kelly gave the officers the phone numbers of Flyers General Manager Keith Allen and coach Vic Stasiuk and asked them to place a call. Of course, the officers returned and said they couldn't reach either.

After letting Kelly stew for about an hour, the police took him to a nearby municipal building for a hearing. Heiskala was there, his leg wrapped in a bandage stained with red ink. And so were the rest of the Flyers, in a small room where they could watch the proceedings, but Kelly couldn't see them.

Surrounded by police, he walked into the courtroom and took a seat before a stern-looking judge. Kelly's jaw dropped when he spotted Heiskala's "bleeding" leg.

The charges were read, some papers filled out, then the judge asked Kelly:

"What do you do?"

"I play for the Flyers," he answered shakily.

"That's a basketball team, isn't it?" asked a court aide.

"Never mind," snapped the judge. "This is a football town. And I was watching a pretty good game on TV before I had to come down here for this."

With that, Heiskala spoke up.

"Sir, I don't think these fellas should have drawn their guns," he said.

"I heard enough out of that guy," roared the judge. "Take him to the hospital, then put him in jail for the night. He can have his hearing in the morning."

Four policemen then dragged Heiskala out of the room. Kelly turned white and the rest of the Flyers broke up. Defenseman Joe Watson had to cover his face with his jacket to keep from being heard. Van Impe and center Jimmy Johnson had to go into a bathroom and close the door.

"How do you plead?" asked the judge.

"Guilty, sir," said Kelly.

"Okay," said the judge, "that will be a $500 fine for hunting snipe without a license, $500 for hunting snipe out of season, $500 for hunting snipe on a private snipe preserve and $32.50 court costs. Can you pay?"

"Yes, sir," said Kelly, "I'll write you a check."

"No checks," roared the judge. "It's either cash or you go to Broadmeadows Prison to work it off at $5 a day."

Kelly seemed in a state of shock until the judge added: "How about those fellas back there? Can't they help you?"

"No, sir," said Kelly.

"How do you know?" barked the judge. "You haven't even looked."

With that, Kelly turned around and spotted his teammates

splitting their sides with hearty guffaws. He looked like he didn't know whether to laugh or cry.

Then Heiskala, minus his bandage, walked in, stuck out his hand and said:

"Okay, now you're in," meaning Kelly had passed his initiation.

"I thought you were done in," Kelly said. "I thought they really got you when they fired that shot. I could just see you showing up for practice tomorrow with a bullet in your leg. I kept wanting to ask you how it was, but I was afraid to say anything in front of that judge."

"I never had any idea this was all a joke. I was never in jail before in my life. The only thing I could think of was that I should be polite to them and they might let me go."

Rookie Bob Kelly was now officially a Flyer.

In this book, you will learn—as Kelly did—that in the world of hockey and the NHL, things frequently are not what they seem to be. I will tell you the inside store of many events, and you will hear things you have never heard before; you will learn that the truth was far different from what had been publicly reported.

I am confident that you will enjoy this unique view from inside the NHL's time capsule. Fasten your seat belt and enjoy the ride.

1

A Bully Pulpit

I called them the Vancouver Seven. They taught me a lot about hockey players. Barry Ashbee, Bill Flett, Ross Lonsberry, Don Saleski, Bobby Taylor, Ed Van Impe, and Joe Watson—all of them Flyers, all of them defendants in a 1973 criminal trial in Vancouver. They were charged with assault for climbing into the seats in pursuit of an unruly Canuck fan at the Pacific Coliseum.

In the 1972–73 season, the Philadelphia press christened the Flyers the Broad Street Bullies. (Their home rink, the Spectrum, was located on Broad Street.) They were one of the most unique and colorful teams in NHL history. Led by their captain, Bobby Clarke—as inspirational a battlefield leader as George Patton at his best—they slashed and marauded their way through NHL cities, to the chagrin of hockey purists like NHL president Clarence Campbell—but always before sellout crowds.

Assembling the Broad Street Bullies was the handiwork of astute General Manager Keith Allen, whose achievement was later recognized when he was both awarded the Lester Patrick Trophy (for contribution to hockey in the United States) and inducted into the Hockey Hall of Fame as a builder. (Builders are elected to the Hall of Fame on the basis of their coaching, managerial, or executive ability; also on the basis of sportsmanship, character, and their contributions to their organization(s) and to the game of hockey in general.)

De rigueur nicknames were the hallmark of the team, and "The Hammer" (Dave Schultz), "Hound" (Bob Kelly), "Big Bird" (Don Saleski), and "Moose" (Andre Dupont) were usually found in the penalty box after one of the frequent on-ice brawls for which the Flyers were famous. Schultz was among the premier fighters of his era, and his teammates derived inspiration from him, dropping their gloves at every opportunity. Philly fans loved them. Other fans loved to hate them. They were coached by Freddie (The Fog) Shero, who specialized in writing obscure motivational messages on the locker-room bulletin board, such as: "Success is a dream in work clothes"; "Pick the shortest route to the puck and arrive in ill humor"; and—on May 19, 1974, the day the Flyers were destined to make history by beating the Boston Bruins to win the Stanley Cup—"If we win today, we will walk together forever." Shero delighted in entertaining the press with tall tales of doubtful historical accuracy. But who cared? The Flyers, and their coach, made great copy.

Owner Ed Snider had retained me as Flyers' general counsel prior to the start of the 1972–73 season. As a corporate-type lawyer, I had no idea my duties would involve getting hockey players out of jail and defending criminal actions. I should have known better. These Flyers were fast gaining a name as the bad boys of the NHL, and it seemed as though they felt obliged to live up to their reputation. The wilder their image, the wilder they became. It was only a matter of time before scrapes with the law would result. The first one was in Vancouver on December 29, 1972.

It all started innocently enough, with a garden variety fight between Bob Kelly and the Canucks' Jim Hargreaves at the 7:31 minute mark of the first period. As the combatants fought, the other players on the ice dropped their gloves and sticks and paired off in the ritual embrace that was then commonplace in the NHL. (Now, of course, noncombatants are required to move themselves to neutral ice.)

Six-foot-three Saleski was grappling with a shorter Canuck, Barry Wilcox, right next to the stands, and with his height and reach advantage, was holding him at bay by squeezing the neck of his sweater with both hands. A Canuck fan, who happened to be both a doctor and a lawyer, seeing Wilcox with a red face and bulging eyes, thought he was being strangled. He ran down to the glass, reached over, and grabbed Saleski by the back of his hair (most players wore their hair long in those days), pulling so hard that Saleski was forced to release his grip on the Canuck. Saleski's teammate Barry Ashbee, who was tied up in a handhold with another player, witnessed the incident and made a beeline for the stands, scaling the glass and chasing the fan, who by now was running for his life up the aisle. Ashbee was followed into the seats by some of the Flyers who were on the ice, and some who went directly into the stands from the Flyers bench, which was located nearby.

The commotion that followed lasted about a minute and thirty seconds. Other fans got involved but no one was hurt, and no one was even struck, except for a police officer who, while tugging at reserve goalie Bobby Taylor, was punched and knocked down from behind by Bill "Cowboy" Flett. Also attacked was Taylor himself, who, after falling down in the seats (he was encumbered by his huge goalie leg pads), actually was beaten over the head with an umbrella by an elderly female fan. Ironically, the policeman did not see that it was Flett who had struck him, and he ended up charging Taylor with the act. After all this died down, the game was completed without further incident (final score, 4–4) and the Flyers left town.

Naturally, the Vancouver newspapers played up the event and demanded something be done. (Hey, we can't let those Flyers get away with coming into our city and beating up our innocent fans.) The Crown (Canadian name for prosecuting attorney's office) responded to the hue and cry, and after an investigation, notified the Flyers that warrants had been issued for the arrest of the Vancouver Seven. Ashbee, Flett, Lonsberry, Saleski, Van Impe, and Watson were each charged with common assault. Taylor was charged with a more serious crime—assault of a police officer. The matter was turned over to me. The good news was that the Crown had elected to lay all charges merely as summary offenses (average fine in Vancouver for a common assault with no one hurt, $50 to $100), rather than as indictable offenses, which would have exposed the players to stiffer sentences. But that was also the bad news, because a defendant facing only summary charges has no right to a trial by jury.

My first task was to find a lawyer in Vancouver to represent our players. On the recommendation of Hal Laycoe, the Canucks general manager, I called a Vancouver criminal lawyer, Tom Fisher, and retained him to represent the players. Fisher had somehow been involved in minor league hockey, which was how Laycoe knew him. Through Fisher, we reached an agreement with the Crown that we would have the warrants served on the players when they arrived in Vancouver for their next scheduled game, February 9, 1973.

In the meantime, I had spoken to NHL President Clarence Campbell about the incident. He was concerned about the prospect of hockey players being prosecuted for what took place during a hockey game, and felt it was far better for the league to enforce its own discipline. I can't say that I disagreed with him. He was also concerned about my having hired Fisher. He didn't know Fisher, but did know Laycoe, and had very little confidence in him. On Campbell's recommendation, I called a prominent Vancouver lawyer, Allan McEachern, who agreed to join the defense team. So as not to bruise Fisher's feelings, I told him the NHL had hired McEachern and that I would make the decision down the road as to who would be lead counsel.

On the morning of the February 9 game, the players were booked on criminal charges, and the Crown agreed to postpone the trial until after completion of the hockey season. The trial date was set for Friday, June 8, 1973.

I had flown to Vancouver with the Flyers on February 9, and asked Shero if I could speak to the team in the locker room before the game. I told them not to let the arrests intimidate them, but to just go out and play their usual physical game. They sure did. In a rollicking, penalty-filled contest, they came away with a lopsided 10–5 victory. In jest, I had also told them that since I had to catch a flight after the first period, I would like it if they had built a four-goal lead by then. They did. The score at the end of the first period was 6–2, with the first two Flyers goals having been scored shorthanded by Bobby Clarke and Rick MacLeish while killing off a five-minute major penalty to Dupont.

For the balance of the season, every time I went into the locker room after a game, Joe Watson would implore me to arrange for them to spend more than one day in Vancouver when we went there for the trial. Joe was a true original—a lovable, fun-loving, boisterous person with a loud voice and contagious laugh. He was a native of Smithers, a backwoods town about six hundred miles north of Vancouver in British Columbia. To him, Vancouver was the big city—the big *fun* city. I remember one game later that season when Joe received a nasty skate blade gash across his cheekbone, just under his left eye. After the game, I saw him sitting at his locker, looking down at the floor, holding a huge ice pack to his stitched-up face. I approached him and asked how he was doing. He looked up at me and roared: "Two days, Gilly, get us two days!" How could I resist? So I directed that the seven players meet me at the Bayshore Inn in Vancouver on Wednesday morning, June 6, two days before the trial. All expenses would be on the Flyers, of course. Joe was ecstatic.

I arrived at the Bayshore Inn around three o'clock in the afternoon on Wednesday, June 6. I had no trouble finding the players. As soon as I entered the lobby, I heard the whooping, hollering and raucous laughter coming from a first floor cocktail lounge. They had been drinking for hours while awaiting my arrival.

I sat down on the end seat of a sofa, next to Bill Flett, who sat staring into space. In the vernacular of the locker room, he was "shit-faced." Across a cocktail table from where I was sitting was Barry Ashbee, who, with a stern face, was looking intently at Flett. The two of them were opposites. Ashbee was from Ontario, and had an Eastern sense of propriety. He was ruggedly handsome, clean shaven, with hair closely cropped, and always dressed in a tie and jacket. "Cowboy" Flett, who hailed from Calgary, had a huge shaggy beard, his hair was unkempt, he probably didn't even own a necktie, and his clothes looked like they had gone to bed with him—for about a week!

Suddenly, without warning, but with a slow and deliberate motion, Ashbee picked up a pack of matches from an ash tray on the cocktail table, lit one, then reached across the table and set Flett's beard on fire. I nearly jumped out of my seat. Ashbee was grinning, the other players were laughing hysterically, and Flett's beard was burning. It smelled like burnt chicken feathers, a smell I remembered from childhood when going with my mother to buy a freshly killed chicken.

"Cowboy!" I yelled, punching him on his left arm, "your beard's on fire!" "Huh?" he grunted, sounding as though I had just awakened him from a deep sleep.

"Your beard's on fire!" I repeated.

"Oh," he said, and proceeded to slowly pat his beard until the fire was extinguished.

Later that evening we met with the lawyers, and one of the first issues confronting us was what to do about Lonsberry. He insisted he had not gone into the seats, and was apprehensive about the charge against him because he had a prior criminal record in Vancouver. While with the Los Angeles Kings, before his trade to the Flyers, Lonsberry and a few teammates had engaged in some after-hours high jinks one night in Vancouver. Annoyed because their barroom advances were being re-buffed by several B.C. lassies, Ross and his buddies followed the ladies out the door, jumped into a car, and drove by the girls with Lonsberry's bare derriere thrust out the window for all to see—including, unfor-tunately, two policemen in a patrol car, who promptly arrested Roscoe by the light of the silvery moon.

We believed Lonsberry when he told us he was not one of the players who had charged into the stands, but he had been positively identified by two eyewitnesses, a man and wife who had season seats in the second row. McEachern knew the man, a respected lawyer, and arranged for Lonsberry to meet with him and his wife that night at their home. McEachern accompanied Lonsberry, and had him bring a helmet. (He was one of only two Flyers who wore helmets. Moose Dupont wore one to protect his head; Lonsberry's was to protect his ego. He was bald as a billiard ball, and wore a toupee off the ice. In games, however, he didn't dare wear the rug for fear it would be pulled off during a fight, so he always wore a helmet. It looked strange during the playing of the national anthem that Lonsberry was the only one who did not remove his helmet.)

McEachern directed that he don the helmet so the witnesses could see him up close. Ross earnestly explained that he was not a fighter, and swore he had not gone into the seats after the fan. "We hear you," said the lawyer, "but the problem is we are absolutely certain that you did." Dejectedly, McEachern and Lonsberry left the meeting, prepared to face the music in court.

The next day, however, Lonsberry got a break. Although the videotape of the game had been inconclusive, showing him neither in the stands nor not in them, newspaper photos told a different story. McEachern contacted the local newspaper's photographer, who had taken a series of photos of the incident and they clearly showed Lonsberry on the ice, looking up at the stands while the melee was taking place.

Faced with this incontrovertible evidence, the lawyer and his wife retracted their prior statements, and the Vancouver Seven became the Vancouver Six. That lawyer went on to have a long and distinguished career as a Supreme Court judge, during which I am sure he was duly circumspect when assessing the reliability of eyewitness testimony. McEachern, too, was appointed to the bench a few years after the incident, and is currently the chief justice of the court of appeal of British Columbia, where he has frequently cited the Lonsberry case to illustrate how misleading the impressions of an eyewitness can be.

On Thursday, while McEachern was running down the newspaper photographs, I chartered a fishing boat for the players, and we spent the day at sea. The weather was cloudy, rainy, and cold. No fish were caught, but there was plenty of food and drink—and at least the players were not in Vancouver getting into trouble. Ed Van Impe spent the voyage teasing and tormenting Watson. Van Impe was a study in contrasts. Off the ice, he was the typical soft-spoken and well-mannered English gentleman, who, when at home with his beautiful wife, dressed for dinner (yes, I mean black tie) every single night. On the ice, though, he was a stay-at-home terror who deftly used his stick as a weapon against any player foolhardy enough to skate onto his turf. Opposing wingers were frequently seen aborting their left-side rushes to cross over to the safer Van Impe-less right side when entering the Flyers' defensive zone.

On the boat, Watson was the perfect foil for his defensive partner's teasing, and seemed to love every minute of it, giggling and guffawing at each barb Van Impe threw his way. But one thing he couldn't stand was the farting. Over and over, Van Impe would trap him in the corner seat of the dining booth in the ship's galley, sliding onto the bench seat next to him. Then he would pass gas loudly, and Watson would go ballistic. "B'Jeezus! He's doing it again!" he would yell. "Oh, m'God, let me out of here!" But Van Impe, who outweighed Watson by at least thirty pounds, physically pinned him against the wall…and everyone laughed.

Thursday night we met with the lawyers. McEachern said he thought we should hire a third lawyer, Maurice Mulligan, to handle the trial. Mulligan had just left the bench and returned to private practice. He had been a magistrate and was the best friend of Chief Magistrate Larry Eckardt, sharing Canucks season tickets with him. Eckardt had decided to preside at the trial of the Vancouver Six himself, rather than assigning another magistrate. I gave McEachern the okay to hire Mulligan, but said: "I'm going to tell you what Joseph P. Kennedy told his son John when asked to finance his campaign for president: 'I'll underwrite a victory, but not a landslide.' Three lawyers will have to be the limit."

The next morning we went to the courthouse. It was a media circus. Press photographers, TV cameramen, and onlookers mobbed us as we approached. At first I was concerned for the safety of the players, but it turned out the spectators only wanted autographs.

The courtroom was equipped with four television sets, strategically placed so that all spectators in the room could view the videotape of the incident. Mulligan was a disappointment. He stumbled over the script McEachern had drafted for him to read, and his alleged friendship with Eckardt was of no help. Eckardt gave a grandstanding type of speech, making it clear he intended to make an example of these ruffians so that Vancouver's streets would once again be safe. His sanctimony made me ill. Here was Vancouver, with one of the worst crime rates in Canada, where drug trafficking was a major problem, and Eckardt was only concerned with getting his name in the papers by dumping on the Flyers.

He found all the players guilty as charged, and fined Ashbee, Flett, Saleski, Van Impe, and Watson the maximum fine for a summary offense: $500 each. He then said he was deferring the sentencing of Taylor, convicted of the more serious crime of assault on a police officer, until the following Monday. Uh-oh, we knew what that meant. He was planning to sentence Taylor to the slammer, and was putting it off until Monday so he could get another day's headlines.

McEachern assured me that on Monday he would have the machinery in place to appeal the sentence immediately to the county court, and was confident Taylor would not have to go to jail. I told Taylor he should expect to hear Eckardt sentence him to serve time, but that we would appeal it immediately and the prospects were good that it would be set aside. My last words to Taylor were to remember he was a Flyer, and not let the judge intimidate him. Watson told me the other players didn't want to leave "Chief" (Taylor's nickname) alone in Vancouver, and asked if the Flyers would pay their expenses to stay with him. Of course, I agreed. I chuckled to myself, knowing how happy it made Joe to get three more days in Vancouver.

I had to go to Montreal to attend the annual meeting of the NHL board of governors. On Monday morning, Taylor was fined $500 and sentenced to thirty days in jail, but was released within an hour as a result of McEachern's successful appeal. The county court judge dismissed the appeal of the conviction, but granted the appeal of the sentence, commuting it to just a $500 fine. I spoke to Taylor by telephone upon his release. He thanked me and the Flyers and wanted me to know he did not give Eckardt the satisfaction of seeing a Flyer cringe when his sentence was pronounced, although he admitted to feeling a bit weak in the knees when it happened.

The Flyers picked a beautiful springlike day in 1975 to have their second brush with the criminal courts. At the tail end of a tiring road trip, on February 23, 1975, they arrived in New York for a Sunday afternoon contest with the Rangers. Their spirit was willing, but they didn't have the legs, and the Rangers beat them, 2–1.

After their postgame showers, the unhappy players streamed toward the team bus, which was parked under Madison Square Garden in the tunnel area, supposedly isolated from the outside throngs by a large chain-lift gate. However, for some unexplained reason, this time the gate was open, allowing Ranger fans free access to an area adjacent to where the bus was parked. About twenty-five New York rowdies had gathered there and were chanting, "We want Schultz!" as the Flyers drifted out of the locker room in single file and headed for the bus. They didn't get him—Dave just boarded the bus. One thing about Schultz—he never got into trouble off the ice. But I can't say the same for his teammates.

Accepting the unspoken but apparent challenge to their machismo, four Flyers—Bill Clement, Bill Barber, Bob Kelly, and Don Saleski—walked toward the crowd. It is ironic that Clement, who now stars as ESPN's elegant and erudite lead NHL analyst, was the one leading the Flyers' foray. He got there first, and found himself belly-to-belly with a boisterous young tough who appeared to be the leader of the gang. He was wearing a black shirt, black pants, and black boots, which were fronted with ominous pointed metal tips. "I don't think you're so tough," he just about spat into Clement's face. Clement responded: "Why don't you show us how tough *you* are?" The invitation was immediately accepted. Just like little boys playing "knock the chip off my shoulder," the challenge had been issued and met.

The jackbooted loudmouth directed a karate kick at Clement's knee, narrowly missing contact, but he followed in immediate succession with a kick at Clement's groin and another kick toward his head. Both missed their marks, but the fight had commenced. Clement grabbed his adversary and pulled him to the ground. Saleski, Kelly, and Barber jumped into the fray, as did some (but, fortunately, only a few) of the other New Yorkers, and a full-fledged brouhaha was quickly underway. It lasted only a few minutes before the Madison Square Garden security guards restored order, and the Flyers repaired to their bus. The bruised and beaten blackshirt left with his cronies—but he didn't head home. Instead, he went to a nearby police precinct and had warrants issued for the arrest of Clement, Barber, Kelly, and Saleski, claiming that he, an innocent bystander, had been the victim of an unprovoked assault by the Flyer thugs. The club was advised of the arrest warrants on Monday, and I was directed to handle the situation.

I went to the team's practice and spoke to the charged players in the dressing room. Not having been in New York when the fracas occurred, I asked them to tell me all about it, starting at the beginning, and pulled out my yellow legal pad to take notes. The boys took this as a signal to entertain me. Kelly started first. "Gil, I swear to you I never once hit him with a closed fist," he said, wide-eyed and innocent. "With my open hand I grabbed his hair and banged his head on the ground." I stopped writing. Kelly was grinning, as were the others. Anything for a laugh.

"Let's get serious," I said, again picking up my pen. "It's important I know the facts if I'm going to help you."

Saleski stepped forward, with a sober look on his face. "Gil, can I sue him?"

"For what?" I asked, "You weren't hurt, were you?"

"No," said Big Bird, "but I ruined a brand new pair of two hundred dollar boots when I was stomping on him."

What clowns! They neither appreciated nor cared that they could be in trouble; they were having too much fun teasing me. Barber wanted a new leather jacket because his had been stained by the big mouth's blood. And so it went.

Two nights later, I went with them in Flyers owner Ed Snider's chauffeur-driven limousine to the New York police precinct where the warrants had been issued, and where, by prior arrangement, they were served. The players were fingerprinted and booked, and then released on their own recognizance to await the scheduling of a hearing. But we did not leave right away; they were having too much fun. The police brought out a ball and chain, had the four players line up together holding it, and took several Polaroid pictures. After autographing the pictures for the cops, we left New York, and they laughed and whooped it up in the limo all the way to Philadelphia.

There was never a trial. We appeared before a judge and took advantage of a New York procedure designed for minor offenses, under which defendants neither admit nor deny the charges, are placed on six months probation, and are left with no residual criminal record. Before going to court, we learned the complainant had withdrawn his statement that Kelly had been one of his assailants, substituting Dupont in his place. This helped us avoid a potential civil action by advising the plaintiff's lawyer that Kelly would sue for false arrest if a lawsuit were filed. That was the end of it.

It is a year later, and there are gorillas in the Gardens. Philly and Toronto are opponents in the opening round of the Stanley Cup Playoffs. Maple Leafs owner Harold Ballard, a P. T. Barnum clone, has decided to whip his team's taciturn fans into a frenzy for game three of the series, which will be played in Toronto on Thursday evening, April 15, 1976. He puts a half dozen men into gorilla costumes, wearing Flyers uniforms, and has them roaming the concourses as patrons file into Maple Leaf Gardens. The fans are up for the game, hoping for a major upset, as the Leafs have not beaten the Flyers in three years. The atmosphere is electric, noisy, exciting, and yes, I'll say it—it is like a zoo.

Seeking a third consecutive Stanley Cup, the Flyers have just emerged from the Spectrum with a 2–0 lead in the series. They fly to Toronto knowing they have to win two of the next five games, three of which will be played in Toronto, to avoid the ignominy of being a defending Stanley Cup champion eliminated in the first round. The Leafs have to win at least one game at home to avoid a 4–0 sweep by the Flyers. Playoff pressure is on both teams.

Something else is going on in Toronto. A local politician, Ontario Provincial Attorney General Roy McMurtry, is waging a headline-grabbing war against violence in hockey. Having previously arrested Detroit Red Wings' Dan Maloney for punching out the Leafs' Brian Glennie, after Glennie had "turtled" (avoided an invitation to fight by dropping to the ice on all fours with his head tucked down like a turtle) on the ice during a November 5, 1975, game at the Gardens, McMurtry has served notice on the NHL that he will be watching future games at Maple Leaf Gardens, and would prosecute all acts of violence. The media has been hailing McMurtry as a hero, and he seems to be feeding on the publicity his antiviolence stand has generated. He directs his staff to be especially vigilant when the bad-boy Flyers come to town. Mindful of the advantage his team would have were the Flyers intimidated into abandoning their usual physical game, Ballard is happily making public comments designed to heighten Philly's awareness of the McMurtry threat.

It may or may not be due to the specter of McMurtry, but referee Dave Newell assesses a total of 42 penalties in the game—28 against the Flyers, a team record. Thanks to their huge advantage in power plays, the Maple Leafs pepper Flyers goaltender Bernie Parent with 52 shots, while the Flyers manage just 28.

Toronto's Scott Garland opens the scoring with a power play goal at 8:27 of the first period, but Bobby Clarke answers with a Flyers power play goal at 12:00. Two minutes later, Claire Alexander gives the Leafs a 2–1 lead, which they take to the dressing room when the period ends.

The second period is played almost completely shorthanded by the

Flyers, thanks to their steady march to the penalty box. The Leafs score two quick power play goals in the opening minutes, Errol Thompson scoring at 3:25, with Joe Watson in the penalty box, and Ian Turnbull scoring at 3:54, with Tom Bladon in the bin. Needless to say, with the Leafs leading 4–1, the crowd is revved up. The decibel count of the nonstop noise is off the meter. And then it happens.

At the 8:38 minute mark, the Flyers' Saleski is given a minor. While sitting in the penalty box, with a uniformed policeman seated next to him, several well-dressed fans in the gold seats pelt him with ice cubes. Although Maple Leaf Gardens's penalty box has eight-foot-high glass separating the sinner from the playing surface, the back of the penalty box has no glass at all. Saleski stands and, turning around, faces his tormentors. He lifts his stick with both hands to chest height and shakes it in their direction. In response, a few of the fans rise from their seats and move toward Saleski. The policeman, who presumably is stationed in the visiting team's penalty box to protect the exposed players from fans, stands up, but, instead of shielding him, grabs Saleski's hockey stick and tries to wrestle it from his grasp. Saleski resists, resulting in a visible tug-of-war for control of the stick. The crowd bellows, and play stops on the ice while everyone's attention is directed toward the box.

Joe Watson is the nearest Flyer on the ice. He skates to the penalty box, and, believing his teammate to be under attack from the fans and in need of a stick to protect himself, instinctively drops his own stick over the top of the eight-foot-high glass, so Saleski can get it. But, on the way down, it grazes the shoulder of the police officer. By then Saleski has wrestled his own stick free from the grasp of the policeman, so he passes Watson's stick back to him over the top of the glass. Order is quickly restored, and the game continues.

The Flyers seem energized by the incident. At 10:58, twenty seconds after his penalty expires, Saleski feeds a pass to Gary Dornhoefer, who scores to make it 4–2. Thirteen seconds later, Jack McIlhargey passes to Jim Watson (Joe's kid brother), who nets the puck to bring the Flyers within one, at 4–3.

But the Flyers rally is snuffed out by a flurry of one-sided calls by Newell. At 12:19, about a minute after Watson's goal, Saleski is assessed a minor and misconduct penalty. At 13:28, Newell sends Andre "Moose" Dupont to the box for a minor and the Flyers are two men short. At 16:24, fifty-eight seconds after Dupont's penalty is killed, he whistles Reggie Leach to the sin bin for a minor. In all this time, no penalties are called against Dave "Tiger" Williams (the NHL's all-time penalty leader) and the other choir boys in white sweaters. The Flyers feel they are getting a classic hosing from Newell, and their frustration is growing.

At 17:29, shorthanded, Mel Bridgman skates into Toronto's defensive zone on a forechecking foray and nails Leaf defenseman Borje Salming against the boards behind the goal, separating him from his helmet. Bridgman then turns his attention to the Toronto goal as the Flyers attack continues. Skating up behind him, Salming cross-checks Bridgman to the ice in front of the Leafs' goal. A crowd quickly gathers in the crease. The whistle blows. The Flyers' Jack McIlhargey confronts Salming. Toronto's Ian Turnbull steps in and engages McIlhargey in fisticuffs behind the Leafs' goal. While that fight is in progress, Salming, still smarting from Bridgman's earlier check, skates toward the Flyers rookie center, who is just then getting up from the ice, and throws a punch at him. Big mistake. Although a great player, Salming is a Swede who has never learned how to fight on ice. Bridgman received his basic training playing for Victoria in the rough and tumble Western Hockey League of Canadian Junior Hockey. He grabs the front of Salming's sweater with his left hand, then answers the Swede's missed punch with nine consecutive hard rights to the jaw, delivered in rapid succession while Salming sinks to the ice. The Toronto crowd looks on aghast as Bridgman pummels their favorite.

When Newell dishes out the penalties, the Flyers find themselves two men down for the rest of the period. They kill the penalties and head to the dressing room. Parent is punchy, but grateful the barrage of shots has finally ended. When the second period body count is totaled, it shows the Flyers received 15 penalties, the Leafs 4. With that advantage, the Leafs have outshot the Flyers in the period, 27 to 5.

At the start of the third period, the still-shorthanded Flyers kill off the carry-over two-and-a-half minutes of a major penalty to Bob Kelly. Less than four minutes later, at 6:21, Newell calls his first third period penalty. Guess who it is against. But the Flyers only have to kill a minute and twenty seconds of it, because Newell calls one against Tiger Williams, at 7:41.

The Flyers do not score during their abbreviated power play, but Bill Barber does at 15:12 to bring the Flyers within one goal. Two-and-a-half minutes later, at 17:27—"tweet-tweet." Off goes Joe Watson—the Flyers are a man short with two-and-a-half minutes left in the game. At 19:16, Newell calls another minor against Tiger Williams. The clock runs out. The Leafs win. Exhausted and frustrated, the Flyers head for their hotel. If they think they've gotten a screwing from Newell, wait till they find out what McMurtry has in store for them.

The next morning, McMurtry calls a press conference and announces he has issued warrants for the arrest of Don Saleski, Joe Watson, and Mel Bridgman. He issues a press release designed to generate headlines, and UPI puts the story on the wires throughout North America that warrants have been issued against Saleski, Watson, and Bridgman, charging them with "offenses involving assault and possession of an offensive weapon—a hockey stick," and noting that one incident "involved a policeman allegedly being hit behind a penalty box at the Maple Leaf Gardens." The UPI story also quotes McMurtry as saying the charges against the Flyers "carry a maximum penalty of five years imprisonment."

McMurtry says the warrants spell out the following charges:

Watson: two charges of assaulting a police officer, two charges of common assault and one dangerous weapons charge (a hockey stick).
(What a joke! All Watson did was pass his stick over the penalty box glass to Saleski, where its light contact with the cop's shoulder was obviously unintended.)

Saleski: two charges of common assault and one dangerous weapons charge.
(Another joke! All Saleski did was shake his stick at Toronto fans, hold it tight when the policeman tried to grab it out of his hands, and pass Watson's stick back to him over the glass. The Crown's half-baked theory is that when Saleski passed Watson's stick back to him, he was attempting to remove evidence so as to conceal the identity of the person—(Watson)—who had "attacked" the cop, therefore Saleski was an accessory to the crime. Yeah, he was trying to hide Watson's identity in front of sixteen thousand eyewitnesses. Give me a break!)

"Bridgman: one charge of assault causing bodily harm."
(Ridiculous! He was being arrested for winning a hockey fight which started when Salming threw the first punch.)

On the recommendation of Maple Leafs counsel Bob Sedgewick, I retain a Toronto criminal lawyer, Austin Cooper, to represent the players. They are taken to a downtown Toronto police station Friday night, where they are fingerprinted and photographed. The next morning they appear in court, and it is determined they will return on June 10 to have a trial date set. The players go from the courthouse to the team's morning skate to prepare for the night's game, which the Leafs win, 4–3. The series, tied after four games, returns to Philly for Tuesday's fifth game. The Flyers win 7-1. The teams go back to Toronto for game six, which will be played on Thursday, April 22.

With their backs to the wall, the Leafs come up big. Captain Darryl Sittler scores five goals as Toronto wins 8–5 to force a seventh game back at the Spectrum. But in the second period there is an incident that gets the attention of McMurtry, who is fast becoming drunk with power in his demagogic crusade against hockey violence.

At 12:57, Dave Schultz has a fight with Toronto's Scott Garland. It ends and the players go to their respective penalty boxes. But when Schultz hears the penalties announced over the P.A. system, he goes wild. In addition to the five-minute majors, referee Wally Harris has given each player an unexpected ten-minute misconduct penalty.

With 15 minutes to serve and only 7 minutes left to play in the period, Schultz throws up his hands and storms out of the rear of the penalty box, heading for the dressing room. He is immediately accosted by Leaf fans, who surround him while the crowd roars. Play stops while everyone, including the players on the ice, look into the stands where the Schultz imbroglio is taking place. Bob Kelly skates to the penalty box to go to his teammate's aid, but can't get the door open—it can only be opened from the inside. Seeing the crowd of Leaf fans menacing Schultz, he reaches up as high as he can and tosses his hockey glove over the tall glass toward them. It hits an usherette in the face. The police disperse the fans and Schultz returns to the box.

After the game, McMurtry issues a warrant for Kelly's arrest, charging him with assaulting the usherette. Hockey violence? Nice going, McMurtry.

The Flyers win game seven in Philly, 7–3, without further incident.

The decision on a trial date for the four Flyers is deferred. To get a feel for how the Crown might prosecute them, I attend the lengthy jury trial of Dan Maloney, which takes place in Toronto in the latter part of June 1976. Maloney had been the first NHL player arrested in McMurtry's public campaign against hockey violence.

I am fascinated by the cool, understated brilliance of the lawyer who represents Maloney, George Finlayson, easily one of the best trial lawyers I have ever seen. The jury acquits Maloney, and I instantly retain Finlayson to represent the Flyers.

Finlayson is a superb strategist. It is clear the Crown's case against the four Flyers is weak. But even though Maloney has been acquitted, McMurtry is still the darling of the Toronto media with his campaign against hockey violence, and as long as the press continues to praise him, it is unlikely he can be dissuaded from bringing the Flyers to trial. "If we can somehow get McMurtry to arrest a Maple Leaf, his honeymoon with the Toronto press will be over," says Finlayson, who then devises a strategy for making that occur. His plan is simple. He will tell the Crown attorney handling the case, Robert McGee, that part of his defense of the Flyers will be to argue that the Crown's position is hypocritical, since violence takes place at both ends of the ice, but they only arrest visiting players. He tells it to McGee every time he sees him, hoping to goad McMurtry into arresting a Maple Leaf.

Sure enough, in a game against Pittsburgh, on October 20, 1976, Tiger Williams accidentally strikes the Penguins' Dennis Owchar in the head with his stick when he loses his balance while being checked in front of Pittsburgh's net. There is blood all over the ice, and Owchar needs twenty-two stitches to close the wound. When the press corps interviews him after the game, Williams shows no remorse, saying Owchar had it coming to him. Sensitivity was never one of Tiger's strong suits.

Two weeks later, after Finlayson continues to prod McGee, McMurtry takes the bait and arrests Williams, charging him with assault causing bodily harm and possession of an offensive weapon. That does it. The local media loved it when McMurtry was intimidating visiting teams, but now he has arrested a Maple Leaf. Editorials start to appear in the Toronto press questioning why McMurtry is spending so much police time prosecuting hockey players when serious crimes are being committed all over the province. There are no more "hockey violence" arrests. The era of McMurtryism is over.

The Flyers never have a trial. Finlayson negotiates an agreement with McGee under which the Bridgman and Saleski charges are dropped, and Watson and Kelly each plead guilty to a single charge of common assault, paying nominal fines.

Finlayson is later appointed to the bench and has an illustrious career as a judge. He is currently a justice on the court of appeal for Ontario.

*   *   *

My experiences with the Flyers were not limited to criminal actions. No, that amazing collection of overachievers left me with many other memories. Let me share one with my readers.

It is a story about an extraordinary human being named Robert Earl Clarke, and, whenever it comes to mind, I think of that wonderfully poignant short story, "The Gift of the Magi," written by William Sidney Porter under his nom de plume, O. Henry.

Shortly after I became Flyers general counsel in 1972, Bobby (he prefers to be called Bob) Clarke asked me to represent him in his local endorsement and promotion activities, but the instructions he gave me were rather unusual. I was to switch all offers for such deals that might come his way to other members of the team, with no mention that they had originally been meant for him. The only exception would be a case in which a deal would go to someone on a different team if he didn't take it.

We're not talking about big bucks. This was 1972. A T-shirt-type deal would come along now and then, and a player could earn $500. But, then again, players did not have megabucks contracts, either, so $500 could look pretty good.

Following Clarke's direction, I passed a number of these offers along to various teammates. At one time or another Bill Barber, Reggie Leach, Rick MacLeish, and Dave Schultz all were beneficiaries of deals they never knew had originally been offered to Clarke. Not that they didn't get offers of their own; they did. But, occasionally, they would receive what had been a Clarke offer, totally unaware their captain had been their secret benefactor.

One day in the summer of 1974, after the Flyers had won their first Stanley Cup, I received a call from a company seeking to produce a Bobby Clarke signature line of street hockey equipment. They made it clear Clarke was the only Flyer they wanted, and if he wouldn't do it, they would get a star from a different team. The deal was attractive. Clarke would be paid an advance of $5,000, and a royalty on all sales. I took it to him for his approval. He agreed to do it, but only if certain conditions were met. I was to find a way to direct some of the money to Barry Ashbee, and Ashbee was not to know it had come from Clarke.

Ashbee had been Clarke's teammate during the Flyers Stanley Cup drive. He was an inspirational and courageous leader, playing game after game in excruciating pain with serious shoulder and collarbone injuries. The other players were in awe of Ashbee's courage and stoicism, watching him suit up for every game with never a complaint, even though he was in such agony he couldn't even lace his skates by himself. In Madison Square Garden, during the third game of the Stanley Cup semifinals, Ashbee's hockey playing career ended abruptly when he was struck in the eye with a puck shot by the Rangers' Dale Rolfe. Afterward, the Flyers hired Ashbee to coach the defense.

The street hockey equipment company was planning to introduce the Clarke line at a New York trade show on a Saturday in early September. At my suggestion, it was agreed they would have Ashbee spend a few hours in their booth at the show, for which he would be paid $1,000 out of Clarke's $5,000 advance. Of course, Ashbee was not under any circumstances to be told the real source of the money. The company agreed to do that. Clarke OK'd the deal.

It was left up to me to tell Ashbee. I went to see him. "Asher," I said, "I have a good deal for you. Bobby has signed with a company to market a 'Bobby Clarke' line of street hockey equipment, and they would like you to spend a Saturday morning in September at a trade show in New York to help introduce the line. They'll pay you $1,000. What do you say?"

"Hell, Gil," he responded, "if it's for Bobby, I'll do it for nothing."

2

Carpe Diem!

John A. Ziegler Jr. was president of the National Hockey League from August 1977, through June 1992. He was far and away the best president the NHL ever had, and the Ziegler era marked the most productive period in the league's history.

When he took office he inherited a badly listing ship. The league was wounded and hemorrhaging as a result of the ongoing war with the World Hockey Association (WHA). Its internal structure was barren of executive talent, as his predecessor, Clarence Campbell, had operated the NHL like a corner grocery store. Ziegler brought a sorely needed business approach to running the league. He hired vice presidents who were experts in finance, law, television, and marketing, where before there had been none. New Vice President of Finance Ken Sawyer, an alert young Canadian chartered accountant Ziegler hired from the Big Eight accounting firm of Ernst and Whinney, brought order to the chaos in the league's accounts and budgets that had existed under Campbell.

Steve Ryan, the new vice president of marketing and public relations, a worldly American business executive recruited by Ziegler through a North American executive search firm, built the league's marketing arm, NHL Services, Inc. (subsequently name-changed to NHL Enterprises, Inc.) to an annual net income of over $10 million, instead of the $600,000 annual loss it had been incurring in Campbell's years. The new vice president of broadcast, Joel Nixon, whom Ziegler "borrowed" from Madison Square Garden, brought years of invaluable U.S. network television experience to the league, filling what had previously been a gaping void.

And then there was me. I had been toiling for the Philadelphia Flyers about ninety miles down the turnpike when John asked me to join the league in New York as its first-ever vice president–general counsel. Prior to becoming Flyers chief operating officer, I had been a litigation partner in Blank Rome Klaus and Comisky, one of Philadelphia's top law firms.

Ziegler gave the title of executive vice president to Campbell's efficient executive director Brian O'Neill, and placed him in charge of the league's hockey-playing operation, including the important role of disciplining players. He elevated to vice-presidential status the job of director of officiating, and later replaced "Scotty" Morrison in that role with widely respected former Toronto Maple Leafs General Manager Jim Gregory. In addition to earning widespread praise for supervising the officials, Vice President Gregory was in charge of the league's Central Scouting Bureau, a department which grew in importance throughout the 1980s.

During Ziegler's presidency, the league grew from eighteen to twenty-four teams, the rival World Hockey Association disbanded, the cost of an expansion franchise rose from $6 million to $50 million, and a strike by NHL players was settled in time to save the Stanley Cup Playoffs. Yet what may have been his greatest personal achievement was to become president of the NHL. The story of how he did it has never been told. It is a tale of intrigue and back-room dealing by certain NHL governors and former President Clarence Campbell that worked to Ziegler's advantage and helped him gain control of the league.

It all started with the World Hockey Association. The WHA was created in 1972 by Canadian promoters after the cost of entering the NHL had skyrocketed to a then-unheard-of expansion franchise price of $6 million. In the 1967 expansion, the cost of a new franchise had been $2 million. "Instead of paying the NHL $6 million," trumpeted the WHA founders, "buy a WHA franchise for $500,000 and use the millions you save to lure players from the NHL." It was an appealing siren song that would lead many would-be hockey impresarios to an early bankruptcy. But, prior to losing their shirts, they got the new league underway, and, before the start of the 1972–73 season, the war had begun.

It turned out to be a nightmare for NHL club owners, who had been reaping the bottom-line benefits of paying major league hockey players an average salary of $25,000. A new species of predator evolved— the player's agent. Salaries began to escalate dramatically. To keep their players, NHL clubs were forced to match inflated salary and bonus offers from the competing league. Those who tried to hold the line on salaries watched helplessly as their players jumped to the WHA. The new league gained instant credibility when Chicago's Bobby Hull, one of the game's superstars, signed with the WHA Winnipeg Jets.

While this was happening, there was turmoil within the NHL. President Clarence Campbell was emphatically advising all governors not to raise player salaries. In the summer of 1972, Philadelphia signed Bobby Clarke to a five-year contract at $100,000 per year. Campbell ridiculed Flyers owner Ed Snider before the other governors at the next board meeting, and said he had information the WHA would fold before the start of its maiden season. When that did not happen, he said they definitely would not last beyond Christmas. At the December 1972, board of governors meeting, Campbell said the WHA would never finish the season. At the June 1973 board meeting, he assured the Governors the WHA would be history before the start of the 1973–74 season. The more his predictions of the WHA's demise proved to be wrong, the more insistent he became that its collapse was imminent.

The public perception of Campbell was that he was a strong and independent president. This was true in the matter of player discipline, where his integrity was unquestioned. In the business end of hockey and the NHL, however, a number of governors felt he was a captive of the owners, particularly two senior ones, Chairman of the Board of Governors Bruce Norris (Detroit) and Bill Wirtz (Chicago). Norris and Wirtz, together with a coterie of loyal followers, constituted a formidable power bloc within the league. It seemed Norris and Wirtz had been around forever. Because of their commitment to retaining the status quo they were referred to by insiders as the Old Guard. Their reputation as longtime hockey mavens intimidated most governors into accepting their lead and following the party line on the WHA articulated by their figurehead spokesman Campbell. Those who did so saw their teams disintegrate, along with Detroit's and Chicago's, as the WHA took their key players.

Teams like the Flyers and Rangers, who defied Campbell and paid what it took to retain their players, prospered on the ice. In 1974, the Flyers won the Stanley Cup after surviving a grueling semifinal series against the Rangers. The thought that the Flyers might win the Stanley Cup was Campbell's worst nightmare. One of the lasting memories of those 1974 Stanley Cup Playoffs is Campbell's morose visage when presenting Lord Stanley's hallowed chalice to Snider's upstart Flyers at the Spectrum's center ice, a scene preserved forever in the NHL's official Stanley Cup film.

After the 1972–73 season, a group of governors had begun to question the wisdom of the league's leadership and, led by Snider and the Rangers' Bill Jennings, they secretly approached WHA leaders and negotiated a plan to merge the WHA clubs into the NHL prior to the start of the WHA's second season. Under the plan, WHA clubs would pay a total of $40 million to the NHL, and, more importantly, player salaries would immediately become stabilized.

When the Old Guard learned of the Snider-Jennings plan, they were furious. The NHL was the establishment. It had been founded in 1917 and had survived two world wars and the Great Depression. Longtime NHL moguls Norris and Wirtz were not about to let some Johnny-come-latelys muscle their way into the venerable NHL through the side door.

At the April 1973 board of governors meeting, Norris and Campbell excoriated Snider and Jennings for what they had done, and the board approved a resolution, which was moved by Norris and seconded by Wirtz, prohibiting all persons connected with NHL member clubs or the league from having any discussions with WHA representatives regarding a possibility of merging the two leagues. The Old Guard still ruled. Snider and Jennings had been effectively silenced. The war raged on.

Contrary to Campbell's prediction, the WHA did not fold after its first year. As it persevered into and through the 1973–74 season, player salaries continued to go up, up, and up—proving the truth of the adage that a war between two leagues makes millionaires out of paupers and paupers out of millionaires.

As the 1973–74 season wore on, with no indication the WHA was terminally ill, some governors began to lose confidence in Campbell. They turned to Snider and urged him to challenge the Old Guard for leadership of the league. The stage was being set for the first contested election in NHL history for the office of chairman of the board of governors.

While all this was going on, Ziegler was at Bruce Norris's side. He was counsel to Norris and the Red Wings, and was Detroit's designated alternate governor. Relatively invisible at board of governors meetings, he served on no league committees except the International Committee, and was generally considered to be innocuous—a likable but light-weight Norris flunky. Unknown to most governors, however, Ziegler had become the Old Guard's key strategic planner. And he was much shrewder than anyone suspected.

Norris's two-year term as chairman of the board of governors was expiring in June 1974, and it was evident he could not be elected to a new term. The NHL constitution prohibited an incumbent chairman from being reelected except by unanimous vote, and Norris had become increasingly arrogant and surly toward his fellow governors. A Norris re-election bid was obviously not in the cards.

As the 1974 annual meeting drew near, Snider agreed to run for chairman. Campbell and the Old Guard knew they were in a battle for control of the league; they decided Wirtz would run against Snider.

On Monday night, June 10, 1974, governors, alternate governors and league officers gathered at the Queen Elizabeth Hotel in Montreal for the NHL's fifty-seventh annual meeting. Each of the eighteen clubs was represented by two or three people, including the California Golden Seals, a club in trusteeship because it had been purchased by the league from Charlie Finley.

The meeting room was an impressive sight. The Queen E's ballroom held a huge conference table, made up of a series of tablecloth-covered 3-by-8-foot tables laid end-to-end to form a giant open-center rectangle, with about fifty chairs set around the perimeter. In one corner of the room was a large buffet table, used for juice, Danish, and coffee in the morning, and sandwiches, soft drinks, and coffee in the afternoon.

With election of the chairman scheduled for Wednesday, Monday and Tuesday nights were devoted to all-night lobbying activity by both the Old Guard and the Snider-led Young Turks. Snider's platform was clear. The league had to shift gears away from Campbell's hard-line approach to the WHA and seek a quick resolution to the war. The Old Guard's platform was equally clear: We were winning the war against the WHA, and if Snider was elected, Campbell's tenure as president would be in jeopardy.

The board disposed of its routine business on Tuesday, and met Wednesday morning to elect its new chairman. President Campbell chaired the meeting. Pittsburgh's Thayer "Tad" Potter nominated Snider. Montreal's alternate governor, Jean Beliveau, seconded the nomination. Toronto's alternate governor, owner Harold Ballard, then nominated Wirtz. The nomination was seconded by Boston's Weston Adams. There were no further nominations. After ruling California, in trusteeship, ineligible to vote, Campbell directed that the voting commence. A majority of the board voted to have a secret ballot, and written ballots were distributed, collected, and counted. Wirtz won by a single vote, 9 to 8. A close call for Campbell and the Old Guard, but they still controlled the league.

One of the chairman's duties was to appoint governors to various standing committees. Instead of seeking to heal the rift within the "house divided" league, Wirtz's first act in office was to remove Snider from the prestigious Finance Committee on which he had served for years. Wirtz announced the new committee appointments in August, and the Young Turks were appalled to find Snider's name omitted from all standing committees. It is said "to the victor belong the spoils," but this was more a case of Wirtz spoiling his victory. A little more than a year later, the resentment engendered by his petty and vindictive purging of Snider would come back to haunt him.

The 1974–75 season got underway, with the NHL featuring two new expansion teams, the Kansas City Scouts and Washington Capitals. The number of clubs was not the only thing growing in the league, however, as the trickle of red ink brought on by the WHA war had turned into a flood. Campbell and the Old Guard remained adamantly committed to a fight to the finish. As more and more governors began to fear that they could end up as discards, they allied themselves with the Snider-led Young Turks.

Snider's team repeated as Stanley Cup champions, providing Campbell with an unhappy deja vu experience. His demeanor was again sullen as he stood on the Buffalo Auditorium ice and once more performed the ritual of handing the cup to Bobby Clarke, the Flyers gap-toothed captain.

The summer of 1975 was not a happy one in la Ligue Nationale de Hockey. Financial losses were mounting at an alarming rate as clubs struggled with a Hobson's choice of either losing fans by letting players go to the WHA or losing solvency by paying the exorbitant salaries needed to keep them. The WHA began its fourth season, and now the Old Guard had something else about which to worry. Wirtz was in the second year of his two-year term as chairman of the board. How were they going to stop Snider from taking control of the league? Norris and Wirtz were starting to feel uneasy and could sense their control of the league eroding. But in their midst was one man to whom the Old Guard's near-paranoid fear of a Snider-led coup spelled opportunity. That man was John A. Ziegler Jr.

It is likely that Ziegler had long secretly coveted Campbell's job. Being a young man who enjoyed the favor of the league's power brokers, he would have felt it was only a matter of time before the elderly Campbell would vacate the office of president and he, with the muscle of the Old Guard behind him, might succeed to the throne. But Campbell, who was seventy, had passed the normal age of retirement and showed no signs of stepping down. Nor did the Old Guard, content with the performance of their revered puppet, show any signs of wanting to replace him.

While the 1975–76 season was being played on the ice, a bigger game was afoot in the boardroom. The Old Guard was looking ahead to the June 1976 board of governors meeting, when a new chairman would be elected. Although it would not have been politic to tell them (a la "The Emperor's New Clothes"), Ziegler no doubt sensed another year of warfare with the WHA might see Norris and Wirtz lose their grip on the governors. An upheaval in the league's power structure certainly would not bode well for a Ziegler agenda of succeeding to the presidency. It was time for action, and the Old Guard hatched a stop-Snider stratagem that I shall call the Ziegler Plan.

The first step under the scenario would be to have Campbell advise the board that the responsibilities of his office had become too much for him to handle at his age, and that he wished to resign as president. This would have to take place fairly quickly, while Wirtz was still chairman, so the Old Guard could control the process of selecting a new president. Step two would have Wirtz, visibly overcome with emotion over Campbell's announcement, offer to resign as chairman so the governors could duly honor Campbell for his many years of sacrifice and service by electing him chairman of the board of governors. Step three would be for Wirtz to take the initiative in appointing a Search Committee to find someone to replace Campbell, and prevail upon him to continue as president until the hiring of his successor. Ever the good soldier, Campbell would of course agree to do so.

As step four, Campbell would be elected chairman, effectively blocking Snider, who would not have the effrontery to oppose the honoring of grand old Clarence after his distinguished career as president. Step five would be to find a man to serve as president who would be responsive to the Old Guard, thus assuring their continued control of the league. If no one else could be found who would be loyal to the Old Guard, Ziegler would volunteer to give up his first love, Norris and the Red Wings, and serve as NHL president.

As Ziegler would have anticipated, Norris and Wirtz bought the plan, hook, line, and sinker. To them it seemed foolproof, and Wirtz, who loved intrigue and high drama, was enraptured. Of course, the only sure thing about the scheme was that it would serve Ziegler's ends by getting Campbell out of office and, hopefully, have the Old Guard control the process of selecting his successor.

Being NHL president was Campbell's life. He had held the job since 1946 and the last thing in the world he ever wanted to do was relinquish it. But he had no choice when Wirtz presented the plan to him. He owed too much to the Old Guard so he agreed to go along, contenting himself with the prospect of assuming the loftier position of chairman and knowing he would have played a key role in stopping Snider.

On November 18, 1975, Wirtz convened a special meeting of the board at the Harbour Castle Hotel in Toronto, ostensibly for the purpose of dealing with mundane items of ongoing league business, such as hearing a finance committee report, reviewing current arrangements for shared feeds in TV pickups in NHL arenas, considering the impact of cable TV, and other nonearthshaking matters. In large part because of the lightness of the agenda, eight governors did not bother to attend, seven of them sending alternate governors in their place, and one club, Vancouver, sending no one. The replacement alternates were Don Cooke (Los Angeles), Sam Pollock (Montreal), Bill Torrey (New York Islanders), Gil Stein (Philadelphia), Wren Blair (Pittsburgh), Jim Cullen (St. Louis), and Peter O'Malley (Washington).

Chairman Wirtz opened the meeting. "Gentlemen, Mr. Campbell has something he wishes to say to the board." Campbell rose and, looking as glum and dejected as he had when handing the Stanley Cup to the Flyers, began to speak. He sadly intoned: "Lately I have found that the demands of the office of president have become too much for me to handle. I have tried to cope with the ever-increasing workload, but my efforts have been in vain. I have given a great deal of thought to what I am about to tell you. After due consideration, I have concluded the course I must follow is to tender my resignation, which with much regret I do at this time."

The announcement was greeted with stunned silence. No one thought to suggest that perhaps what was needed was to hire one or more vice presidents, executives to whom Campbell could delegate some of his administrative responsibilities.

Instead, Wirtz said: "This is a sad day for the National Hockey League. Mr. Campbell has given so much of himself all these years. We cannot just let him leave. We must find a way to keep him active and honor him for all he has done for hockey. I move that we immediately elect him chairman of the board of governors, and I will resign so we can do that."

I was sitting next to Sam Pollock when Wirtz made his startling proposal. The ever-perceptive Canadiens general manager was not fooled for even one minute. Turning to me with a quizzical look on his face, Sam lowered his eyebrows and, sotto voce, uttered six words I shall never forget: "My name is Tucker, not Sucker!"

Peter O'Malley, Washington's alternate governor, objected to further action being taken on the motion, reminding Wirtz that the NHL constitution would first have to be amended to permit a nongovernor to be elected chairman, and that the constitution required proposed amendments be circulated to all governors at least ten days in advance of a vote. Wirtz concurred, and then proposed that the constitution be amended to permit Campbell to be elected chairman, with appropriate amendments circulated to the governors after the meeting. He announced there would be a special meeting of the board on January 20, 1976, to vote on the amendments.

New York Rangers Governor Bill Jennings then proposed the constitution be amended to create an executive committee, which would be vested with most of the powers presently reserved to the board of governors, with the specific language of the amendment to be sent to the governors along with the other amendments. Wirtz then invited anyone else wishing to offer amendments for the January 20 meeting to file them with the league prior to January 3 so the appropriate ten-day notice could be given. Most of the other items on the November 18 agenda were then deferred to January 20, and the meeting was adjourned.

It had been a momentous meeting. Afterward, Sam Pollock and I spoke briefly. He had immediately and correctly identified the Campbell and Wirtz announcements as the Old Guard's latest stop-Snider move. I could hardly wait to get to the telephone to tell Snider what had occurred, and he was flabbergasted to hear that one of the Young Turks' highest priorities—getting rid of Campbell—had been achieved by Campbell taking himself out of the presidency. What we did not realize at the time was that Wirtz had orchestrated it as step one of the Ziegler Plan. But step two would not be so easily accomplished.

The Young Turks geared up to defeat Wirtz's effort to amend the constitution. Amendments required a 75 percent majority, which meant

Wirtz had to get affirmative votes from fourteen of the eighteen clubs. All Snider's group needed was five votes. It was a piece of cake. The core of the Young Turks included Philadelphia, Montreal, the New York Islanders, Pittsburgh, and Washington. Reacting to Wirtz's purge of Snider after the 1974 election, Kansas City Scouts owner Ed Thompson had quietly joined their ranks. Based on the results of that election, there had been two other unidentified governors who also supported Snider's agenda. Notwithstanding the 1974 election results, the Old Guard was unaware Snider had such strength, and was cocky in the belief they could pull off the Campbell caper.

The board met on January 19 and 20, 1976, at the Marriott City Line Hotel in Philadelphia. All eighteen clubs were represented. A great deal of time was spent on other items of business, so a vote on the constitutional amendments was deferred to a special meeting to be held on February 27. But one of the things that was accomplished on January 20 was step three of the Ziegler Plan, as the board approved Wirtz's motion to appoint a special committee to search for and screen potential candidates for the position of president. Appointed to the search committee were governors Bruce Norris (Detroit), Bill Jennings (New York Rangers), Jacques Courtois (Montreal), Roy Boe (New York Islanders), and Clarence Campbell. The Old Guard could depend upon a majority of the committee—Norris, Jennings and Campbell—to do the right thing. Ziegler had to be pleased. His personal interest was being served.

The next meeting of the board was held on February 27, 1976, at the Sheraton LaGuardia Hotel near LaGuardia Airport in New York. It was chaired by President Campbell, who opened the meeting by stating its purpose would be to consider a number of amendments to the constitution that primarily concerned the eligibility for election to office and the establishment of an executive committee of the league.

Wirtz then made a motion, seconded by Jennings, to approve as a package a number of amendments to the constitution that Jennings had proposed. They were referred to as the Rangers Amendments, and included the creation of a league executive committee that would have most of the powers and authority of the board of governors. The motion was soundly defeated, with more than half of the clubs voting against it.

Vancouver's governor, Bill Hughes, then made a motion to create a special position called honorary life chairman, and that Clarence Campbell, in recognition of his contribution to the NHL, be appointed to the post. As honorary life chairman, Campbell would be paid and would serve as a nonvoting member on the board of governors and all league committees. In short, this would provide for Campbell everything Wirtz had said he wanted to do for him, except Campbell would not be eligible to hold the position of chairman of the board.

Ah, that was the rub. If Campbell could not be elected chairman, the whole elaborate stop-Snider scheme would have been for naught. I loved it, and seconded Hughes's motion. Wirtz hated it, and moved that it be tabled. In America, a "motion to table" is a motion to remove a matter from consideration at that time. In Canada, a "motion to table" is just the opposite; it is a motion to bring a matter forth for consideration. In the NHL, the American interpretation applies. Wirtz's motion to table the Hughes motion was seconded by Washington's Peter O'Malley and approved by a vote of 12 to 5. It was to be Wirtz's last victory that day.

Wirtz then made a motion to approve the constitutional amendments that would have made Campbell eligible to be elected chairman of the board. They were referred to as the Chicago amendments. There was no discussion on the motion. It was moved immediately to a vote and was defeated, with roughly half the clubs voting nay. It was a firm rejection of the Old Guard and a personal contretemps for Campbell and Wirtz. Campbell's resignation as president was irreversible, and Wirtz had suffered a humiliating defeat—his stop-Snider locomotive had been derailed. But there was one winner among the Old Guard—Ziegler. With Campbell out of the way and a favorable search committee in place, Ziegler's presidential caboose was still on track.

The Old Guard had to regroup. A chairman would be elected in a few months against the background of a continuing WHA war, so a new strategy would be needed to stop Snider. Norris and Wirtz remained confident in their ability to muster a majority of votes to elect a new chairman, but they needed a good candidate, and not all governors were eligible. The constitution stated a person could be elected chairman only if he were a governor, and provided he had been a governor or an alternate for at least five years. It also prohibited an incumbent chairman from being reelected except by unanimous vote, which ruled out Wirtz. The Old Guard reviewed the list of governors and realized there were very few choices available to them:

Atlanta—Charles Loudermilk. Ineligible, less than five years.
Boston—Paul Mooney. Ineligible, less than five years.

Buffalo—Seymour Knox. Eligible.
California—Munson Campbell. Ineligible, less than five years.
Chicago—Bill Wirtz. Eligible, but would need unanimous vote.
Detroit—Bruce Norris. Eligible.
Kansas City—Ed Thompson. Ineligible, less than five years.
Los Angeles—Jack Kent Cooke. Eligible.
Minnesota—Walter L. Bush, Jr. Eligible.
Montreal—Jacques Courtois. Eligible.
New York Islanders—Roy Boe. Ineligible, less than five years.
New York Rangers—Bill Jennings. Eligible.
Philadelphia—Ed Snider. Eligible.
Pittsburgh—Al Savill. Ineligible, less than five years.
St. Louis—Sid Salomon III. Eligible.
Toronto—Harold Ballard. Eligible.
Vancouver—Bill Hughes. Ineligible, less than five years.
Washington—Abe Pollin. Ineligible, less than five years.

Only ten governors met the constitution's five-year experience requirement. Of that ten, two were known members of the Young Turks—Snider and Courtois. Five were deemed nonelectable—Wirtz, because of the unanimity rule; Norris, because his surliness had turned off many governors; Cooke, because he was even more arrogant than Norris and rarely came to board meetings; Salomon, because he was very young and considered a lightweight by most governors; and Ballard, who so relished his role as league curmudgeon that he had long ago forfeited all leadership potential. That left three possibilities—Knox, Bush, and Jennings. Bush and Jennings were not acceptable to Wirtz because they had voted against his constitutional amendments. That left only Knox. He would be their man.

The Old Guard were not the only ones doing their homework. Under the astute direction of the Capitals' Peter O'Malley, who had cut his eye teeth on Washington politics, a similar analysis of potential stop-Snider candidates was underway in the Young Turks camp. The collective judgment of O'Malley, Snider, Courtois, Pollock, and Stein had narrowed the likely candidates down to two—Jennings and Knox. Sam Pollock was convinced it would be Knox; he doubted Jennings would run the risk of losing a contested election. Gulf and Western had recently acquired Madison Square Garden Center, Inc. (owner of the Rangers) and, in an effort to help Jennings keep his job, the Old Guard had gotten him inducted into the Hockey Hall of Fame. Having impressed Gulf and Western with how highly regarded in hockey he was, it would not do for Jennings to risk coming out the loser in an election for chairman. As usual, Sam was right on target.

The board held an emergency meeting on May 25, 1976, at the O'Hare Hilton Hotel in Chicago to deal with two looming crises. Mel Swig, the new owner of the California Seals, had served notice on the league that, due to the collapse of the proposed Yerba Buena redevelopment project, he was planning to exercise his previously granted option to sell and move the Seals. (The Yerba Buena project included the building of a state-of-the-art arena in downtown San Francisco. It was killed when its leading proponent, Mayor Joseph Alioto, failed in his reelection bid.) And, Kansas City Scouts owner Ed Thompson was going broke, had failed to pay his league dues, and was a candidate for bankruptcy.

While attending this meeting, Snider dropped a small bombshell in private conversations with his most loyal supporters. He was upset at having lost the 1974 election and did not want to run the risk of losing a second time. Therefore, he had decided not to run for chairman at the upcoming annual meeting, which was then only a fortnight away. They beseeched him to sleep on it for the next two weeks and reconsider his decision. He agreed to do so, but held out little hope that he would change his mind.

Meanwhile, the Old Guard had met with Seymour Knox and informed him they sought his leadership and would throw their full support behind getting him elected chairman. Knox was a bit uneasy about having to run in a contested election against Snider. On the other hand, he was flattered to learn how much his colleagues respected him. Having been taught by his father to always do the right thing, he told himself it was his duty to provide help to the league in its time of crisis. Expressing appreciation to the Old Guard for the honor they had bestowed upon him, he agreed to run for chairman.

On Monday night, June 7, 1976, more than forty governors, alternate governors, and league officers converged upon the Queen Elizabeth Hotel in Montreal for the NHL's fifty-ninth annual meeting. After dinner, Snider met in his suite with Canadiens governor Jacques Courtois and Sam Pollock, one of Montreal's alternate governors. Also present were Washington's alternate governor Peter O'Malley and me.

Snider reiterated his earlier statement that he was not going to run for chairman: It was strictly a matter of pride. He was unhappy with having lost the 1974 election and was not willing to chance another defeat. Unable to change his mind, we decided to pursue another strategy. Having deduced that Knox would likely be the Old Guard's candidate for chairman of the board, we would approach him and offer our support in return for his agreement to appoint Snider chairman of the Finance Committee. Knowing how relieved he would be to avoid a contested election and have the league united behind his leadership, we felt Knox would agree. Believing it was imperative that the Old Guard not learn of the deal until after the vote, we agreed to keep mum about it and not even talk to Knox until Tuesday night, the eve of the election.

On Tuesday morning, Wirtz opened the meeting and announced the governors would meet in executive session, which, under the league's procedures, meant only two representatives per club would be present. Once the room was cleared of the extraneous people, Wirtz reminded everyone that the search committee was actively seeking a replacement for Campbell, who would continue to serve as president until the committee's job had been completed and a successor elected. Other business then consumed the day, including dealing with the pressing problems in Kansas City and Oakland. Thompson was given three weeks to sell the Scouts, and Swig was given the same deadline to determine where he would move the Seals. Each discussed the possibility of relocating his franchise to New Orleans.

At the close of the day's business, Jacques Courtois asked Seymour Knox to join him and me for a drink, and we met in my hotel room. Courtois told Knox he was speaking on behalf of a number of clubs who felt the league would benefit by eliminating the internecine divisiveness that had existed for several years. To accomplish unity, he proposed that the clubs he spoke for swing their weight behind Knox the next morning, electing him chairman of the board in return for a commitment from Knox that after his election he would appoint Snider chairman of the Finance Committee. Knox said he thought it would be wonderful for the league to heal its internal wounds, and agreed to the deal. We shook hands. Before Knox left, Courtois cautioned him that it was essential he tell no one about what we had discussed until after the election. Unfortunately for Knox, he failed to heed that advice.

Knox left the meeting exhilarated. He had previously been filled with a sense of foreboding over the impending election. Now, Wednesday would bring a coronation rather than a confrontation. He could hardly contain his joy at the good hand fate had dealt him, and could not wait to share the good news with his Old Guard supporters. True, Courtois had advised him not to tell anyone about it, but Courtois did not know the Old Guard had come to him, asking him to provide the leadership the league so sorely needed.

After a few phone calls he located Wirtz, who was having cocktails with Norris and Ziegler in his suite. At Wirtz's invitation, Knox joined them. He proceeded to tell them about his conversation with Courtois, knowing how thrilled they would be to learn Snider would not be running for chairman of the board, and that the league would be united under his leadership. But when he got to the part about appointing Snider chairman of the Finance Committee, they did not take it very well.

Norris had made no secret of his disdain for Snider, who was brash, Jewish, progressive, and successful in business—all the things that Norris was not. There was also a tinge of jealousy, since newcomer Snider's Philadelphia Flyers had won two Stanley Cups while Norris's legendary Red Wings had sunk to the bottom of the league. He ranted and fumed about how bad it would be for the league to have Snider chairing the powerful Finance Committee.

Wirtz, who was Norris's best friend, said a great number of their followers could not stand Snider, and would feel Knox had betrayed their trust in him were Snider appointed. By the time they finished their harangues, Knox acknowledged he had made an error and said he would tell Courtois he was backing out of the deal. Wirtz complimented him for having seen the light, and Norris told him he was doing the right thing. Then Knox left to keep a dinner engagement.

As soon as he left the suite, Wirtz looked at Norris and Ziegler and said: "We picked the wrong man. We've got work to do." They had been stupefied by the news Knox had brought. Even though he had pledged to back out, the fact that Knox had made the deal in the first place did not sit well with them. Wirtz said they would have to dump Knox, and Norris agreed. But what could they do at this late date? An eleventh-hour plan of action was developed. It was ingenious, and by coincidence, would help Ziegler become president. Once again, fate and the Old Guard's "Snideroia" had presented Ziegler with an opportunity.

The Old Guard stayed up most of the night notifying friendly governors, and President Campbell, of their changed plan. Knox was not told. Not unlike Charles Evans Hughes, he went to sleep believing he was the Old Guard's candidate. (On election night in 1916, Hughes retired to bed thinking he had been elected president of the United States. During the wee hours of the morning, California narrowly went for Democrat Woodrow Wilson. A reporter came to Hughes's front door and was told, "The president-elect is still asleep." The reporter replied, "Well, tell him he's no longer president-elect.")

Early the next morning, while I was dressing, there was a knock at my door. It was Knox. After entering my room, he quickly got to the point.

"I came to tell you I cannot agree to appoint Snider Finance Committee chairman," he said, adding, "You know, there are a lot of governors who don't like him."

"From your sudden change of heart," I replied, "it appears you're not your own man, as we had thought you were. It looks like you are just taking orders from Norris and Wirtz. I thank you for coming to tell me before the meeting, but I hope you understand we will have to oppose your election."

"I understand," he said, and left.

I quickly spread the word to the others, and we held a brief meeting in Snider's room. The consensus was that Snider would have to stand for election. He agreed.

A short while later, we assembled with the other governors, alternate governors, and league officers in the Queen Elizabeth ballroom where the board meeting commenced, chaired by President Campbell. Only seventeen clubs were represented, as Kansas City's Ed Thompson had flown to New Orleans to meet with Al Hirt in a last-ditch attempt to sell his hockey club. Without saying a word to anyone, he had just disappeared. We were stunned by his absence, but could do nothing about it.

Campbell announced the first order of business would be the election of officers, starting with chairman of the board. As we expected, Bill Jennings nominated Seymour Knox. Jacques Courtois then nominated Snider. Then a completely unexpected thing happened. Harold Ballard, a committed follower of the Old Guard, nominated John Ziegler. Knox got the picture quickly and announced he was declining his nomination. No other nominations were made and Campbell declared the nominations closed.

I could not understand the Ziegler nomination. Surely Campbell realized that, as a nongovernor, Ziegler did not qualify. "Point of order, Mr. Chairman," I said, addressing Campbell. "I believe Mr. Ziegler is not eligible for this election, since the constitution provides only a governor may be elected chairman."

In response, Campbell engaged in a remarkable charade which proved beyond all doubt what the Young Turks had long believed, that he was nothing more than a willing tool of the Old Guard.

"Well, let us see, Mr. Stein," said Campbell, picking up a copy of the constitution, "we certainly are obliged to follow the letter of the constitution, aren't we." Turning to the appropriate page, he began to read aloud: "'The chairman of the governors and vice chairman of the governors shall be appointed from among the governors for two-year terms at the annual meeting of the league in 1966 and each second year thereafter, provided that no governor shall be eligible for any such office unless (a) he was a governor or alternate governor on June 14, 1966, or (b) he shall have been a governor or alternate governor for at least the five years preceding his appointment.' Well, Mr. Stein, it appears you are correct. Only a governor may be elected to the office of chairman. But it so happens, Mr. Stein, that I have here a very interesting piece of paper."

With that, Campbell reached into his breast pocket and pulled out a piece of yellow legal paper. Unfolding it, he held it in front of him and read aloud. "'I hereby appoint John A. Ziegler Jr. governor of Detroit Hockey Club, Inc., effective this eighth day of June, 1976.' It is signed by Bruce A. Norris."

Campbell was smirking. Snickers and snorts could be heard from Old Guard followers around the conference table. But I was not through yet. Long before that, I had made it my business to become an expert on the league's constitution and by-laws. Picking up my copy of the constitution, I said: "Another point of order, Mr. Chairman. According to the constitution, the letter of which you have confirmed we are obliged to follow, the governor of a club owned by a corporation cannot be appointed by a mere note handwritten on a piece of yellow paper. I refer you, Mr. Chairman, to Article Five, section 5.2, which provides, and I quote: 'such appointment shall be by resolution of the directors of the member club and a certified copy thereof shall be filed with the president.'"

Campbell's smirk disappeared. His face turned red and he appeared to be bordering on apoplexy. I knew I had him. Ziegler had not been appointed Detroit's governor in accordance with the constitution. Snider would be elected without opposition. But then Snider arose and, standing beside me, whispered in my ear: "Don't fight it."

"I can win this," I whispered in return.

"I don't care," Snider said. "Number one, Ziegler is my friend; number two, I don't want to be chairman unless a majority want me. Don't fight it." Snider was my boss; I had no choice but to comply.

"Point of order withdrawn," I said.

A visibly relieved Campbell then proceeded with the election. After the board voted to have a secret ballot, written ballots were circulated, collected, and counted. With Kansas City's Thompson absent, Snider was missing one of his supporters, for Thompson had not left an alternate governor behind to cast Kansas City's vote. Ziegler won the election by one vote, 9 to 8.

Ziegler's election as chairman of the board provided him with the impetus he needed to become president, for being chairman gave him visibility and stature, which he had previously lacked. It also provided him with a forum in which to display his considerable leadership talent, as he chaired all board of governors meetings. His vision and personal integrity impressed all the governors as he wrestled with the day-to-day internal problems of the league. When it was time to elect Campbell's successor, Ziegler had become an eminently acceptable candidate, and won easily.

Over the years, I have often thought back to that day in June 1976, wondering what might have been had Snider not stopped me from invalidating Ziegler's nomination. Had Snider been elected chairman that day, I believe Ziegler would not have been elected president and the course of NHL history would have been changed forever. In a Snider-led league the WHA war would have been brought to a speedy close. With Ziegler's conservative approach, the debilitating struggle dragged on for three more years. Under Snider, the emphasis would have been on network television and seeking a salary cap with the union. These were never Ziegler's priorities.

The NHL prospered under Ziegler. His years at the helm were very productive and the league's fortunes rose considerably. Yet, based on Snider's unbroken line of business successes, I cannot help but wonder whether the league under his stewardship might have soared to new heights of prosperity. We will never know.

3

Lords of the Rinks

The National Hockey League board of governors—who are these men who serve as the lords of hockey? From where do they come? What attracts them to hockey? Beyond dollar signs, do they give a damn about the fans?

The first thing you should know is that traditionally the governors are the owners of the hockey clubs, except where a club is owned by a corporation, in which case a corporate officer who is not an owner is designated to serve as the governor, or where multiple corporate owners own the club and appoint a nonowner as governor. Under the league's constitution, each member club is entitled to one seat (and therefore one vote) at the board of governors table. Each club designates a governor and several alternates. Since there are twenty-six National Hockey League clubs, the board of governors consists of twenty-six people.

The board of governors controls everything that happens in the National Hockey League. Although the commissioner is the league's CEO, with very broad powers, including the power to discipline member clubs and players, it is the board of governors that hires, and can fire, the commissioner, and determines what powers he should be given. The board also decides whether to expand the league, and, if so, on what terms expansion teams will be admitted. The board decides what changes will be made in the playing rules, and what terms the league will approve in a collective bargaining agreement with the players. If no agreement has been reached in collective bargaining, the board decides whether hockey will be played without an agreement (as in 1991–92) or if, instead, there will be a lockout of the players (as in 1994–95). The board is also responsible for deciding the amount of money to be spent on league operations, how the clubs will be aligned into conferences and divisions, the number of games each club will play against its division rivals, and more.

National Hockey League owners consist of two basic groups—the Haves and the Have-Mores. Do not be misled by public utterances during collective bargaining negotiations. There are no poor owners in the NHL.

Almost all NHL franchises lose money, but the Have-Mores are so wealthy that they have staying power, regardless of the profitability of their hockey clubs. The individual owners of the Have-More clubs, nine of whom are listed by *Forbes* among the four hundred wealthiest men in America, each have personal fortunes in the half billion dollar range or more. The same is not true for the Haves. And so, herewith are the first annual S. P. ("Stein Perception") ratings (in alphabetical order):

The Haves	*The Have-Mores*
Buffalo Sabres	Anaheim Mighty Ducks
Calgary Flames	Boston Bruins
Carolina Hurricanes	Chicago Blackhawks
Colorado Avalanche	Detroit Red Wings
Dallas Stars	Florida Panthers
Edmonton Oilers	Los Angeles Kings
New Jersey Devils	Montreal Canadiens
New York Islanders	New York Rangers
Ottawa Senators	Philadelphia Flyers
Phoenix Coyotes	St. Louis Blues
Pittsburgh Penguins	San Jose Sharks
Tampa Bay Lightning	Toronto Maple Leafs
Washington Capitals	Vancouver Canucks

THE HAVE-MORES

Anaheim: Through its wholly-owned subsidiary, The Mighty Ducks of Anaheim, entertainment colossus Walt Disney Company owns the Mighty Ducks hockey club. 'Nuff said. Disney Chairman Michael D. Eisner (himself an entertainment colossus) runs the show, although hired hand Tony Tavares serves as Anaheim's president and NHL governor. Although known for carefully guarding his company's assets,

Eisner abhors mediocrity and there is no doubt that if money is needed to build the Ducks into a winner, hockey fan Eisner will do it.

In an effort to woo Eisner and stimulate his interest in joining the league, Bruce McNall and I had two dinner meetings with him in Hollywood in the fall of 1992. McNall and Eisner were friends and Bruce set up the meetings. I was then NHL president and McNall was chairman of the board of governors. At the initial meeting, Eisner impressed me as a sincere and smart hockey fan, but lived up to his reputation for being tight with a buck. Because of the 1992 expansion, in which the price of a new franchise was $50 million, we told him there was no way the league would agree to a lower fee. Eisner balked at this, insisting that having Disney join the National Hockey League would enhance the stature of the league—which we agreed was true—and that the league should pay Disney to join—which we told him was completely unrealistic.

Interestingly, when I later brought the prospect of bringing Disney into the NHL to the league's Advisory Committee, the first words out of Stanley Jaffe's mouth were "We should pay *them*!" (Jaffe was the New York Rangers governor and a longtime Hollywood producer, quite familiar with the power of the Eisner and Disney names.) His fellow governors quickly disabused Jaffe of that notion, however, and Disney ended up paying $50 million for its franchise. (Twenty-five million dollars was paid to the Los Angeles Kings for territorial indemnification and $25 million was shared by all NHL clubs.)

In our California meetings, I was struck by Eisner's simplicity and candor. *The Mighty Ducks* had been a very successful movie for Disney, he asserted, and therefore his instincts told him a real-life Mighty Ducks NHL team would also succeed. "That's the extent of my market research," he said. Time has proved his genius once again, and the Mighty Ducks have produced mighty bucks as the marketing success story of the league. And, in 1997, they qualified for the Stanley Cup playoffs after their first winning season.

Boston: Owner Jeremy M. Jacobs represents the Bruins hockey club on the board of governors. His far-reaching financial empire, the Delaware North Companies, Inc., is one of the largest privately held companies in the world. It includes more than two hundred operating units in thirty-nine states and six countries, with assets in the billions. Jacobs is an astute businessman whom his fellow governors respect. He is rarely aggressive at board meetings, but when he does speak his views receive careful attention and most governors often follow his lead.

Jacobs relies heavily on Bruins president Harry Sinden, who handles the operation of the hockey club. This reliance is well placed. Sinden is one of two hockey geniuses with whom I was privileged to work during my years with the league. The other was Montreal Canadiens wizard Sam Pollock.

Frequently owners and general managers stand up at board of governors meetings and try to convince their colleagues that what they are proposing is in the best interest of the league, when they are transparently just trying to get an edge for their own hockey clubs. Jacobs and Sinden are different. They have consistently demonstrated a willingness to set aside the Bruins' interest while advocating what is truly best for the league. I believe this stems in part from their complete confidence in Sinden's hockey management skills. It is almost as if they say, "Go ahead and set whatever rules you like. We'll play the game by those rules, and the Bruins will always come out on top." (Based on results, they have been right. The Bruins hold a professional sports record of making the playoffs twenty-nine consecutive years—an incredible streak which came to an end in the disappointing 1996–97 season.) An example of the Jacobs-Sinden league-first style was the fight over the 1993 expansion draft regulations. Bruce McNall and I had given our word to Michael Eisner and Wayne Huizenga, on behalf of the NHL, that the expansion draft for their two new 1993 teams (the Mighty Ducks and the Panthers) would provide them with a fair chance to be competitive in their first year—unlike the fate that had befallen our 1992 expansion teams (and all previous expansion teams in other sports).

We charged a committee of owners with the responsibility of drawing up such a plan. With Jacobs providing committee leadership, a new set of expansion draft regulations was crafted and submitted to the board of governors for approval. Sure enough, when the liberalized regulations reached the full board, hard-line general managers like Chicago's stone-faced Bob Pulford and sunnier Cliff Fletcher of Toronto sprung their anticipated ambush. Had they succeeded, we probably would have rewarded our glittering new partners from Disney and Blockbuster with an Ottawa Senators–like inaugural campaign (10–70–4, dead last in the league). But a number of governors and general managers stood up to the hard-liners—none more eloquently than Jacobs and Sinden, who cajoled and shamed their colleagues into approving the new regulations. And the results were worth it, as the Mighty Ducks finished fourth in the six-team Pacific Division with a respectable 33–46–5 record, while the Panthers missed the playoffs by just one point, finishing fifth in the seven-team Atlantic Division with a record of 33–34–17. By 1995–96, the Panthers had reached the Stanley Cup Finals.

I believe the kind of progressive leadership provided by Jacobs and Sinden had fallout throughout professional sports—not just in the NHL—changing expansion forever. It must be more than mere coincidence that the National Football League and Major League Baseball expansion plans implemented after our Disney-Blockbuster moves were far more generous to incoming teams than their predecessors. Look how quickly the NFL's Carolina Panthers and Jacksonville Jaguars, and Baseball's Colorado Rockies, became league powers.

Chicago: The owner and governor of the Blackhawks is William W. Wirtz, the most charismatic and enigmatic person in hockey's hierarchy. The senior owner and governor in the league, Wirtz is the only governor who was on board prior to the original expansion of 1967. He grew up in hockey, a son of the legendary Arthur Wirtz, one of the truly powerful individuals in the history of the National Hockey League. Arthur, the son of a Chicago cop, began buying real estate in 1922. Within five years, he owned or managed eighty Chicago lakefront properties, then cleaned up during the Depression, investing heavily in then-cheap real estate with his partner, grain speculator Jim Norris. Together with Detroit's Norris, the elder Wirtz kept the NHL alive through the Depression and war years, when they actually owned three of the six teams in the league. Arthur Wirtz also branched out into other entertainment areas, and was the one who brought figure skater Sonja Henie to the United States in 1936.

As the chief executive and principal owner of the Wirtz Corporation, Bill Wirtz controls one of the largest family fortunes in North America. Some people who are born into wealth spend their lives squandering it. Not Wirtz. Under his stewardship, the size and power of the Wirtz Corporation have increased dramatically.

The Wirtz empire includes a piece of the NBA (National Basketball Association) Chicago Bulls, 50 percent of the new United Center arena, and widespread holdings in real estate, banking, liquor distributorships, and food concessions. Not surprisingly, Wirtz is politically powerful in Chicago. Without question, however, Wirtz's passion and first love is hockey—and that means the National Hockey League and the Black-hawks. Called Dollar Bill by fans in Chicago for his love of the buck, Wirtz is a hard-nosed businessman who never loses sight of the bottom line. But few who know him doubt he would sacrifice whatever it took to win the Stanley Cup.

The Dollar Bill side of him is very real. I was with Wirtz before the start of the 1992 All-Star Game in Philadelphia when we were approached by Flyers owner Ed Snider, who had just been booed on the ice by a number of fans. "I hate when they boo me," said Snider. "Don't let it bother you, Eddie," Wirtz laughed, "just do what I do. Every time Chicago fans boo me, I raise their ticket prices."

There is much more to Wirtz than his business persona. He is an exceptionally warm and gracious human being who is generous and caring with his friends. I personally experienced that side of him, and loved him for it. I also was impressed with his talent as a strategist. He is the kind of leader I would want were I headed off to war.

However, there is a dark side to Wirtz which I have also experienced. And this Bill Wirtz also cares—cares to crush opposition, almost casually. In response to slights, real or imagined, he can become petulant and vengeful. He had no closer friend in the league than John Ziegler, yet often he would actually refuse to take or return the league president's phone calls. It was this petty and angry side of Bill Wirtz that contributed to the governors replacing him as chairman of the board with Bruce McNall in 1992. Nonetheless, he still possesses residual power and influence on the board among a number of longtime governors.

Detroit: Michael Ilitch and his wife, Marian, own the Red Wings, with Michael serving as its governor.

Ilitch is a self-made man who built his fortune in the pizza business. His company, Little Caesars, has become a billion-dollar enterprise through his genius for franchising, an amazing achievement for this first-generation American and his family.

A former minor league baseball player, Ilitch's background and orientation are therefore in baseball rather than hockey. For a period after his acquisition of the Detroit Tigers in the early 1990s, he devoted more of his time and attention to baseball than hockey. However, his disgust with Major League Baseball's disastrous labor relations and excitement over the ascendancy of the Red Wings brought his focus back to hockey.

Although the other NHL governors respect him, he has not shown an interest in seeking a leadership role on the board. He will frequently line up with Bill Wirtz on controversial hockey issues.

An honest and trusting person, Ilitch never quite recovered from the personal betrayal he felt at the hands of Bob Goodenow during the 1991–92 collective bargaining negotiations, when the NHL Players' Association executive director (and a fellow Michigan resident) led the players out on strike after assuring Ilitch he would not. It clearly dampened his enthusiasm for continued personal involvement in the affairs of the league.

However, his commitment to his team never wavered, and his willingness to invest whatever it took to build a winner paid off in 1997 for Ilitch and the long-suffering Detroit hockey fans as the Red Wings won their first Stanley Cup since 1955.

Florida: The owner of the Panthers hockey club is Florida Panthers Holdings, Inc., a company created by H. Wayne Huizenga that is publicly traded on the New York stock exchange.

A self-made billionaire, Huizenga built the hugely successful Waste Management, Inc. (now called WMX Technologies), then sold it and retired. He soon came out of retirement to buy control of Blockbuster Entertainment Corp., rapidly building it into a billion-dollar company. He later merged Blockbuster with media superpower Viacom, Inc., in the process of which he sold his interest in Blockbuster.

Along the way, he also acquired Joe Robbie Stadium, the Miami Dolphins football club, the Florida Marlins baseball club, and the Panthers. Wow!

So far he has opted to remain in the background in the NHL, appointing longtime hockey executive William A. Torrey as Panthers president and governor. As a result, Huizenga has not yet assumed a leadership role in the NHL. He has a unique and pragmatic approach to league activities, which he recently articulated to author Gail DeGeorge (*The Making of a Blockbuster*, John Wiley and Sons, 1996):

I have a rule that I don't sit on an advisory board. When you sit on an advisory board your vote doesn't count. When you're on a committee in baseball or any other sport, your vote doesn't count. Your committee turns in its report but after that you have no authority, right? There's more important things to do than sit on an advisory board.

Although the NHL board of governors is a decision-making board, the lack of control inherent in having just one vote out of twenty-six apparently holds little appeal for Huizenga. However, the other governors hold him in such awe because of his fabled accomplishments in the business world that he could easily assert leadership were he so inclined.

Bringing Huizenga and Eisner into the National Hockey League were key accomplishments of my administration as president. You will learn how I did it in chapter 4.

Los Angeles: A franchise in turmoil for years, and particularly since former owner Bruce McNall was indicted and pleaded guilty to major bank fraud for duping banks out of a quarter billion dollars through false financial statements, the Kings have undergone a series of rapid and unsettling ownership changes. The most recent was in September 1995, when the club was purchased by Majestic/Anschutz Ventures, a partnership of billionaire Denver rail baron Philip F. Anschutz and Los Angeles real estate developer Edward P. Roski Jr., whose Majestic Realty Co. is the largest commercial real estate operation in Los Angeles, with a portfolio of 2.2 million square feet. Anschutz and Roski plan to build a new 20,000-seat arena to house the Kings and the NBA's Los Angeles Lakers by the end of the century.

The new owners paid a record price of more than $113 million for the Kings, and may have to pay even more to free the club of residual McNall obligations. This remains a franchise of unlimited potential, but, to date, very limited achievement. Hired executive Robert Sanderman serves as governor.

Montreal: Toronto-based beer giant Molson Companies Ltd. owns the Canadiens hockey club, which is well represented on the NHL board of governors by Canadiens president Ronald L. Corey. Corey is a French-Canadian (a decided asset in Montreal) who has a genius for public relations.

An accomplished speaker, Corey wields influence with governors by often being the most articulate man in the board meetings. He is handicapped, though, because he is not among the upper echelon in Molson's executive suite, and so the respect the governors have for Molson has not been transferred to Corey. Molson's potential for leadership on the board is significant but will likely remain dormant under the present lineup of governors, despite the Canadiens standing as the most successful of all NHL franchises on the ice and their long record of dominance in league affairs.

New York Rangers: Like Colorado, Dallas, Los Angeles, the New York Islanders, Philadelphia, Phoenix, and Vancouver, the Rangers hockey club has undergone recent ownership changes. First Paramount (parent of Madison Square Garden L.P., which owns the Rangers) was acquired by Viacom, Inc., then Viacom sold Madison Square Garden L.P. to a partnership of ITT Corp. and Cablevision Systems Corp. for a rather astronomical $1.06 billion, then Cablevision bought out ITT's partnership interest, then Cablevision sold 25 percent of Madison Square Garden L.P. to NBC. What next?

It is too early to tell how the new cast of characters will fare at the board of governors table, but the Rangers governor is brilliant Cablevision entrepreneur Charles F. Dolan, who has a number of strong friends on the board. Dolan, who owns the SportsChannel cable network, sued the league in 1992 to prevent NHL games from being broadcast on ESPN, rather than SportsChannel. He lost the suit, but, amazingly, never lost his friends on the Board of Governors.

Money has never been an object in the Rangers' quest for the Stanley Cup. There are more millionaire players on the Rangers' bloated payroll than on any other NHL club. When Phil Esposito was the Rangers general manager in the 1980s, his friend and fellow general manager Lou Nanne (Minnesota North Stars) said, "Phil was given an unlimited budget, and he exceeded it." One thing for sure, the New York Rangers have always epitomized what it means to be a Have-More, and they have never been shy to use that advantage.

Philadelphia: The Flyers are owned by Comcast/Spectacor, a joint venture formed in 1996 between cable TV giant Comcast Corp. and Spectacor, a sports, entertainment, and communications company. The joint venture is operated and managed by its principal minority owner, Edward M. Snider, founder of Spectacor and former majority owner of the Flyers. Snider represents the hockey club on the board of governors. Second only to Bill Wirtz in seniority on the board, he has owned the Flyers since the league granted Philadelphia an expansion franchise in 1966.

Snider built the Flyers into one of the strongest sports franchises in North America, while at the same time elevating their home arena, the CoreStates Spectrum, to its position as one of the premier privately held entertainment and sports facilities in the United States. This was accomplished after he bought the Spectrum out of bankruptcy by agreeing to pay creditors one hundred cents on the dollar. Along the way

Snider created PRISM, a premium cable channel, pioneering the concept of combining movies and local sports teams' home games into a single pay package. He later sold PRISM for millions of dollars.

Capitalizing on the expertise he had developed in operating the Spectrum, Snider created Spectrum Management Group (SMG), an arena and convention center management company that now is the biggest in North America, responsible for managing sixty other major arenas, stadiums and convention facilities in the United States. Moving to California, he jumped into the motion picture business, successfully producing profitable low-budget movies for the European market through his company, Spectacor Films.

Prior to his negotiating the Comcast deal, Snider's latest achievement had been to finance and construct the new $210 million, 20,000-seat CoreStates Center, the colossal state-of-the-art sports and entertainment palace that became home to the Flyers in the 1996–97 season. As part of his Comcast arrangement, Snider's company, Spectacor, manages both the CoreStates Center and its adjacent "little brother," the CoreStates Spectrum.

The governors hold Snider in high regard, in part because of his apparent Midas touch, but primarily because he has demonstrated unerring good judgment in the business of hockey. He is also a spellbinding orator at board meetings, having few equals when it comes to persuasively expressing his views. His inability to attend many board meetings due to the time demands of his multiple coast-to-coast business interests has, frankly, reduced his once-powerful leadership role in the league.

A self-made multimillionaire, Snider had been a Have with an impressive business empire. By partnering with Comcast, he gained admission to the exclusive Have-More club.

St. Louis: The Blues are owned by Clark Enterprises, Inc., a limited partnership of twenty-nine individual and corporate investors, including beer giant Anheuser-Busch, Inc. and other corporations that could constitute a "Who's Who" of *Fortune* 500 companies in the St. Louis business community. Its chairman and governor is former Anheuser-Busch chief financial officer Jerry E. Ritter. Until his firing last year as part of the Mike Keenan purge, previous governor Jack Quinn had been onboard since Harry Ornest bought the franchise from the league in 1983, in the aftermath of Ralston Purina's aborted attempt to move the Blues to Saskatoon. He was bright, witty, and personable, and gave a good account of himself at board of governors meetings. However, the Blues' aggressive spending in signing free-agent hockey players for huge salaries and bonuses made the club a pariah to the other governors. Regarded as financially reckless, St. Louis had been somewhat isolated at the board. This will likely change under Ritter.

San Jose: George Gund III is the owner and governor of the Sharks hockey club, and the Gund family fortune is one of the largest in the United States. The initial building blocks of that wealth were provided by George's late father, George Gund Jr., a self-made multimillionaire who founded the Cleveland Trust Co. bank. After his death, it was not George, but rather George's brother Gordon who was the financial whiz responsible for building the family's wealth to its present size. The Gunds are very private and guarded about their holdings, maintained through their Gund Investment Corp. *Forbes* estimates the Gund brothers' wealth at $2 billion. It is said they own the largest privately held share of Kellogg's, the cereal company. It has also been said that Gordon's genius for making money is rivaled only by George's genius for spending it.

Prior to selling the Minnesota North Stars and acquiring the Sharks, Gordon was a prominent and greatly respected member of the NHL board of governors. Afflicted with retinitis pigmentosa, Gordon lost his eyesight as a young man, but never let it get him down. Instead, he founded the RP Foundation to conduct research and help others avoid that fate. He is so perceptive and tuned in to everything that's going on, you can sit with Gordon at a meeting, or even at a hockey game, and never realize he is sightless. He is a remarkably keen businessman and a caring friend, husband, father, and brother. Since the advent of the Sharks, Gordon has concentrated on his ownership of the NBA Cleveland Cavaliers, and no longer plays a role in NHL affairs—a big loss to the league.

Shy and good-natured, George is treated with affection by just about all the governors, but none look to him for leadership, as they did to Gordon. George is an authentic sportsman who loves hockey. Look for him to spend whatever it takes to build the Sharks into a Stanley Cup winner.

Toronto: The storied Maple Leafs, considered by some to be the most valuable franchise in the NHL, has fans who literally leave season ticket rights to their children in their wills. It is wholly owned by Maple Leaf Gardens Ltd., a privately held corporation whose shares were traded on the Toronto Stock Exchange until August 1996, when majority owner Steve A. Stavro took the company private. Maple Leaf Gardens Ltd. also owns Maple Leaf Gardens arena.

Grocery tycoon Stavro indirectly controls Maple Leaf Gardens Ltd. through his interest in MLG Ventures, which holds 95 percent of Maple Leaf Gardens Ltd.'s stock. Stavro owns 51 percent of MLG Ventures through his holding company, MLG Holdings.

Stavro is the governor for the Leafs. He is a conservative businessman who prefers remaining in the background, unlike his late predecessor as Leafs owner, the relentlessly rambunctious Harold Ballard. Not only is Stavro shy in dealing with the media in hockey hotbed Toronto, but at NHL board of governors meetings he chooses to be virtually invisible, speaking out on only the rarest of occasions. He has a few good friends and no enemies among the governors and is more likely to follow, rather than lead, at their meetings.

Vancouver: The Canucks governor is former cellular telephone mogul John E. McCaw Jr., a Seattle native, who early in 1996 replaced then-minority owner Arthur R. Griffiths on the board. (In November 1996, he purchased Griffiths's remaining minority interest.) As a rookie governor, McCaw will not wield a ton of influence.

Griffiths's late father, Frank A. Griffiths, had amassed a fortune while building Western International Communications, Inc., an electronic media empire. As a result, young Griffiths had influence and wealth thrust upon him, rather than achieving it himself. One of the things he did achieve, however, was stealing hockey guru Pat Quinn away from the Los Angeles Kings and turning the Canucks hockey operation over to him. It was a very clear-sighted move, albeit handled in such a clumsy manner that then NHL president Ziegler felt compelled to impose a lengthy suspension on Quinn. At the board of governors, Griffiths was looked upon as just "young Arthur," son of admired Hall of Famer Frank A. Griffiths, and was not held in very high esteem by the governors.

McCaw made his fortune when he and his brothers sold their McCaw Cellular Communications to AT&T in 1994 for $11.5 billion. His company, Orca Bay Sports and Entertainment, owns approximately 87 percent of Northwest Sports Enterprises Ltd., which, through its wholly-owned subsidiary, Vancouver Hockey Club Ltd., owns and operates the Canucks.

Orca Bay Sports and Entertainment also owns 80 percent of Vancouver's new NBA team and the sparkling new arena, General Motors Place. McCaw's financial strength assures the Canucks a place on the list of the Have-Mores.

THE HAVES

Buffalo: The Sabres are owned by Niagara Frontier Hockey, L.P., of which 34 percent is held by cable television big leaguer Adelphia Cable Communications, one of the ten largest cable TV operators in the United States. John Rigas, the CEO of Adelphia, is the team's largest single owner.

Controlling minority owner Seymour H. Knox III, who died in May 1996, at the age of seventy, was the longtime governor of the Sabres. He was born into old wealth, with his family's vast fortune having been built upon the foundation of large holdings of Woolworth stock, and much more. The story is told of the time his late father, Seymour H. "Shorty" Knox Jr., was a student at Yale and one of his classmates hatched the idea of publishing a magazine, but lacked the financial wherewithal to do it. Shorty Knox put up a significant portion of the needed capital in return for a healthy share of equity in the venture. That classmate was Henry Luce, and the venture was *Time* magazine. The rich get richer.

Seymour III was a true sportsman whose love for the city of Buffalo and hockey kept him committed to the Sabres despite the club's losing a ton of money. He could always be depended on to provide a voice of moderation and reason in the midst of sometimes heated and unruly board debates, as he did during the 1992 strike, when the league's hawks wanted to gas the season "to teach the players a lesson." Knox, with gentlemanly eloquence, prodded them to focus on how important it was for hockey and the league that the strike end and the long tradition of Stanley Cup Playoffs be continued without interruption. It's apparent that Major League Baseball did not have enough Seymour Knoxes when they allowed the 1994 World Series to be canceled in a labor dispute. He brought dignity to the board of governors, and I am proud my nomination of him led to his election to the Hockey Hall of Fame.

Minority owner and longtime NHL activist Robert O. Swados, vice chairman of the board of Niagara, succeeded Knox as governor. Swados, a Harvard Law School graduate, served for many years as secretary of the league, and the old-line governors respect him. Interestingly, perhaps Bob Swados's greatest claim to fame is his daughter Elizabeth, the brilliant singer, composer, and playwright, long a fixture off-Broadway.

Seymour's son, Seymour H. Knox IV, a bright young man with a bearing much like his dad's, serves as alternate governor.

Calgary: The Flames are owned by nine wealthy partners, one of whom, Harley N. Hotchkiss, serves as its chairman, CEO, and governor. Hotchkiss is president of Spartan Resources Ltd., a private Canadian oil exploration company. Other principal partners include the Seaman brothers—Daryl "Doc" Seaman, chairman of Dox Investments, and Byron J. Seaman, chairman of Ballantrae Resources Ltd.—Ronald V. Joyce, senior chairman and cofounder of Tim Horton Donuts, and N. Murray Edwards, president and CEO of EDCO Financial Holdings Ltd.

Hotchkiss is a man of quiet dignity who has earned the respect of the other governors through his deep personal integrity and years of intelligent and constructive participation at board meetings, culminating in his election as chairman of the board of governors in 1995. He is reserved, rather than assertive, and is unlikely to make waves during his tenure as chairman. He will, however, be a potent advocate on behalf of the Haves. Despite the recent $30 million renovation of the Saddledome, Calgary remains a small market. Although the owners are men of means, they cannot match the huge wealth and awesome power of the Have-Mores.

Everyone knows that in the present environment, help is desperately needed for the Haves to be able to compete on a level playing field with the Have-Mores. Hotchkiss was instrumental in creating the NHL's Canadian Assistance Program in January 1996, under which, depending upon the percentage of season tickets sold and other criteria being met, Canadian clubs can each get a subsidy of up to $5 million a year from a pool of funds drawn from league-generated television, licensing, and sponsorship revenues. The esteem in which Hotchkiss is personally held by the governors may be the Haves' best hope, but it is unlikely to be enough to convince the Have-Mores to budge from their long-standing resistance to the concept of shared local revenues.

The large-market versus small-market debate plagues all major sports leagues. Teams in big markets like New York and Chicago generate much more money from ticket revenue and local TV than those in small markets such as Calgary and Edmonton. The result is an imbalance in resources that permits wealthy clubs to spend more for their players, which can lead to a competitive imbalance on the ice. One method of counteracting this would be for all clubs to share equally in each club's local "gate" and TV revenues. But the powerful big market teams have never agreed to do this—and probably never will.

Carolina: Peter Karmanos Jr., through his KTR Limited Partnership, owned the Hartford Whalers hockey club and moved it to Raleigh, North Carolina, after the 1996–97 season, paying the City of Hartford more than $20 million to get out of the last year of his arena lease. He also changed the name of the team to the Carolina Hurricanes. Karmanos serves as governor of the club.

Corporate chairman and CEO of Compuware Corp., a computer software company, Karmanos and his minority partner, former NHL goaltender Jim Rutherford, have been active in amateur hockey. In 1989 they acquired the first U.S.-based franchise in Ontario Hockey League history, the Detroit Ambassadors (subsequently renamed the Whalers). Having long sought to buy an NHL franchise before purchasing the Whalers, Karmanos failed in his bid to obtain a 1992 expansion franchise for St. Petersburg, Florida. Insiders had considered him the favorite to win the 1992 competition over the Tampa group headed by former hockey star Phil Esposito, but Karmanos blew it at the last minute. On the day the board of governors was to make its decision, he appeared before them and tried to lowball the NHL, withdrawing his application for a $50 million expansion franchise. Instead, he asked that the board reject the Esposito group's $50 million application and give him a six month exclusive option to buy an expansion franchise in the Tampa Bay area for only $29 million. Affronted by his chutzpah, the governors coldly showed him the door.

A number of the governors have long memories and might still resent Karmanos for what he did in the 1992 expansion, and it may take a long time for him to live it down. Do not expect to see a leadership role for him in the foreseeable future. Compuware has deep pockets, but Karmanos must be responsive to shareholders, so for now the Hurricanes belong on the list of Haves.

Colorado: Ascent Entertainment Group, Inc. owns the Avalanche hockey club—the Quebec Nordiques until 1995. COMSAT Corp. (formerly Communications Satellite) purchased the Nordiques hockey club for $75 million and moved it to Denver, where it got off to a rollicking start, winning the Stanley Cup in its first season by sweeping the Florida Panthers in the 1996 finals. In December 1995, COMSAT spun off its entertainment group as Ascent Entertainment Group, Inc. in an initial public offering. Its shares are traded on the NASDAQ stock exchange, with 80 percent of its outstanding common stock owned by COMSAT. Ascent holds interests in on-demand multimedia entertainment, professional sports franchises, major motion pictures, and television products. The Avalanche governor is corporate executive Charlie Lyons, who headed COMSAT's entertainment group before the creation of Ascent.

COMSAT had announced plans to build a new $132 million arena, the Pepsi Center, in partnership with the Anschutz Corp. (see Los Angeles), but has become disenchanted with the sports business because of the team's sizable financial losses. Despite its success on the ice, with a club that boasts some of the best young talent in the league, COMSAT is actively seeking a buyer for its stake in Ascent.

Dallas: Until his 1996 sale of the Stars to wealthy Dallas investment banker Thomas Hicks (Hicks, Tate, Muse, and First) for $84 million, Norman N. Green had been the governor and owner of the Stars. Owner Hicks is now the governor.

Green is a Canadian who became wealthy through commercial real estate in Calgary and was one of the early minority owners of the Flames. While enjoying the success of that franchise, Green made no secret of the fact that he longed to own and control his own NHL team. He got the chance in 1990 when the new (and brief) owners of the Minnesota North Stars, Howard Baldwin and Green's boyhood friend, Morris Belzberg, ran short of capital prior to the 1990–91 season. Green sold his share of the Flames and purchased a controlling interest in the North Stars, subsequently buying out Baldwin and Belzberg completely.

An enthusiastic marketer, Green brought a fresh, innovative approach to the selling of hockey in Minneapolis, and enjoyed early success when the team General Manager Bob Clarke built for him advanced to the 1991 Stanley Cup finals. That success was short-lived, however. Over the following two seasons, Green lost more than $15 million—a sizable chunk of his personal net worth—when high player payroll costs greatly exceeded the gate receipts and local TV revenue available in the small Twin Cities market. He learned the hard way that Minnesota is not Canada.

Desperate to stop the financial bleeding, Green spent most of 1992 secretly shuttling between the Twin Cities and Anaheim, California, attempting to lease the new Anaheim arena so he could move the North Stars there at the start of the 1993–94 season. He was thwarted when the board of governors granted Walt Disney Co. a franchise for Anaheim at its December 1992 meeting. As consolation, Green was given the right to relocate the North Stars to any North American city of his choice, provided the decision was made within one year. He elected to move the Stars to Dallas in advance of the 1993–94 season. His exit from Minneapolis was rancorous. Press and fans vilified him for leaving, and, as a parting gift, a former employee charged him with sexual harassment. After two seasons in Dallas, Green learned that Texas was also not Canada, and he was forced to sell the team in order to survive. Because he had accumulated approximately $70 million in debt, Green is believed to have gained little or nothing from the sale.

Green developed friendships with some governors, but his flamboyant style and penchant for constantly blabbing to the media turned off the more conservative element in the league. He was not highly regarded as a hockey operator, and had very little influence with his peers. However, one move Green made may prove to have lasting benefit for the transplanted Stars. He wooed Jim Lites away from the Detroit Red Wings (ironically owned by Lites's father-in-law, Michael Ilitch). Lites is a progressive and agile marketing maven, who, as president of the Stars, provides stable continuity for the new owner. Under his administration, the club has progressed on the ice, becoming one of the league's powerhouses.

Plans are under way for a new arena in Dallas that will house the Stars and the NBA Mavericks, although differences between the ownership of the two teams will first have to be resolved.

Edmonton: The Oilers governor is owner Peter Pocklington, one of the true bon vivants of North America. Most governors do not regard him as a hockey heavyweight, but credit him with having had the good judgment to employ a brilliant and ferocious general manager, Glen Sather, whose acumen built the Oilers into one of the greatest teams in hockey history.

Unfortunately for Edmonton fans, the financial needs besetting all small-market Canadian teams, coupled with his other business reverses, led Pocklington to convert the superpower to a supermarket, and star after star was sold to Have-More clubs for cash and window dressing. Sather's perspicacity has been sorely tested as he has struggled to keep the Oilers competitive on the ice.

Early in 1997, Pocklington announced plans to take the Oilers public in a new company that would own 45 percent of the Oilers and his other sports and entertainment ventures. If underwritten, the stock would likely have been traded on the Alberta and Toronto stock exchanges. Pocklington's continued ownership of the Oilers in Edmonton would seem to have been dependent upon the success of the proposed stock sale. With the continued squeeze of today's hockey economics, Pocklington could not long own the Oilers in Edmonton without this infusion of capital.

In June 1997, Pocklington declared he had lost between $6 million and $7 million on the Oilers in the 1996–97 season and was putting the team up for sale. Although local ownership remains a possibility, the more likely scenario will be the move of the Oilers to one of the localities in the United States interested in securing an NHL franchise, such as Houston, Seattle or Oklahoma City.

New Jersey: Dr. John J. McMullen has been the majority owner and governor of the Devils since he purchased the foundering Colorado Rockies in 1982 and moved them to the Meadowlands.

A committed reactionary, McMullen just cannot understand why hockey players should be paid a lot of money. Extremely personable, he is a persuasive speaker with the ability to attract other governors to his point of view. In 1994 he convinced a majority of the board to engage in a lockout of the players, which nearly cost the league the entire season.

In June 1992, shortly after I was elected president, McMullen took me to lunch and shared with me his views on how we should approach the upcoming collective bargaining negotiations. He was adamant that the players should be locked out.

"When they miss two paychecks, they'll agree to anything we want," he said.

"That's what you said in baseball, John," I replied. (McMullen had been the owner of the Houston Astros during Major League Baseball's collective bargaining wars.)

"That's right," he said, "and it proved to be true."

"But John, in 1981 the players stayed out fifty-one days, and didn't come back until the owners threw in the towel after their fifty days of strike insurance ran out, and gave the union everything it wanted."

"That's true," he conceded, "but if we had waited two more weeks we would have had them." He was not being facetious.

Aside from his hard-line collective bargaining views, McMullen is a great dinner companion and fabulous conversationalist. He has a sharp mind and a complete grasp of the issues involved in sports ownership. I appreciated the support he provided me during my presidency.

Although a man of considerable wealth, he is not in the same ballpark as most of the Have-Mores. The McMullen Group, a company owned by McMullen, owns several other entertainment assets—U.S. independent broadcast network America One Television, Prime Sports Interactive, and Prime Sports Radio.

McMullen has benefited from the tireless and tightfisted leadership of his general manager, Lou Lamoriello, and the Devils were able to win the Stanley Cup in 1995 while operating under a stringent budget. His position reinforced by this on-ice success, McMullen remains a man of considerable influence on the board of governors.

New York Islanders: In June 1997, the board of governors formally welcomed new Islanders majority owner John Spano into their midst. It was hoped he would provide stability for a franchise that had been drifting ever since league power John Pickett abandoned Long Island for Florida and became an absentee owner. But a month later, Spano was out and Pickett was back in after Spano defaulted on a $17 million payment due Pickett as part of Spano's $165 million deal.

Pickett has once again put the franchise up for sale. In the meantime, its league affairs will be well handled by its new governor, William M. Skehan. The last remaining founding father of the Islanders, Skehan is a savvy lawyer who has been general counsel for the franchise since its birth. The Isles have sailed through some troubled waters lately, and more storms may loom on the horizon. Skehan's experienced hand on the tiller will be a stabilizing influence.

Ottawa: The governor of the Senators is majority owner Roderick M. Bryden. As part of a sixty-seven-member ownership group, Bryden and the Stormont Entertainment Corp. (previously Terrace Corp.) own a 70 percent stake in the team. The Senators play in the $200 million Corel Center, which opened in January 1996.

I met Bryden in Ottawa at a private dinner with then-majority owner Bruce M. Firestone during my 1992 North American tour, and he wowed me with his iconoclastic views on hockey and the world in general. Rod has a laser mind and is one of the true original thinkers in the NHL. He delights in challenging conventional thinking. One example: "Why should a referee skate? If we put him in an elevated chair, like a tennis referee, he would have a more commanding view of the ongoing play, there would be one less official on the ice to get in the way of the action, and we would be able to utilize the maturity of judgment developed by veteran referees, instead of having them retire just because they can no longer skate."

Sounds good. But I believe most of his views may be too radical for conservative governors to digest and they will not pay him much heed unless, and until, the Senators become a power on the ice. It is a curious phenomenon in the NHL that the degree to which governors respond to words of wisdom from one of their number is frequently directly proportionate to the position of that governor's team in the standings. Based on the Senators record to date, it will be a long while before Bryden has an audience.

Phoenix: One of the handful of WHA survivors who entered the NHL in 1979 (along with Quebec's Marcel Aubut, Hartford's Howard Baldwin, and Edmonton's Peter Pocklington), Barry L. Shenkarow owned and was governor of the Winnipeg Jets until he sold the franchise in 1995 to BG Hockey Ventures, owned by Richard T. Burke of Minneapolis and Steven Gluckstern of New York. Burke and Gluckstern moved the Jets, renamed the Coyotes, to Phoenix in 1996. Burke, whose wealth springs from the health-care industry (he formerly served as chairman and CEO of United HealthCare Corp., a company he founded in 1974), serves as governor. Gluckstern is the chairman of Zurich Reinsurance Centre, one of the largest broker market reinsurers in the United States. Shenkarow will serve as a consultant for ten years. He, and especially his comely wife, Rena, will be missed. They were two of my favorite friends in the league.

Although Shenkarow is personable and self-effacing, with an easygoing demeanor that tends to mask his gifted intellect, he is a shrewd deal-maker who twice used opportunistic leverage over his fellow governors to enrich himself by extracting money from them—no mean feat.

In 1982 the league was considering McMullen's bid to buy and move the failing Colorado Rockies to the Meadowlands in New Jersey. One of McMullen's conditions was that the team be moved from the Smythe Division to the Patrick Division, which made sense geographically. The NHL's four divisions were the Smythe (Calgary, Colorado, Edmonton, Los Angeles, Vancouver), Norris (Chicago, Detroit, Minnesota, St. Louis, Toronto, Winnipeg), Adams (Boston, Buffalo, Hartford, Montreal, Quebec) and Patrick (New York Islanders, New York Rangers, Philadelphia, Pittsburgh, Washington).

There were only five teams in the Smythe Division, and, with four teams in each division assured of a playoff berth, removing Colorado/New Jersey would leave the Smythe with only four teams. Someone had to move into the Smythe to replace Colorado—otherwise all clubs in the division would automatically make the playoffs, an unacceptable result in pro sports. The logical solution was to move Winnipeg from the six-team Norris Division to the Smythe. However, President Ziegler ruled that, because 1982 was the second year of a two-year cycle of rotating the odd home game between opponents who played three games each year against each other, a unanimous vote would be required to move a team out of its division.

Shenkarow would not approve Winnipeg's move to the Smythe until a deal was made in which the other governors agreed to: pay Winnipeg an $800,000 share out of McMullen's $5.1 million transfer fee, to which the Jets and the other former WHA franchises were not otherwise entitled; relieve Winnipeg of close to $4 million of debt it owed to the league on its original expansion note; and give Winnipeg a commitment that it would be returned to the Norris Division when the league next expanded.

When the NHL expanded to San Jose in 1991, Shenkarow expected Winnipeg would be returned to the Norris Division, as had been agreed. This was resisted within the league, however, with all Norris Division owners—including powerful board chairman Bill Wirtz—dead set against it. Traveling to Winnipeg was a long and tough road trip for the Norris Division teams, four of which were located in midwestern American cities. Taking a team across the border frequently meant long customs-clearing delays. Also, experience had taught that the uniformly dull image of the name Winnipeg had virtually no appeal to fans in Chicago, Detroit, Minneapolis, and St. Louis, so gate receipts fell dramatically when the Jets came to town.

Once again, Shenkarow made a deal which brought him money from the pockets of other club owners. He first agreed Winnipeg would remain in the Smythe Division for one year, then, in 1992, consented to stay in the Smythe, but only after the other clubs agreed to pay the Jets $1.5 million per year out of the league's playoff revenues.

One would expect new ownership to begin with a clean slate. However, it would not be surprising in the sometimes illogical world of the NHL that some governors will remain resentful of Burke and Gluckstern over Shenkarow's pecuniary adventures. After the honeymoon in Phoenix is over, the club's financial strength will be reevaluated. But for now, list the Coyotes among the Haves.

Pittsburgh: The Penguins are owned by Pittsburgh Sports Associates Holding Co., of which Howard L. Baldwin is the chairman and majority owner. Baldwin serves as governor. One of the more experienced and perceptive hockey operators, Baldwin's entrepreneurship has taken him from a lowly start as Philadelphia Flyers ticket manager to becoming owner of the Penguins, operator of the Pittsburgh Civic Arena, and marketing managing agent for the Red Army team in Russia. He began that long journey in 1972 as an early pioneer in the World Hockey Association with the New England Whalers. While operating the Whalers, he also had to run the entire league, having been elected WHA president by the other owners. It is an everlasting tribute to Baldwin that he was able to hold the WHA together despite its many vicissitudes. Every season franchises moved or went bankrupt, yet Baldwin saw to it that the league endured. When the seven-year war ended in 1979, Baldwin's hockey club was among the four survivors brought into the NHL—a survivor because he willed it so.

After selling his minority interest in the Whalers, Baldwin set his sights on bringing a 1992 NHL expansion team to San Jose, California. When he was preempted in San Jose by Gordon and George Gund, who convinced the league to grant them an expansion team there in 1991, Baldwin and his partner Morris Belzberg purchased the Minnesota North Stars from the Gunds. Before the 1990–91 season began, however, Baldwin and Belzberg found themselves short of cash. Turning that problem into an opportunity, they sold the North Stars to Norman Green. A year later, they reinvested their North Stars capital gain, buying the Penguins in November 1991. As the Pittsburgh Sports Associates Holding Co., they oversaw the Penguins return to financial solvency while the team was winning a second Stanley Cup. Baldwin simultaneously pursued a long-standing fascination with Hollywood, involving himself in the production of movies through his Baldwin Entertainment Co. In many ways, he is like a younger Ed Snider. In April 1997, Belzberg sold his 50 percent interest to Boston investor Roger Marino for a reputed $40 million.

As president, I could not have asked for a more supportive or helpful owner than Baldwin. Though he is many years my junior, I appreciated his counsel. Because of his relative youth, his WHA background, and lack of a large personal fortune, most old-line governors do not look to him for leadership—despite the Penguins' consistent prowess on the ice. Maybe some day they will see the light.

Tampa Bay: The Lightning is owned by Lightning Partners Ltd. The governor is David E. LeFevre, a New York lawyer who has for years represented significant business interests in Japan. LeFevre brought one of his Japanese clients, Takashi Okubo, chairman of Kokusai Green, into the picture as the principal owner when Phil Esposito was scrambling to find the capital needed to fund Tampa Bay's 1992 expansion bid. The financial strength of this Japanese developer of golf courses and other recreational facilities was the vital factor leading to Tampa Bay's franchise award. Since then, Kokusai Green has acquired 100 percent ownership of the team. The Lightning began play in the new 19,500-seat Ice Palace at the start of the 1996–97 season.

Although he is an able and constructive member of the board of governors, LeFevre operates on the outer fringes of the league's power structure. There are several reasons for this. For one thing, he is a hired hand, not an owner. Secondly, there is seemingly intractable bad blood between him and John McMullen, which dates back to an incident in Houston, when LeFevre found himself pitted against McMullen in a very public power struggle after owner McMullen fired popular Astros general manager Tal Smith. Thirdly, there is that peculiar NHL losing-team syndrome: Governors generally do not get respect from their colleagues on the board if their teams do not do well in the standings.

Washington: Virginia attorney Richard M. Patrick, a 20 percent owner of the Capitals hockey club (along with longtime majority owner Abe Pollin), serves as its governor. Pollin, generally more interested in basketball than hockey, had served as governor for many years, but recently elected to take a back seat and concentrate his time and effort on his NBA franchise and other ventures.

Patrick's strong hockey background serves Pollin well on the board of governors. He is a member of hockey's royal family—the distinguished NHL hockey clan that began with legendary New York coach and general manager Lester Patrick, continued with Lester's progeny Lynn and Muzz, and remains prominent with Lester's grandsons Richard (son of Muzz) and his cousin Craig (son of Lynn), who is Pittsburgh's general manager. Affable and good-humored, Richard Patrick is respected and well-liked by the other governors, who consider him a good citizen and team player at the board level. They do not see him as a leader, however, and gave short shrift to his campaign to become commissioner in 1992.

Abe Pollin is one of a vanishing breed in the NHL—the sportsman and individual owner of a small-market team. He has steadfastly maintained the Capitals since their inception in 1974, despite consistent financial losses. He is hopeful of seeing some light at the end of the tunnel when the new 20,000-seat MCI Center in downtown Washington's Gallery Place is completed—which is expected to be in time for the Capitals 1997–98 season.

The governors of the NHL are, with very few exceptions, super-wealthy men who enjoy the unique personal comportment of the rich and famous, far removed from the daily financial problems which beset the hockey fans whose hard-earned dollars make their franchises so successful. During the twenty-one-year period from 1972 through 1992, they met each December (or November) in Florida, the winter playground of the affluent. In the early seventies, the meetings were either at the Golden Strand Hotel in Miami Beach, the property of St. Louis Blues governor Sid Salomon Jr., or at a hideaway resort in Homosassa owned by Detroit Red Wings governor Bruce Norris. In the latter part of that decade, they shifted to the exclusive Ocean Reef Club in Key Largo.

Starting in 1980, they held December meetings for thirteen consecutive years at the fabulous Breakers hotel in Palm Beach. Meetings were held only in the morning. In the afternoon and evening, it was playtime—rich man's style. There were organized tournaments in golf, tennis, and croquet—yes, croquet—that occupied every afternoon. A cocktail party was held one night each year on Bill Wirtz's ninety-foot yacht, the $20 million *Blackhawk*. The meetings closed with an evening of fun at the annual dinner dance, where dozens of expensive Oscar-like trophies were handed out to participants in the golf, tennis, and croquet tournaments. Meanwhile, in a scene right out of *Sabrina*, the governors and their ladies, entertained by intermittent skits, poems, and speeches, danced the night away to sophisticated music provided by a live fifteen-piece band.

Having grown up in a working-class environment, I had never experienced anything like the sybaritic lifestyle of the NHL's governors. I soon got into the spirit of it, however, dressing in my finest whites for the croquet tournament and, each year at the dinner dance, penning and reading a poem that parodied the morning sessions. Ziegler dubbed me the Poet Lawyerate of the NHL. This annual poem became known as the Informal Minutes of the meeting.

During the Great Depression, the famous conductor Leopold Stokowski approached the Du Pont Company about sponsoring a series of Sunday afternoon concerts. Surprisingly, he was able to see Pierre Du Pont himself, to whom he made his pitch. "Nonsense," said Mr. Du Pont firmly, "at three o'clock on Sunday afternoon, everyone is out playing polo." Pierre would have been right at home on the NHL board of governors.

4

Take the Money and Skate

Ideally, the NHL's reputation throughout the hockey world should be akin to that of a powerful King of the Jungle. Viewed from the outside, its board of governors should be seen as a well-oiled machine, a powerful group of sagacious businessmen who steer the NHL ship with a firm hand on the tiller and a cool eye on the horizon. But in reality, the antics of the governors sometimes resemble those of the Gang That Couldn't Shoot Straight. A case in point was the 1990 Plan of Sixth Expansion.

THE EARLY EXPANSIONS

There are different reasons for a professional sports league to expand its membership, but they all have a common denominator—money. Selling expansion franchises is a tried and true way to make quick up-front money. In part, that reason motivated the NHL's first expansion in 1966, when the six-team league doubled its size for the 1967–68 season by granting franchises to Los Angeles, Minnesota, Oakland, Philadelphia, Pittsburgh, and St. Louis. The new members were each charged a fee of $2 million, which of course put $2 million into the pockets of each owner of the original six—Boston, Chicago, Detroit, Montreal, New York, and Toronto. And $2 million was serious money thirty years ago. It reminds me of what Everett Dirksen (longtime Republican leader in the U. S. Senate from Illinois) was fond of saying: "A billion here, a billion there, pretty soon you're talking real money."

But the primary reason for that initial expansion was not the divvying up of expansion fees; it was to obtain major U.S. network television dollars. By expanding to the West Coast, with giant TV markets in Los

Angeles and the San Francisco Bay area, and adding to its lineup other American cities that were among the twenty biggest in the country— Philadelphia, Pittsburgh, Minneapolis-St. Paul, and St. Louis—the NHL was able to get the attention and the dollars of CBS, which signed on for a game-of-the-week package.

The second expansion was effected solely for the purpose of grabbing expansion loot, as the league agreed to grant franchises in Buffalo and Vancouver in 1969 at a per-franchise price of $6 million, thus providing a million-dollar windfall for each of the then twelve members. Adding Buffalo to its U.S. television footprint did very little for the NHL's TV profile. Adding Vancouver did nothing for it. When it comes to calculation of Neilsen ratings, Canadian cities count for zero. It's as if no one lives in them.

By 1971, a new reason for expansion had surfaced: There was talk about the formation of a competing league. A new arena was being built on Long Island, the giant suburban sprawl east of New York City that had suddenly appeared after World War II. A similar threat loomed in Atlanta and in other U.S. cities. To discourage potential owners in major U.S. cities from joining the new league, the NHL board of governors announced an unprecedented three-phase Plan of Third Expansion, which would add teams from Long Island and Atlanta in 1972, two more teams in 1974, and two more in 1976. In case that were not enough to preempt all the good U.S. hockey venues, in 1971 President Clarence Campbell announced that the leading candidates for 1974 Phase II franchises were Cleveland, Kansas City, Miami, Seattle-Portland, and Washington-Baltimore (all among the top twenty-five U.S. television markets), and that the NHL planned to expand to "at least twenty-four teams in North America during the 1970s." Hmm...there were only fourteen teams in the league in 1971. Adding six teams during the three-phase Plan of Third Expansion would bring the total to twenty by 1976. This meant that, in order to reach the twenty-four-team target in the 1970s, four more would be added between 1976 and 1979. The franchise fee to be paid by each of the Third Expansion entrants would still be $6 million, except for Long Island, which was required to pay the $6 million plus an extra $4 million as compensation to the New York Rangers for territorial invasion.

In June 1997, the NHL followed the precedent of the Plan of Third Expansion when it announced a new three-phase plan, expanding to Nashville in 1998, to Atlanta in 1999 and to St. Paul, Minnesota and

Columbus, Ohio, in 2000. Like the Plan of Third Expansion, one of the effects of the 1997 announcement was to preempt the named cities for league expansion and thereby remove them from consideration as targets for relocation by existing teams. Another effect, of course, was to infuse $320 million of added capital into the coffers of the existing NHL clubs, which will provide short-term relief from rising player costs.

The NHL's preemptive strategy achieved initial success early in 1972, leading a number of latent WHA candidates to apply for an NHL franchise instead. The board of governors met at the Gotham Hotel in New York City on May 24 and 25, 1972, and heard presentations by NHL wannabees from Cincinnati, Cleveland, Dallas, Indianapolis, Kansas City, Phoenix, San Diego, and Washington, D. C. At their annual meeting from June 6–8, 1972, at the Queen Elizabeth Hotel in Montreal, the governors awarded Phase II conditional 1974 expansion franchises to Edwin Thompson for Kansas City and Abe Pollin for Washington, D. C. The rejected applicants from Cincinnati, led by William O. DeWitt, said they would be willing to wait until 1976 provided they received a commitment from the NHL that they would be awarded a Phase III franchise. Their request was denied, with no reason given. Cincinnati, Cleveland, Indianapolis, Phoenix, and San Diego subsequently became WHA member cities.

Phase III of the third expansion was an abject failure. At its annual meeting on June 11 and 12, 1974, at the Queen Elizabeth Hotel in Montreal, the board of governors awarded conditional 1976 expansion franchises to Ivan Mullinex for Denver and Vince Abbey for Seattle. Neither could meet the monetary conditions of their franchise grants, however, and there was no expansion for 1976. The "golden age" of expansion had ended prematurely.

The next expansion was in 1979 (and in reality was more a merger than an expansion), when the World Hockey Association disbanded and WHA teams Edmonton, Hartford, Quebec, and Winnipeg were absorbed into the NHL. Although the new teams paid a fee to join, the real purpose of this expansion was to terminate the WHA. The four markets being added did nothing for the league's TV network prospects in America, since three were in Canada and one was in Hartford, which was already an integral part of the New York and Boston area of TV influence. The likelihood of long-term survival of NHL teams in those small markets was rather slim, and the franchises in Quebec, Winnipeg, and Hartford have now moved. Most NHL-watchers believe Edmonton is on deck. It is a very real possibility that the millennium will arrive with none of the former WHA cities left in the NHL.

Forgetting they had called the 1974 expansion Phase II of the Plan of Third Expansion, the board of governors labeled the 1979 expansion the Plan of Fifth Expansion, thus creating this burning question: Did we miss the fourth expansion? Only in the NHL...

PRESSURE BUILDS TO EXPAND AGAIN

And then in 1989 came the Plan of Sixth Expansion, motivated solely by the short-term greed of a majority of NHL governors.

In the late 1980s, new arenas had been built, financed principally through the sale of luxury boxes to corporate buyers. This phenomenon stimulated expansion of the National Basketball Association, which added two teams in the 1988–89 season (Charlotte and Miami) and two more in the 1989–90 season (Minnesota and Orlando). Each of the new teams paid a whopping $32 million for its fledgling franchise. NHL governors were envious and wanted a shot at this new bonanza—and the time was ripe for the next NHL expansion. It had been a full decade since the last one.

Responding to the governors' clamor, President John A. Ziegler Jr. included expansion on the agenda of the board's semi-annual meeting to be held December 7–9, 1989, at the Breakers hotel in Palm Beach, Florida.

In 1968, Burt Bacharach wrote a haunting melody, Hal David penned the lyrics, and Dionne Warwick sang the ballad that was to become one of the greatest hits of the 1960s. None of them knew, however, that two decades later their song—"Do You Know the Way to San Jose?"—was destined to become the unofficial theme song of the NHL's Plan of Sixth Expansion.

On December 7, 1989, the governors gathered at the Breakers with expansion on their minds. The atmosphere was laced with strong San Jose undercurrents. It was known to Ziegler and several governors that Howard Baldwin, who had recently sold his ownership interest in the Hartford Whalers, had been working the hustings of Silicon Valley, and, along with his newly found partner, former Budget Rent-A-Car mogul Morris Belzberg, was prepared to bid on an expansion franchise for the mushrooming California city of San Jose. This gave comfort to Ziegler, since the last thing the NHL needed was to make a big splash announcing it was expanding and then have no takers. That would be embarrassing—like bringing your bass fiddle to a party and no one asks you to play.

Unknown to Ziegler and Baldwin, however, Gordon and George Gund also had their sights set on San Jose. The Gunds had been enduring immense cash losses in Minneapolis and were secretly mapping plans to move their North Stars team to the San Francisco Bay Area, where George resided. The likeliest venue for construction of a new hockey arena in the Bay Area was, you guessed it, San Jose. The Gunds could not afford to let their targeted area be awarded to Baldwin for an expansion team. On the other hand, Ziegler could not afford to lose his one fail-safe expansion site, the San Francisco Bay Area, for fear the league (and Ziegler) might end up humiliated by having no expansion applicants.

The plot thickens. Back to the Breakers and the December 1989 board of governors meeting. The semiannual soiree was always well attended, but this one seemed especially so. After all, there was a smell of money in the air. Sixty governors and alternate governors showed up on Thursday morning, Pearl Harbor Day, to represent the twenty-one member clubs. Add to that, Ziegler and eight league officers. The giant meeting room at the Breakers was bursting at the seams.

Before getting to the business of expansion, let me give you a taste of what goes on at a typical board of governors meeting.

Anticipating a long day, Ziegler had scheduled an 8:30 A.M. start. He called the meeting to order, and, as was his usual custom, made some opening remarks. To no one's surprise, he announced there would be a cocktail party that night at a local mansion, with chauffeur-driven limousines providing transportation. He also described the social activities that would be held at the Breakers on Friday—the golf, tennis, and croquet tournaments in the afternoon, followed by the annual "Jack Krumpe Dinner-Dance" (so-named in fun after the New York Islanders alternate governor, who always objected to it). Bill Wirtz interposed that thirty-four participants had signed up for the croquet tournament, and that they would be entertained on the patio by a string quartet while enjoying their mid-game snack of shrimp and champagne. Ziegler said the morning session would be devoted to a variety of league business matters, and that expansion would be taken up after lunch.

Washington general manager David Poile, chairman of the general managers committee, put through a playing rule amendment increasing the distance from the end boards to the goal line by one foot—a change some felt was aimed at reducing the effectiveness of Flyers goaltender Ron Hextall, whose virtuoso stickhandling ability had enabled him to score a goal into an open net against Poile's Capitals in the 1989 playoffs.

Poile also proposed that eligibility for the Calder Trophy (rookie-of-the-year) be amended to provide that "a player must not have attained the age of twenty-six by September 15 of the season in which he is eligible." The purpose of this amendment was to preclude veteran Iron Curtain players, such as Calgary's thirty-one-year-old import, two-time Soviet Olympic gold medal winner Sergei Makarov, from walking off with "rookie" honors in unfair competition against eighteen- and nineteen-year-old North Americans. For Olympic and world championship eligibility purposes, the Soviet Union and Czechoslovakia had always hypocritically labeled their seasoned hockey pros "amateurs." Poile's proposal received a vote of 14 in favor and 7 opposed, but because of the NHL's policy of requiring a unanimous vote to make an in-season rule change, the motion was defeated. (At season's end, Makarov was awarded the Calder Memorial Trophy, recognizing him for being "the player selected [by the Professional Hockey Writers' Association] as the most proficient in his first year of competition in the National Hockey League." Minnesota's brilliant rookie, nineteen-year-old Mike Modano, was runner-up.)

League Vice President of Broadcast Joel Nixon then reported on the NHL's TV sales outside North America, describing the twice-weekly edited game broadcasts (Monday and Friday) being distributed via European satellite, and NHL games being shown in Sweden, Finland, West Germany, and Italy, with plans to start showing them in Japan and other Pacific rim countries in January. Next, Ziegler reported on the status of the dispute the league was having with the Swedish Ice Hockey Federation over its failure to give recognition to the validity of NHL contracts. He had met with the president of the Swedish Federation in the hope of ironing out the problem, and said one of the obstacles was that NHL clubs were entering into separate agreements with Swedish clubs, which courts or arbitrators could interpret as violating NHL bylaws. At Ziegler's request, a motion was unanimously approved that all agreements between NHL clubs and European clubs or federations that relate to players must be approved by the league and must contain a provision that requires NHL approval for the agreement to be effective.

Calgary's alternate governor, Norman Green, cochairman of the league's Marketing and Public Relations Committee (MPRC), then gave a slide presentation to a darkened meeting room, showing the progress the league had made in building royalty revenues. He said each club would receive $80,000 for fiscal year 1989, which was 50 percent higher than fiscal 1988; that next year was expected to produce $125,000 per club; and that earnings should reach $200,000 per club in the not-too-distant future. He then called upon other members of the MPRC to describe two very significant anniversary celebrations planned for the league. Minnesota alternate governor Lou Nanne spoke of the upcoming 1992 celebration of the seventy-fifth anniversary of the NHL, and Montreal governor Ron Corey discussed the following year's celebration of the one-hundredth anniversary of the Stanley Cup.

The board then approved a motion giving NHL Services, Inc. complete control over All-Star Weekend, after a somewhat heated debate over which seats the host club would be required to make available for league sponsors. (NHL Services, Inc. was the league's profit-making business corporation whose name has since been changed to "NHL Enterprises, Inc."—the National Hockey League itself is a nonprofit corporation.) The MPRC wanted NHL Services to have preemptive rights to purchase "top price" tickets. The compromise voted by the board was that NHL Services would have the right to buy "good" seats.

Ziegler then brought NHL Players' Association executive director R. Alan Eagleson into the meeting room to speak to the board in his capacity as cochairman of the league's International Committee. Eagleson reviewed the history of the NHL-NHLPA partnership in international competition, and described the upcoming year's schedule of Soviet teams' games to be played in North America and NHL preseason games to be played in Russia.

At 1:00 we broke for lunch. Ziegler announced we would reconvene at 2:00 in "executive session" (which in NHL parlance means a limit of two representatives per club) and devote the rest of the day to expansion. Soon the expansion fun would begin.

The afternoon session got underway at 2:10. Ziegler made an introductory statement in which he reviewed written material which had been sent to the governors in advance of the meeting. It had contained findings and recommendations from the Franchise and

Market Analysis Committee relevant to expansion, and also a financial model which league Vice President of Finance Ken Sawyer had structured.

The Sawyer model looked at optimum revenues an expansion club might be able to generate, and showed that, using price-earning ratios of 10 percent to 14 percent, the sale price in the open market of a successful hockey franchise in a state-of-the-art arena could be in the vicinity of $50 million. There is an old saying: Figures don't lie, but liars figure. Sawyer was not a liar, by any means, but neither did he have a crystal ball. His model anticipated a significant revenue stream from the leasing of corporate suites in a newly built arena, but did not take into account that those revenues would likely have to be pledged to the banks to obtain the financing necessary to build the arena. Nor did the model anticipate the astronomic rise in player salaries in the 1990s. (Salaries in the NHL then averaged close to $300,000. At this writing, the average is $1 million, and it continues to climb dramatically each year. The cost of an expansion franchise has also gone up. The NHL is now receiving $80 million for new franchises.) I got the impression none of those monetary realities really mattered to the governors. They seemed concerned only with how much money they could get from an expansion applicant, not whether the new franchise would be financially viable.

In the world of business franchising, a company selling a franchise will generally seek an up-front rights fee and a subsequent cash stream derived from products and services to be supplied to franchisees. I have always advised my clients who were seeking to buy a franchise from a specific franchising company (e.g., McDonald's) to check the percentage of that company's franchises that were operating at a profit after their first, second, and third years. What I have learned is that there are some franchisers, like McDonald's and Little Caesars, who charge fair franchise fees and nurture their franchisees to be sure they succeed. These franchisers measure their own success by the success of their franchisees. Then there are the franchisers who care only about how much up-front money they can grab, and don't give a hoot whether their franchisees survive or go bankrupt. Let's just say that—in this area—the NHL will never be mistaken for McDonald's.

Ziegler referred to a business plan the board of governors had approved a year ago entitled "A Vision for the '90s," in which three basic principles for expansion consideration had been articulated. First, all present teams should be healthy; second, the league should define its markets; and third, the league should make a commitment to growth. He called for a poll to determine whether the governors still supported that plan. (Ziegler's style was to informally poll the governors on controversial issues, to determine the lay of the land before proceeding with formal on-record voting. Polls were conducted by roll call. Each club's name was read aloud, and its governor or alternate governor would respond, asserting his club's view.) The poll results were 19 yes votes, 0 no votes. Two clubs, Detroit and Philadelphia, abstained. The strong support for "A Vision for the '90s," particularly its first principle—that all clubs should be healthy before expansion would be considered—was good news for the Gunds, whose Minnesota franchise was in financial trouble. As they were later to learn to their dismay, however, most governors were merely giving lip service to the "Vision's" principles, and the North Stars' financial woes would not deter their expansion gold rush.

Ziegler next said it was important to establish a critical date path for expansion and recommended that no new team be admitted to play prior to the 1992–93 season. A poll of the members produced unanimous acceptance of his recommendation.

Next, he called for a poll to have the members express their views as to whether they believed the NHL should or should not expand, and why. He cautioned that, to be on the safe side legally, no one was to express an opinion as to whether the prospect of a new league was part of the consideration to expand. He also asked everyone to agree to a gag rule, muzzling themselves regarding any comments to the media for the duration of the meetings, leaving him to be the sole spokesman.

The poll on whether the league should or should not expand, and why, then commenced. For the sake of variety, Ziegler directed that the roll be called in reverse alphabetical order. (The quotes are from personal notes I took at the time.)

Winnipeg (Bill Davis, Jets alternate governor, Winnipeg-based executive with firm owning North American TV and cable companies): "We don't think it can hurt. We're in favor. But we have concerns about divisional realignment."

Washington (Abe Pollin, Capitals owner and governor, who also owned the Washington Bullets in the National Basketball Association): "When the proper time comes for expansion, it is a mistake *not* to expand. The time is now. We should learn from the NBA experience, and consider what is the real value of an NHL franchise. We're awarding not just the right to play in the league, but real estate opportunities and other business tie-ins. Generally, I think the time has come."

Vancouver (Arthur Griffiths, Canucks alternate governor, son of owner Frank A. Griffiths): "We echo the views of Washington and Winnipeg. It's an opportunity to expand our business opportunities."

Toronto (Rosanne Rocchi, Maple Leafs alternate governor, a Toronto attorney who represented owner Harold Ballard): "Harold Ballard feels it is premature to consider expansion. He feels expansion would lead to less competitive games."

St. Louis (Mike Shanahan, St. Louis businessman who was Blues governor, president, and CEO): "We're generally in favor of it. The time is right."

Quebec (Marcel Aubut, Quebec attorney who was Nordiques governor, president, and CEO): "I'm one hundred percent for it. But first, all present teams should be healthy. First choice of sites should be given to existing franchises who wish to move. And we should keep in mind that the next CBA [collective bargaining agreement] may be impacted by expansion considerations."

Pittsburgh (Bill Strong, Penguins alternate governor, who was an accountant in Pittsburgh): "Yes. We're in favor of expansion. New areas in the United States are developing arenas. We could increase our TV exposure."

Philadelphia (Jay Snider, Flyers president and governor, son of owner Ed Snider): "We're in favor. We feel we should have a long-range plan. TV is an important factor. We would like a TV discussion to be part of it."

New York Rangers (Dick Evans, Rangers governor, who was president and CEO of Madison Square Garden Corp., owner of the Rangers and the New York Knicks in the National Basketball Association): "Yes. We're in favor. And we have the same TV concern as Philadelphia."

New York Islanders (John Pickett, owner and governor): "In favor. We should expand where we find teams and territories that qualify. We should profit from past mistakes. It would be foolish to hold back. I agree with Jay Snider that we should look beyond 1992—for eight or ten years—give other cities hope. We should let them know the qualifications are going to be fair—but steep."

New Jersey (John McMullen, Devils owner and governor): "I'm generally in favor, but a lot of things have to be considered. For one, the rule on eighteen-year-olds. We should be able to use our draft picks on our farm teams, instead of having to send them back to Junior hockey. Also, it's very important who the new owners are—the owner is more important than the city."

Montreal (Ronald Corey, Canadiens governor, president, and CEO): "In favor. I agree with what John Pickett said. We should take note that more and more people are putting up buildings."

Minnesota (Gordon Gund, North Stars owner and governor): "No. It's premature. Primarily because condition number one is not in place today. All franchises are not healthy."

Los Angeles (Bruce McNall, Kings owner and governor): "We'd like to see expansion. We'd like to see new cities."

Hartford (Emile Francis, Whalers general manager and alternate governor): "Yes. We'd like to see us get to twenty-four teams. But we're concerned about salaries, travel, single trips to the West Coast. A team has to have a chance to be competitive. We have parity now. It's something to be concerned about. Why not have new franchises start with their own farm team before their NHL franchise starts?"

Edmonton (Peter Pocklington, Oilers owner and governor): "In favor. For all reasons that have been stated."

Detroit (Jim Lites, Red Wings alternate governor, son-in-law of owner Michael Ilitch): "Unequivocally in favor. We prefer *not* to bring in three in one year—we should plan on steady growth. In determining the expansion fee, we should remember that the NBA undervalued their expansion franchises."

Chicago (Bill Wirtz, Blackhawks owner and governor, chairman of the NHL Board of Governors): "In favor of expansion. We must learn from prior mistakes and from the success in the NBA. Realignment must all be laid out in advance. We must get cash up front—no notes. We must be careful about partnership and joint venture agreements. Franchises should be debt free."

Calgary (Cliff Fletcher, Flames general manager and alternate governor): "In favor. Attractiveness of an NHL franchise has never been greater. It will not be as good after the next CBA."

Buffalo (Bob Swados, Sabres minority owner and alternate governor, who also served as NHL secretary): "In favor."

Boston (Harry Sinden, Bruins president, general manager and alternate governor): "In favor. But we should proceed cautiously."

Note that each of the governors and alternate governors who spoke after Gordon Gund of Minnesota ignored the concerns he had expressed, even though this poll was taken within minutes after the board had unanimously agreed to support the three basic principles for expansion consideration, the first of which was "all present teams should be healthy."

But Ziegler picked up on it, and he called on Gund to discuss his concerns. "Look at our basic beliefs," said Gund. "All franchises should have an opportunity to make a profit with good management. All franchises should be concerned. Salary levels in sports have been going up at an accelerated rate. Any slide down the scale of free agency is going to create salary problems for all of us. Player costs will be our largest cost.

"We don't have the luxury of NBC and Turner Network deals, which will provide each NBA club with $9 million per year. The difference in revenues between big-market teams and small-market teams must be addressed. It is being addressed in the NBA now—a committee has been formed to deal with it.

"The problem in the NBA and the NHL is that smaller markets who do not have the opportunity for big dollars from local TV and cable, as larger markets do, cannot compete.

"Minnesota is the smallest area in the United States that has four major league franchises. There are other cities that I suggest share our concern—Winnipeg, Hartford, Los Angeles without Gretzky, St. Louis, and Pittsburgh, to name some.

"There are few components of revenue for a hockey club. It is clear that league-generated revenues are not going to move ahead at the same pace as payroll. Therefore, locally generated revenues, such as gate receipts, have to be shared. Likewise, the revenue generated from local TV and cable.

"The key components of revenue are league-generated revenue, local cable and TV revenue and local gate receipts. A meaningful way has to be found to share these revenue sources."

How ironic it was that Gund, who had no eyesight, was the most prescient person in the room. But you didn't really think his plight would slow the governors' rush for the pot of expansion gold, did you?

Abe Pollin (Washington) asked for the floor. "I'd like to speak to some of the things Gordon spoke about," he said. "The NBA has a salary cap. It's a good thing to limit salaries. But where are our revenues going to come from? There is a definite problem with certain markets in all leagues. There are inequities in the size of markets…and," he said, pausing for effect, "*in the way people run their franchises.*"

Ouch! That hurt. It seemed to be a direct slap at Gund, whom certain governors had criticized (behind his back, of course) for being too extravagant in the administrative overhead of the North Stars.

Pollin continued: "I would suggest that a committee made up of big and small markets be formed by John [Ziegler] to look into this problem. But that should *not* stand in the way of moving ahead with expansion, because the timing is right *now* for expansion."

John McMullen (New Jersey) then spoke. "There's no question that players' salaries is the major problem," he said, invoking one of his favorite themes, "and we don't need a salary cap to maintain salaries at a decent level." (He had long been an advocate of collusive "self-control" among owners.) "But Gordon has a unique problem. And I am against revenue sharing."

John Pickett (New York Islanders) took the floor. "It's unfortunate that Gordon's situation is brought up at the same time as expansion. The issues do not relate. I'd support letting Gordon move at no cost to another city if he so desired. But it's unfair in this set of circumstances to have Minnesota's unfortunate situation related to the issue of expansion. I cannot take my business and project it with doom and gloom re the next CBA.

"I'd support any help for Gordon, other than revenue sharing, whether in conjunction with expansion or otherwise, but it should not interfere with going ahead with expansion."

Dick Evans (New York Rangers) was the next to speak. "I am also on the planning committee of the NBA," he said, "and I can tell you the salary cap does not help the small-market versus big-market problem. We're recognizing that there may be certain markets that will not support a franchise. I would support Abe Pollin's suggestion that a separate committee be formed to study the problem."

Ronald Corey (Montreal) gave his view: "The real question is what is the potential of the Minnesota market, viewing it on the average of good years and bad years. The issue does not relate to the question of whether we expand or not."

Bill Wirtz (Chicago's governor, and chairman of the board of governors) then said: "I feel if any of our present owners wishes to move his franchise, he should discuss it with the president on a confidential basis."

Ziegler then added: "With respect to the Meadowlands, the principle was established that valuation of what a franchise for a new area is worth would be the basis for determining what the franchise transfer fee would be."

Gund could read between the lines. What Ziegler was telling him in NHL-speak was: "Don't be misled by the expressions you are hearing of people willing to let you move. A move will cost you. If you think you are going to be allowed to pick off an NHL expansion site (like San Jose) and deprive your fellow owners of their anticipated expansion fee, think again!"

Jerry Jacobs (Boston) then added his thought to the mix. "I caution everyone to keep in mind that potential transfer by present owners becomes a stalking horse for municipalities seeking an NHL franchise." A sound observation. Why would anyone pay a big fee to the NHL to get an expansion team if an established team could be lured for less money?

Sensing that the mood of the board was to move ahead with expansion, Ziegler called for another poll. "Thinking in terms of no sooner than 1992," he said, "tell us whether you favor expanding by one team only or by more than one team, and if more than one, what do you feel as to the timing?"

This time the roll call started with Washington, still going in reverse alphabetical order.

Washington (Abe Pollin): "Three teams at one time. I would also consider future additional teams."

Vancouver (Arthur Griffiths): "Three at the same time."

Toronto (Rosanne Rocchi): "One. Preferably on the West Coast."

St. Louis (Mike Shanahan): "Three. All at once."

Quebec (Marcel Aubut): "Three at the same time. Plus plan for future expansion."

Pittsburgh (Bill Strong): "Three at the same time."

Philadelphia (Jay Snider): "Three at the same time in Hockey Country [an expression used in "Vision of the 90's" to describe geographical locations where hockey was popular]. Into the '90s on a missionary basis."

New York Rangers (Dick Evans): "Three at the same time, with the possibility of additional teams at a later date."

New York Islanders (John Pickett): "Three for 1992. Target a group for the '90s. Consider an additional four teams."

New Jersey (John McMullen): "Three at once. No more in the '90s."

Montreal (Ronald Corey): "Three at once."

Minnesota (Gordon Gund): "No more than one."

Los Angeles (Bruce McNall): "Three at once. Possible future expansion."

Hartford (Emile Francis): "Three for '92–'93, with a plan to expand further in the '90s. Encourage all cities."

Edmonton (Peter Pocklington): "Three in '92, four or so more in the '90s. Take option fees from cities."

Detroit (Jim Lites): "Three at the same time."

Chicago (Bill Wirtz): "Three at once."

Calgary (Cliff Fletcher): "Three at once. Same as Hartford, encourage others for the future."

Buffalo (Bob Swados): "Three in '92–'93, and further plan for expansion to approach the number of markets of other leagues."

Boston (Harry Sinden): "Three at once. Reserve judgment for the future to see how they work."

Winnipeg (Bill Davis): "Three in '92–'93. More later if there are available markets and owners."

It was clear where the sentiments lay. Everyone but Gund was eager to expand. The consensus was to go for three in 1992.

The hour was getting late, and the cocktail party awaited. Ziegler adjourned the meeting for the day.

The next morning the board convened at 8:00 A.M., but the first hour was devoted to hearing a report from SportsChannel officers Marc Lustgarten and Jeff Ruhe, who painted a rosy picture of the growth they anticipated in their network's distribution of hockey programming. The board then moved into executive session to continue its expansion deliberations.

Ziegler reviewed one of the recommendations of the Franchise and Market Analysis Committee (FMAC), which was that a nonrefundable application fee of $100,000 should be required of each expansion aspirant, with the money to be used to cover the expenses of a thorough examination of the applicant and the proposed franchise site. He directed that the board be polled to determine if clubs supported that recommendation. The roll was called in reverse alphabetical order, starting with Vancouver.

Vancouver, Toronto, and St. Louis voted yes. Then Marcel Aubut of

Quebec voted no, expressing his belief the application fee should be refunded if a franchise were not granted.

Pittsburgh then voted yes, but Jay Snider of Philadelphia voted no, saying he could accept a portion of the application being nonrefundable, but not the full $100,000. Thereafter, the New York Rangers, Minnesota, Los Angeles, and Hartford all voted yes, but the New York Islanders, New Jersey, Montreal, Edmonton, Detroit, Chicago, Calgary, and Boston agreed with the Aubut-Snider position and voted no. Buffalo abstained. The final tally showed only nine clubs favored a nonrefundable deposit.

Ziegler then discussed another FMAC recommendation, that one of the conditions for granting an expansion franchise should be a requirement that at least ten thousand season tickets be sold before final grant, and that such requirement remain in force for a designated number of years. A poll showed this idea had unanimous support, with the consensus that the requirement should remain in effect for the new franchise's first three years. The next poll showed unanimous approval for requiring that the ten thousand season tickets sold must have an average price no less than the league's projected average ticket price.

There was then a discussion of the FMAC's concern over what ownership investment structure should be required of applicants. A poll showed the clubs felt the league should only indicate the "preferred" structure, capitalization, and debt-to-equity ratio, rather than make anything a rigid requirement. The meeting was then adjourned for the day so the Friday afternoon golf, tennis, and croquet tournaments could commence.

On Saturday morning, the board started in executive session to address the key question of what the expansion fee should be. No one talked about how an expansion franchise could earn enough to justify paying a huge fee, although Ziegler did review the Sawyer model. No, they never talked about *how*, only *how much*—and all of it would have to be in U.S. dollars, no notes.

Knowing the NBA had received $32 million in expansion fees from each of its newest members, Buffalo governor Seymour Knox thought he was reaching for the moon when he stood up and suggested: "Since we have twenty-one clubs, why not ask $42 million, so we would have $2 million per club?" It turned out he was a piker. His colleagues wanted more. A Ziegler poll produced the following suggested prices for an NHL expansion franchise:

$40 Million		$40 to $50 Million	$42 Million
New York Rangers		Minnesota	Buffalo

$45 Million	$50 Million	$60 Million	$65 Million
Philadelphia	Calgary	Boston	Pittsburgh
	Detroit	Edmonton	
	Hartford	New Jersey	
	Los Angeles	New York Islanders	
	Montreal		
	Quebec		
	St. Louis		
	Toronto		
	Vancouver		
	Washington		
	Winnipeg		

Bill Wirtz of Chicago abstained, stating his view would differ depending upon whether there were one, two, or three teams.

The meeting adjourned after the governors approved a resolution proposed by Ziegler that the league would grow to twenty-eight teams by the year 2000, and that the first step would be expansion by one or more teams for the 1992–93 season.

Take a good look at the nuance of Ziegler's resolution. By saying the first step would be expansion "by *one or more* teams," Ziegler had covered his flank. He was banking on former Hartford Whalers owner Howard Baldwin to apply for an expansion franchise for San Jose. If no one else applied, Ziegler and the league would not lose face because they had stated publicly one of the options they were considering was to expand by only one team ("one or more") in 1992.

OTTAWA OR BUST

A year later, the governors again converged on the Breakers in Palm Beach, Florida, for what would be one of their more momentous semi-annual meetings. Expansion franchises were to be awarded for 1992–93, but Baldwin was not an applicant. Expansion sites were to be considered for 1992–93, but San Jose was not among them—a San Jose expansion franchise for 1991–92 had already been awarded to Gordon and George Gund. How come? What happened to the Minnesota North Stars? You'll find out later, in chapter 6. For now, let's concentrate on expansion developments at the semiannual meeting which was held on December 4–8, 1990.

The board of governors had approved the formal Plan of Sixth Expansion on May 8, 1990, and application packages had thereafter been made available to potential applicants upon request. The deadline for submitting applications was August 15, 1990, with each one accompanied by a check for $100,000. If the board were to reject the application, $65,000 would be returned. Were an application to be withdrawn prior to the board's acceptance or rejection, up to 100 percent of the application fee, but not less than 35 percent, would be retained by the league as compensation for the expenditure of cash and personnel time in processing the application up to the time of withdrawal.

By the time of the semiannual meeting in December, nine applications were under review by the board. Expansion franchises were being sought for two Canadian cities in the province of Ontario: Hamilton and Ottawa; and six U.S. cities: Miami, St. Petersburg, Tampa, Seattle (two separate applications), San Diego, and Anaheim. Ziegler and the governors could not believe their good fortune. A year ago, they had been apprehensive that no one would pay them $50 million for an expansion franchise. Now, nine applicants were clamoring to do so. Could it be $50 million was too low?

Prior to the meeting, league consultants, staff, and counsel had reviewed the applications and done market research into the viability of the proposed sites for hockey, but, just like the Miss America pageant, the board would make the final decision based on personal interviews with the applicants. The board set aside the entire day of Wednesday, December 5, to hear presentations by the nine applicants, whose interviews were scheduled forty-five minutes apart:

    9:00—Miami: Godfrey Wood and John Henry
    9:45—Seattle: Bill Lear and Bill Ackerley
   10:30—Seattle: Christopher Larson and Bill MacFarland
   11:15—Ottawa: Bruce Firestone and Randy Sexton
   12:00—San Diego: Ballard Smith and Scott Wolfe
   12:45—Lunch Break
    1:45—Hamilton: Ronald V. Joyce and Gerry Patterson

2:30—St. Petersburg: Peter Karmanos Jr. and Jim Rutherford
3:15—Tampa: Phil Esposito and Mel Lowell
4:00—San Diego/Anaheim: Jerry Buss and Ken Doi

The atmosphere at the Breakers was wild and wacky. The media were there in hordes—not just from applicant cities, but from all the NHL cities in North America. A full-time hospitality tent was set up on the hotel's side lawn to accommodate them with a place to hang out during the long hours between Ziegler's twice-daily press briefings. The air was filled with loud and festive music from a marching band and cheering section that Bruce Firestone's Ottawa group had flown down to Florida.

The furniture in the board of governors' meeting room was reshuffled from its normal long conference table format to an amphitheater-type setting, arranged so the applicants would sit at their table facing three circular stepped-up tiers of tables, each tier elevated by two feet over the one in front. On the tables were large name cards facing the applicants table, which identified the governors and their clubs, and also told the governors where to sit. It was a very impressive sight, and reminded me of the meetings of the United Nations Security Council usually shown on TV when important world political events were taking place.

The first to appear were Godfrey Wood and John Henry, who had applied for a franchise in Miami. Wood was a former Harvard All-American hockey star and a present promoter. Henry was the man with the money, and thus he did all the talking. It soon became evident there were serious problems with this applicant. Henry had no commitment for an arena in which to play hockey games, although he hoped to become a tenant in a new arena that he expected the NBA's Miami Heat would build. He had no answer when asked what his plans for a building would be if the Heat decided to stay put in the Miami Arena. The capper came when Henry proclaimed he was unwilling to pay $50 million in cash for an NHL franchise, but would be willing to enter into negotiations with the league for a lower fee, part of which would be contingent upon his franchise making a profit. We all heard a giant but silent "Gong!" as Ziegler thanked him and said, "We'll get back to you after the board's deliberations have been concluded." One down, eight to go.

Next up were the first Seattle applicants, Seattle businessmen Bill Lear and Bill Ackerley. Ackerley did the talking, and made it clear his only interest was in building and operating a new arena, in which an NHL team in Seattle would play. He described his plans for a new

(Left) NHL President John A. Ziegler Jr. (left) shakes hands with NHLPA Executive Director Robert W. Goodenow upon termination of the 1992 player's strike, which cost Ziegler his job. (Bruce Bennett Studios)

(Below) A grim-faced Bob Goodenow as executive director of the NHLPA (left) appears uncomfortable attending a hockey game alongside his predecessor, Alan Eagleson. On Eagleson's left is NHL President John Ziegler's wife, Kay. (Bruce Bennett Studios)

Michael Eisner welcomes Paul Kariya after the Mighty Ducks make him their first pick (fourth pick overall) in the 1993 Entry Draft. (Bruce Bennett Studios)

Gary B. Bettman became the NHL's number 1 man when he took office as the league's first commissioner on February 1, 1993. (Bruce Bennett Studios)

Ottawa boosters engage in one of their many parades at the Breakers hotel during the December 1990 Palm Beach meeting of the board of governors. Their enthusiasm enlivened the atmosphere as the governors pondered who would be awarded expansion franchises. (Bruce Bennett Studios)

"I'm going to Disneyland!" Minnie Mouse holds Blockbuster video cassettes in her lap while (left to right) Michael Eisner, Bruce McNall, Gil Stein, and Wayne Huizenga join Mickey Mouse in the December 1992 announcement that expansion franchises have been awarded to Anaheim and Florida. (Andy Stein memorabilia)

Participants in the NHL governors' annual croquet tournament pose for a team picture at the Breakers hotel in Palm Beach. Men, left to right, (standing) Richard Patrick, Jack Krumpe, Gil Stein; (kneeling) Barry Shenkarow, Michael Wirtz, Scotty Morrison, Bill Wirtz. (Bruce Bennett Studios)

Kansas City Scouts owner Edwin G. Thompson (left) and Washington Capitals owner Abe Pollin (right) join NHL President Clarence Campbell in celebrating the birth of their 1974 expansion franchises. (Bruce Bennett Studios)

Longtime NHL President Clarence Campbell (left) poses alongside his youthful successor, John A. Ziegler Jr. (Bruce Bennett Studios)

High-powered club presidents convene on the floor of the Hartford Civic Center during the 1994 NHL Entry Draft. From left: Phil Esposito (Tampa Bay Lightning), Bill Torrey (Florida Panthers), Glen Sather (Edmonton Oilers). (Bruce Bennett Studios)

Francis "King" Clancy (left) joins with Toronto owner Harold Ballard (right) during the 1977 playoffs in spoofing Ontario attorney general Roy McMurtry's campaign against hockey violence. (Philadelphia Flyers Archives)

Sam Pollock, president and general manager of the Montreal Canadiens, was not taken in by the Old Guard's 1976 attempt to make Clarence Campbell chairman of the NHL board of governors. Said Pollock: "My name is Tucker, not sucker." (Bruce Bennett Studios)

The Broad Street Bullies achieved a worldwide reputation when they defeated the Soviet Red Army team, 4–1, at the Spectrum on January 11, 1976. Two days later, this cartoon appeared in Moscow in the Soviet youth newspaper "*Komsomolskaya Pravda*." (Andy Stein memorabilia)

Flyers defenseman Joe Watson had one thought in mind after he received a nasty skate cut under his eye in 1973: "Two days, Gilly, get us two days!" He wanted an extra day to party before his upcoming criminal trial in Vancouver. (Philadelphia Flyers Archives)

Philadelphia Flyers winger Bill "Cowboy" Flett, one of the Vancouver Seven facing criminal charges in Vancouver in June 1973. While awaiting trial, his beard was set on fire by fellow defendant Barry Ashbee. (Philadelphia Flyers Archives)

Flyers center Bill Clement (number 10) was never one to shy away from violent confrontations. Now an urbane hockey color commentator for ESPN, he was arrested in February 1975 after battling with New York Rangers fans outside Madison Square Garden. (Philadelphia Flyers Archives)

Enigmatic Flyers coach Fred Shero—shown here at the end of the Flyers bench during pregame cogitation—maintained that coaching was the loneliest of all professions. (Philadelphia Flyers Archives)

Seattle arena that would seat 16,000-plus for hockey, but said he could not offer a lease on the terms outlined in the Plan of Sixth Expansion. (One of the plan's requirements was a favorable lease for the expansion team, which would insure an adequate cash flow along the lines projected in the Sawyer model.) He outlined generally what terms he could offer a hockey tenant, which did not include any revenue from corporate suites. He said all suite revenues were pledged in order to obtain construction financing.

Lear's interest was the concession business in the proposed new arena. He said he had a concession contract with Sports Service of Buffalo, but disclaimed any interest in obtaining an NHL expansion team and formally requested that the Lear-Ackerley application be withdrawn. He said, "If you'd like to hear Larson's presentation, you're welcome to do so," but advised us Larson (the other applicant for a Seattle franchise) was no more interested in getting an expansion franchise than he was. As they were about to head for the exit, Ziegler acknowledged the withdrawal of their application and thanked them for the interest they had shown. We were 0 for 2. Things were not looking good. The best thing we had going for us was the hope that those outside the room did not know what was going on.

Soon after the second Seattle applicants, Christopher Larson and Bill MacFarland, entered the room, we learned that Lear's appraisal of their lack of serious interest was on all fours. Larson was a young executive who had worked for Bill Gates at Microsoft and had made a lot of money with his Microsoft stock. Bill McFarland, a former minor league hockey executive, was in the insurance business in Phoenix. Larson stated immediately that, although he had an interest in seeing NHL hockey come to Seattle, he was not prepared to pay $50 million for an expansion franchise. 0 for 3!

Next came Ottawa. Their delegation, headed by upbeat Ottawa real estate promoter Bruce Firestone, was the clear winner of the "Most Enthusiastic Applicant" award, with their marching band, cheerleaders, banners, and literature being almost as ubiquitous in the Breakers as the little signs that said "Gentlemen must wear ties and jackets after 5 P.M." But, based upon the premeeting sentiment of the governors, it seemed that was all they would win. A number of governors were against adding another team from a small Canadian city, and even among those who felt political expediency required that if we were to add three teams, one should be from Canada, most favored Hamilton over Ottawa. Yet, one never knows. Games are won on the ice, not in the newspapers. As we say in hockey, that's why the games are played.

Firestone brought his energy and enthusiasm into the meeting room, and delivered a first-class offering to the governors, starting with the showing of a special videotape extolling Ottawa's virtues. He described in very optimistic terms the relative affluence of the fan base, and had Ottawa's mayor on hand to assure the NHL of the cooperation Firestone would receive from the local government in his plan to build a new arena. At least he was making a major league effort, unlike the others who had preceded him.

Firestone's message was positive and to the point. He wanted a team in 1992. He'd be ready to play in 1992. And, of course, the best part was that which was unspoken. He was the first applicant who raised no question about the $50 million fee. At last, a live one! Maybe our luck was changing.

Energized by Firestone's positive presentation, an eager welcome greeted the first of the San Diego aspirants, a nine-man delegation headed by California promoters Ballard Smith, Scott Wolfe, and Harry Cooper. The air quickly went out of this particular balloon, however, when these gentlemen made it clear they were not serious applicants for a 1992, or even a 1993, expansion team. What they were seeking was a strong statement of support from the NHL for: San Diego as a hockey city; and secondly their group, so they could work on getting a new arena built. One of their members, Ron Hahn, said they were hoping for a 1996 start, although he allowed it was possible they might be prepared to start a year or two earlier, in a small building, provided we were to send a public message that we saw San Diego as an NHL city, that we felt theirs was a strong group, and that if they were to build a new building, the NHL would be there.

Cooper said they would allow the NHL thirty days to give them the commitment they sought, and if we did, they would make a $5 million down payment and hope to firm up the deal in March of 1994. Was this guy for real??

Next!

It was lunchtime. The morning had been almost a complete washout. We had seen our hopes dashed that major U.S. cities Miami, San Diego, and Seattle might be joining the NHL. All we could do was hope the afternoon would be better. It could hardly be worse.

At 1:45 P.M. we welcomed the Hamilton applicants, promoter Gerry

Patterson and deep-pocket Ronald V. Joyce, owner of the successful Canadian donut chain, Tim Horton Donuts. Hamilton is a major city in Ontario, located within forty miles of Toronto. They made an excellent impression on the board—up to a point. They had all the right credentials: ownership, market, fan support, and a favorable lease with an excellent NHL-quality playing facility. (Long before the Kevin Costner film *Field of Dreams*, the NHL experienced the "Build it and they will come" phenomenon when Hamilton's city fathers built the Victor K. Copps Trade Center, a.k.a. Copps Coliseum, in hopes of attracting an NHL team.)

But Joyce did himself in by falling into the trap of questioning the expansion fee. Someone must have misled him into believing a purpose of the interview was to negotiate price with the league. So he tarnished what was an otherwise sterling presentation by telling the board he was not prepared to pay the $50 million the league was demanding.

Instead, he proposed to pay $5 million now, $10 million in March 1992, and $10 million more on September 1, 1992, for a total of $25 million by the time his team would start to play, and thereafter he would pay $5 million a year for each of the following five years.

Ziegler thanked him and said the board would consider his proposal. When Joyce left the room, Ziegler breathed a sigh of relief. He had been concerned about the Joyce application, because the Toronto and Buffalo owners were both claiming Hamilton was located within their exclusive territory and therefore each felt he had the right to either veto a Hamilton franchise award or at the very least receive a substantial payment from the applicants as territorial indemnification. Denying Hamilton a franchise under the terms of the Plan of Sixth Expansion for either of those reasons would have likely triggered an uncomfortable lawsuit. Now that Joyce had chosen to back away from the terms he had agreed to when he filed his application, Ziegler knew the league was off the hook. After Joyce had gone, Ziegler quietly said to me, "He made it easy for us."

We may have avoided a bullet, but with six down and only three to go, we were still left with a big void in expansion candidates, and we had come up dry in our target U.S. cities. The battle of Tampa Bay was coming up next.

First in was the St. Petersburg applicant, Peter Karmanos Jr., the principal owner of Compuware Corp., whose contingent included Jim Rutherford, Lou Beer, and Ralph Caponigro. Rutherford, a former

NHL goalkeeper, had played 465 games for Detroit, Pittsburgh, Toronto, and Los Angeles between 1970 and 1983. In those thirteen seasons he had never been called upon to make a more important save than the one Karmanos would need before this day ended.

Karmanos came into the meeting room brimming with confidence. He had become well acquainted with Board of Governors Chairman Bill Wirtz, and the confidential feedback Wirtz had given him convinced him he was set. The NHL was seeking a presence in Florida, and his competitor for a Tampa Bay franchise, former hockey superstar Phil Esposito, was generally considered too thinly capitalized to merit serious consideration. In addition, Karmanos had a secret weapon— NHL Players Association Executive Director Alan Eagleson. Eagleson had clout with Ziegler and Wirtz, and had actively lobbied governors on Karmanos's behalf. (A lengthy indictment issued against Eagleson in 1995 by the U.S. Attorney's office in Boston included an allegation that Eagleson had an undisclosed secret agreement with Karmanos under which Eagleson was to be paid a fee of $1 million for helping Karmanos obtain an NHL franchise. That agreement may not have been applicable to the NHL's Plan of Sixth Expansion, but clearly Karmanos had friends in high places. Eagleson, who refused to waive extradition, has not yet been brought to trial in Boston).

Rutherford was the leadoff batter for team Karmanos. He spoke about the state of the economy, which was experiencing a downturn. He said the ongoing competition within the Tampa Bay market between Tampa (Esposito) and St. Petersburg (Karmanos) inhibited their opportunity to mount a season ticket drive. He discussed St. Petersburg's new arena, the Sundome. It was no secret many governors did not consider it adequate for NHL play. Still, Rutherford praised it and said the Karmanos group felt it was a great facility, but, in deference to what they had heard about the governors' views, they were prepared to address any concerns the league had about the building.

Next up was Beer, who seemed to be Karmanos's marketing person. He startled everyone by saying what Karmanos was seeking was a conditional franchise for six months. He said they fully understood the league's desire for a $5 million down payment, but they were not yet prepared to give it, and would first have to conclude a firm deal on a new permanent building were the league to tell them they needed one. He disclosed that their Suncoast Dome lease provided that if they were required by the

NHL to play in a different facility, they were permitted to exit the lease. I got the impression they were hoping the league would do so.

Beer laid out four reasons why Karmanos wanted the league to reject the Esposito group's Tampa application and give him the six month exclusive option he was seeking. First, he could conclude, in principle, a firm building deal. Second, he could conduct "due diligence," testing the corporate market for the sale of luxury boxes. Third, he could conduct a market analysis for hockey in the Tampa Bay area. Fourth, with competition from the Esposito group eliminated, he could establish a season ticket drive and do other presales. Beer assured the governors that, in not more than six months, they would be in a position to know whether an NHL franchise could be successful in Tampa Bay.

We next heard from Caponigro, whom I gathered was Karmanos's financial man. He reiterated Rutherford's gloomy view of the downturn in the economy, citing a number of factors, including the new tax laws and the increase in the gasoline tax.

"We want to respect your desire to receive $50 million," he said, "and we think we have a solution. We will pay $50 million for the franchise, but not in up-front cash. Instead, if we decide after our six-month exclusivity period to purchase the franchise, we will pay you $5 million on July 1, 1991, $10 million on December 13, 1991, and $14 million on July l, 1992, so you will have been paid $29 million by the time our team starts to play. Then, for the next seven years, we will pay you $3 million at the end of each year, provided it has been earned from a 50 percent share of profit or gross advertising revenues."

Karmanos then summed up. He confirmed what those before him had said—that he wanted a conditional six-month franchise to be extended to him by the NHL, after which, if he so elected, he would pay $29 million in cash, with the balance of $21 million to be paid over the following seven years, but only if certain profit and revenue contingencies were met.

The governors were pissed. Wirtz looked particularly glum. He liked Karmanos, and had spoken up for him to a number of governors. Now it seemed he had been used. Karmanos had not breathed a word to him that he was going to try to parlay the Wirtz-created goodwill into a bargain-basement deal so he could get a franchise for $29 million plus smoke and mirrors.

Ziegler politely, but grimly, thanked Karmanos and told him the governors would give his request due consideration. Karmanos and his party left the room.

Next up were the Tampa applicants, a group headed by Phil Esposito. They passed the Karmanos party on their way in. Phil had no way of knowing it, but his stock had never been higher.

They showed a videotape about Tampa. Mel Lowell, a former New York Rangers financial officer, said they had raised $124 million, and $80 million had been committed to finance a new arena. He talked about another $44 million that would be raised by the Tampa Bay Hockey Group. He described the Japanese businessmen who were underwriting the project. But with all that was said, what was unsaid was most important. As in the Ottawa presentation, no one said anything about not paying the $50 million.

After what the governors had heard all day, it was becoming clear that was all it would take. Like in that old Groucho Marx TV show, *You Bet Your Life,* I could see the little duck pop into view and hear Groucho's voice, "Say the magic words, win an expansion franchise." And what were the magic words? "We'll pay the $50 million!"

The final presentation was a nonevent. Former Los Angeles Kings owner Jerry Buss was seeking to control the rights to two 1993–94 conditional franchise areas—San Diego and Anaheim—in speculation that by doing so, he could position himself to become a player in potential new building deals in those sites. But he was not seeking a franchise under the terms of the Plan of Sixth Expansion. So, it was nice to see you again, Jerry—keep in touch.

The long day was over. The governors went to their hotel rooms, dressed, then headed for the sumptuous Florida estate of Boston's Jerry Jacobs, who was hosting a posh dinner party for the governors and the applicants. There was a lot of glad-handing during the cocktail hour, but the applicants received no insight as to what the governors might decide the next day.

AND THEN THERE WERE TWO

At 9:00 A.M. on Thursday, December 6, 1990, the governors met to witness the birth of two new franchises.

Ziegler opened the meeting by reviewing the status of the applications. The two Seattle applications had been withdrawn. The San Diego and Anaheim-San Diego applicants were seeking commitments for 1993 and beyond. The Ottawa and Tampa applicants had agreed to meet the terms of the Plan of Sixth Expansion. The Hamilton, Miami, and St. Petersburg applicants did not accept the NHL's terms and had made counteroffers. Ziegler called for a discussion to determine whether there was any sentiment for amending the Plan of Sixth Expansion.

Calgary (Cliff Fletcher): "I am against making any changes."

Detroit (Mike Ilitch): "My feeling is that up to now we've done a good job. But we've got to look to the future—new arenas, and television. We should be the ones directing to what markets we wish to go. We have the ability to select our cities, go in, and make it happen. We should look at the ADIs [TV areas of dominant influence] and place teams in those markets which will place us in an advantageous position for television." (Mike had the right idea. Instead of casting a huge net on the waters in the hope of catching some fish, the NHL should direct its focus to where franchises are needed to create a better product for network television. And, of course, that is exactly what the league has since done, with new franchises now in place in Anaheim, Miami, Dallas, Denver, and Phoenix—all big television markets—and with Atlanta, Nashville, St. Paul and Columbus soon to follow.)

Wasington (Abe Pollin): "I'm puzzled. I don't understand applicants coming in here and trying to negotiate with us. I think that's bullshit. In the NBA, we did not consider varying and taking less than what our plan called for. I wouldn't waste any time even considering any of them other than the two which applied under our terms."

Boston (Jerry Jacobs): "By and large, I would say that the committee had the obligation to filter the applications for you. You should not have had to listen to all that stuff."

President Ziegler: "The board did not authorize the committee to reject applicants."

Quebec (Marcel Aubut): "We should learn for the future from the process."

Minnesota (Norman Green): "We should accept at least one for $50 million, to send a message for the future that $50 million is the price. I would *not* change the process."

Edmonton (Peter Pocklington): "We'd get a black eye if we turned down Hamilton." (Peter was up to something with Hamilton, but no one could figure out what.)

Montreal (Ron Corey): "What I have seen yesterday is that there are not too many businessmen willing to pay $50 million. We should answer the question whether the $50 million is our first priority, or is it getting the right cities for TV."

Philadelphia (Jay Snider): "I agree with what Ron said, and also Mike Ilitch. We have to adjust to the law of supply and demand. The NBA got $32 million. If we had set $32 million as the price, we might have had eight or ten applicants. We should consider revising our terms—taking less up front, more in notes on the back end."

Calgary (Cliff Fletcher): "Miami, St. Pete, and Hamilton lowballed us."

Chicago (Bill Wirtz): "A year ago we made our statement that we wished to expand to twenty-eight teams. We awarded one." [San Jose—to the Gunds. But that's another story.] "We have other applicants. There's a group in Miami that wants to build a new building next to Joe Robbie Stadium. There's a group in Houston willing to go. I think there's good stuff out there. My notes say there are too many holes in the Ottawa and Tampa situations. I could not vote for them." (Maybe William W. Wirtz could not vote for them, but "Dollar Bill" Wirtz could—and did.)

Boston (Jerry Jacobs): "All teams that went into the NBA controlled their own destinies. I think there's something to be said for having the expansion committee develop target markets. We need to identify the markets we want, and equally important, we need to identify the people we want in those markets." (Bulls-eye! Just like Mike Ilitch, Jerry had the good business sense to put his finger on a key to sound expansion—target the cities we want and go after them. But he added another ingredient—target the people we want as owners and go after them! It is the path I would follow in 1992 in bringing Blockbuster's Huizenga [Florida Panthers] and Disney's Eisner [Anaheim Mighty Ducks] into the league.)

Pittsburgh (Paul Martha): "Just what do we want to accomplish during the next few days. Do we want to award conditional franchises?"

Edmonton (Peter Pocklington): "If we do not grant two franchises to Tampa and Ottawa, we'll look like complete idiots." (Should we have been shocked at Peter's quicksilver—or, should I say "quick gold"—abandonment of Hamilton?)

Washington (Richard Patrick): "I agree with Peter. We have two real good applications here. I'm all for identifying markets for future expansions. But we have to deal with what's before us."

Montreal (Ron Corey): "I think we have to look at the two teams.

Ottawa will be successful—no doubt—it's a strong hockey market. Tampa is a nonhockey market, but it is a strong TV market." (Earlier, Ron had said we must decide whether our priority was getting the $50 million or getting the right cities for TV. Having thought about it, he concluded Ottawa and Tampa met both tests.)

Winnipeg (Barry Shenkarow): "Ten years ago, if we had looked only at TV, we would not have approved Edmonton and Calgary—yet they are strong members of this league. Ottawa has worked for two years—they will be a strong partner—we have to look at them on the merits of their application. If we simply reject Ottawa because they are in Canada, we're going to have a real problem." (No chance that they'll be rejected, Barry. They said the magic words.)

Hartford (Emile Francis): "If bullshit were music, we had a couple of brass bands march through here yesterday. We've stirred the pot. If we were to tell the people out there we're not interested after telling them for a year that we were, we'd have a real problem."

NY Islanders (John Pickett): "TV is important, and will be someday, but maybe not in our lifetime. If you look at the map, you know we're going to need to add Tampa, Miami, Atlanta, Houston, San Diego, Seattle, and someone from Canada. We're going to have to take some of these. I'm taking on face value what Ottawa and Tampa say." (John was never one to turn up his nose at 100 million big ones.)

Washington (Abe Pollin): "I agree with John [Pickett]. This board set a price. We have two teams that I'm impressed with. If we postpone a decision, that will be a terrible message to the rest of the world. We cannot tell these two teams that we don't accept them. Ottawa definitely should come in. They've got the money. Let's go with them."

Ziegler: "Let me suggest a hypothetical scenario. What about thinking in terms of Ottawa for 1992, and granting Tampa a franchise today for 1993? And then we could give authority to the expansion committee to work on bringing in Houston, Miami, San Diego, and others."

Mixed Chorus: "No." "Do them both now." "Take the money now." "Deal with the future later."

Ziegler: "Hokay, hokay, I hear you. Let's take a poll. I would like an expression of opinion on whether you are in favor of Ottawa coming in now under the terms and conditions of the Plan of Sixth Expansion."

A roll call poll was taken. The vote was unanimous, 20–0–1 (Philadelphia abstained), in favor of granting Ottawa a franchise for 1992.

At Ziegler's direction, a poll was then taken on Tampa. The approval vote was unanimous, 21–0.

Abe Pollin then made a formal motion that the Ottawa and Tampa applicants be granted conditional memberships for commencement of play in the 1992 season, under the terms of the Plan of Sixth Expansion. Peter Pocklington seconded the motion, and it was unanimously approved by a 21–0 vote.

And that was how the Ottawa Senators and Tampa Bay Lightning came to be, and why the applicants from Miami, San Diego, Anaheim, Hamilton, and St. Petersburg got the gate. As some Washington politicians have been known to say, "Money talks and bullshit walks!"

But that was not to be the last expansion while I was with the league. As president, I steered the league to another expansion in December 1992. The way I did it had never been done before.

THE MICKEY MOUSETRAP

The 1990 process highlighted the shortcomings of the league's haphazard approach to expansion. Jerry Jacobs and Mike Ilitch knew the right way to do it was to first ascertain why, and where, the league needed to expand. I got the chance to do that when I became president of the NHL.

On the morning of June 22, 1992, in the midst of the Seventy-Fifth Annual Meeting of the Board of Governors, at the Radisson Gouverneurs Hotel in Montreal, the board met in extraordinary executive session. The only ones present were Ziegler, Board Secretary Robert O. Swados and one governor (or alternate governor) per club. Along with the other league vice presidents, I was excluded from the meeting room, but directed to be available "on call" at my hotel room.

Ziegler had told me and the other vice presidents a week before the meeting that he was going to resign as president, and had negotiated an agreement with the board on his severance package. After hearing that, I called Board Chairman Bill Wirtz and asked if I should be out looking for a job. "No, Gil," he said. "Your job is safe. Just stay where you are."

About 11:30 on the morning of June 22, I was called on the phone and told to come immediately to the board's meeting room. When I entered, the governors were standing around in four small groups, engaged in informal discussions. Ziegler was not in the room. Los Angeles owner Bruce McNall met me at the door. He told me he had been elected chairman of the board of governors, Ziegler had resigned effective October 1, 1992, and I had been elected to succeed Ziegler as president, and was being given all the powers of the president, effective immediately. He said both his election as chairman and mine as president had been by unanimous vote. He also said he would be chairing a search committee whose job it would be to find someone to become the league's first commissioner. It was a lot for me to digest on such short notice.

He called the meeting to order and introduced me as the new president. Everyone stood and applauded. Present were Jerry Jacobs (Boston), Seymour Knox III (Buffalo), Harley Hotchkiss (Calgary), Bill Wirtz (Chicago), Jim Lites (Detroit), Peter Pocklington (Edmonton), Richard Gordon (Hartford), Norman Green (Minnesota), Ron Corey (Montreal), John McMullen (New Jersey), Bill Torrey (New York Islanders), Stanley Jaffe (New York Rangers), Bruce Firestone (Ottawa), Ed Snider (Philadelphia), Howard Baldwin (Pittsburgh), Gilles Leger (Quebec), Mike Shanahan (St. Louis), George Gund (San Jose), David LeFevre (Tampa Bay), Steve Stavro (Toronto), Arthur Griffiths (Vancouver), Barry Shenkarow (Winnipeg), and Bob Swados (Secretary).

I made a brief acceptance speech and the meeting was adjourned so Bruce McNall and I could meet with the media representatives, who, not surprisingly, were clamoring for a face-to-face meeting with the league's sudden new power structure. I accompanied McNall to a mammoth press conference which Gary Meagher, the league's very efficient public relations officer, had arranged on short notice. With no opportunity to plan my remarks I winged it, laying out for the press what would be my goals as president. Without hesitation or equivocation, I said that moving NHL hockey onto U.S. network television would be my number one priority, and that expansion into major TV markets would be a means toward that end. My remarks on that day and the days that followed were reported by the press. I said:

> We need to get the League up and running. Obviously, we have to add national television in the United States. The league is seventy-five years old, and hockey is still the best-kept secret in the United States. We have a dazzling display of stars, but stars in the sky can be obscured by clouds. Our job is to blow away the clouds and get the game out where it deserves to be—on national networks.

A reporter from the *Detroit News* asked a series of smart questions:

> Q: You said most of your franchises are strong. Obviously,
> franchises such as Hartford are not. Why choose expansion when
> you could move Hartford?
> A: That would be expanding. The normal expansion indicates
> that you're adding teams. But what I'm talking about is expanding
> our market, where we are going in the U.S. Where do we need to
> go to build what we need in the U.S. to make our sport attractive
> to network television?
> Q: Where will you have to go?
> A: There are some obvious population centers we can see.
> Texas—
> Q: Houston?
> A: Yes. If Houston, then you may end up looking at Dallas. You
> may have to look at New Orleans. Certainly Miami—the South is
> very important. Certainly California. There are more people in
> California than in Canada, and we only have two franchises there.
> Every other league has four.

Less than six months later, I led a whirlwind expansion into Miami,
Florida and Anaheim, California. In order to accomplish it, I had to
break with the NHL's traditional means of expanding.

My first target was California. But location was only half the battle.
"Who" was just as important as "where." I trained my sights on Walt
Disney Co.'s fabled chairman, Michael Eisner. Chairman of the Board of
Governors Bruce McNall, who owned the Los Angeles Kings, set up a
dinner meeting for the three of us in Hollywood on Monday night,
October 12, 1992, while I was in California to do an interview with Roy
Firestone for ESPN. We went to a small restaurant which was apparently
a haunt of Disney execs, one of whom, Jeffrey Katzenberg (now Steven
Spielberg's partner at Dreamworks), showed up at a different table while
we were there.

A beautiful new arena was being completed in Anaheim, and McNall
had told me he had stimulated Eisner's interest in exploring the
possibility of acquiring an NHL expansion team to play there. The
meeting went well. We discussed what it would cost for Disney to get an
expansion franchise. Michael suggested we give him one free of charge,
because of the good it would do the league for Disney to join. I told him
the minimum he would have to pay was $50 million. It didn't appear to

scare him. We finished the meeting on a high note, agreeing to give the idea some thought and reconvene in a few weeks when I would be returning to California for a November 6 session of the league's Marketing Committee in Palm Springs. Later, McNall and I spoke on the phone about the upcoming meeting. Assuming Eisner remained interested, it would be up to me to create a mechanism for making it happen.

All prior NHL expansions had involved a lengthy process that took two years to complete. First, a committee of owners would be formed, which would hold a number of meetings to develop a plan of expansion. Then several board of governors meetings would be needed to review, criticize, modify, and ultimately approve the plan. After that, the league would publicly announce it was expanding, with interested parties encouraged to request application forms. Next, applicants would submit a complex and lengthy form, along with a $100,000 deposit. The league would then conduct market surveys to determine the viability of the applicants' venues for hockey, and investigations would be made into the background and financial wherewithal of the applicants themselves. Finally, each applicant (or some might say supplicant) would appear before the board of governors to be questioned, after which the board would make its decision, accepting some and rejecting others.

I knew instinctively that if we went the usual route, we could kiss Disney goodbye. For one thing, Eisner was hot to trot now; I did not know how long he would remain interested. Also, the owners of the plush new arena being completed in Anaheim would not let it sit idle for two years waiting for Disney to obtain an expansion franchise. Norman Green was already negotiating to move the North Stars to the new building.

On November 6, 1992, I met again with Michael Eisner and Bruce McNall in Hollywood. I sensed the timing was right, but only if we could move quickly. Eisner expressed his reluctance to get involved at all if there were any chance he would be rejected. McNall and Eisner turned to me to get it done.

As we spoke, I conceived a plan of action which called for a bold new approach. Eisner would confidentially submit to me a letter making an irrevocable offer to purchase an expansion franchise under the terms and conditions of the 1990 Plan of Sixth Expansion, subject to such changes as the board of governors would deem appropriate. I would then promptly, in confidence, seek the approval of the league's Advisory

Committee and, thereafter, the board. I said the entire process—from application to approval—could be completed in less than a month, and Disney's expansion team could begin play in the new building by the start of the 1993–94 season.

One sticking point was territorial indemnification for McNall, since Anaheim was within a fifty-mile radius of Los Angeles, and thus fell within the Kings' exclusive area. Eisner made it clear he would not pay a dime more than $50 million. McNall was sitting on an offer from Norman Green to pay him a $25 million indemnification fee to let him move the North Stars to Anaheim. It was a dilemma, sure enough, but I had to think of a way to get it done. I simply could not let us lose Eisner and Disney.

I suggested the problem be solved by allocating $25 million of the $50 million expansion fee to McNall. That way the league's expansion price of $50 million would be preserved and McNall would get his indemnification. After all, there was nothing written that said expansion fees had to be divided equally among all the clubs; the allocation was up to the board of governors. I was confident the governors would agree to those terms if it meant bringing Disney into the NHL.

Eisner and McNall welcomed my solution, and Michael agreed to do it. I said I would draft a letter for him in which he would offer to buy an expansion franchise whose team could start play as early as the 1993–94 season, on essentially the same terms as had applied to the 1990 Plan of Sixth Expansion, except for the expansion draft, which would be revised by the board of governors.

I was very excited as I took the red-eye back to New York. Wow, Disney, Michael Eisner—it was very heady stuff. But another goal was in reach. A few weeks earlier, McNall had told me I would be getting a call from Wayne Huizenga, the celebrated chairman of Blockbuster Entertainment Corp. Bruce said Huizenga might be interested in bringing NHL hockey to Miami, one of my targeted expansion sites. I had met with Huizenga in my office, and agreed to get back to him should the NHL be considering further expansion. Now, I told Bruce, I felt Huizenga could become a candidate for entry under the fast-track plan I had created for Michael. He certainly met our criteria for Eisner-caliber ownership. McNall concurred. I called Huizenga, and we met again in my office.

Huizenga later told *Business Week*'s reporter Gail DeGeorge about our meetings, and she described them in her 1996 book *The Making of a*

Blockbuster. He told her that in October 1992, he had gone shopping for an airplane and ended up buying a hockey franchise. While in California on business, he had met Bruce McNall, owner of the Los Angeles Kings and then chairman of the NHL's board of governors, who was seeking to sell his 727 airplane. While looking over the plane, Huizenga told McNall he thought hockey would do well in South Florida and asked when the NHL would next be considering expanding. McNall told him to speak to me. Within several weeks, Wayne came to see me in my New York office and told me of his interest in acquiring a hockey franchise.

A few weeks later, after returning from my meeting with Bruce McNall and Michael Eisner in California, I called Huizenga and asked him back to my office. We met at 9:30 A.M. on Monday, November 16, 1992, and I told him I had a plan under which he could be awarded an expansion franchise within three weeks, but he'd have to tell me right now: "Do you want it or don't you?"

He thought about it for a minute or two, then said, "Yes, I want it."

I had him put in writing a formal request for a franchise under the basic terms of the Plan of Sixth Expansion, and drafted the letter for him—the same letter I had drafted for Eisner. Less than a month later, the Panthers would be his.

The semiannual meeting of the board of governors was scheduled to be held from December 10–12, 1992, at the Breakers hotel in Palm Beach. Huizenga and Eisner had each sent me their offer letters, pursuant to my plan. Bruce and I felt it was important that Huizenga and Eisner be there to be presented to the governors. Huizenga agreed to come, but Michael balked. He didn't want to risk the loss of face should he come and be turned down. It was like the chicken and the egg. I was confident, as was Bruce, that if Eisner were there, he would not be turned down. We also knew that the governors might get their collective nose out of joint if they believed Eisner thought he was too good for them, and would not come to meet them in person. Were that to happen, the risk of his being rebuffed would increase.

The night before the meeting, Bruce and I spoke to Michael on the phone. We each told him his approval would be a sure thing if he came to the meeting, but if he did not come he might be creating a needless risk. He was convinced, and flew in the next morning. We arranged to have Eisner and Huizenga hide out in my suite until after lunch, when we would present them to the board. My wife, Barbara, along with

Shirley Sawyer (vice president Ken's wife) and Rena Shenkarow (Winnipeg governor Barry's wife) made a quick trip to the hotel store and bought giant Mickey and Minnie Mouse dolls, which they sat in chairs facing the entrance to my suite. In the arms of the dolls were Blockbuster video cassettes. Eisner was the first to arrive. He loved the dolls.

The rest, as they say, is history. The board was flabbergasted when McNall and I produced Eisner and Huizenga, in person. The approval vote was a mere formality.

As the day's momentous meeting came to a close, the governors paraded past me, offering congratulations for my achievement. Governor after governor shook my hand and thanked me. Remarks such as "This is the greatest day in the history of the NHL," and "You have just increased the value of our franchises by millions" were commonplace utterances by my grateful bosses.

It was to be my last hurrah. The next day I turned the reins of the league over to newly elected commissioner Gary Bettman.

5

Arm Wrestling With Jingle-Nuts

In December 1977, I was elected vice president and general counsel of the National Hockey League. Although I had practiced law for more than twenty-five years, which included three years on the staff of the Pennsylvania Labor Relations Board, I had never seen anything like what passed for collective bargaining in the NHL.

The players' union, called the National Hockey League Players' Association (NHLPA), was strictly a one-man band, and that man was R. Alan Eagleson, a talented Toronto lawyer who wore many hats. As the original—and only—executive director of the NHLPA, it was his duty to represent all NHL players in collective bargaining with the league. But at times he would put on his player's agent hat and represent an individual player (client) in contract negotiations with his club. At the same time, he might put on another hat and represent management personnel, as when he negotiated Chicago General Manager Bob Pulford's deal with the Blackhawks. And all the while, he would be wearing his Hockey Canada hat, functioning as the de facto czar of international hockey. It was often a dizzying display.

Putting it mildly, Eagleson was enmeshed in serious conflicts of interest, but there appeared to be full disclosure of these conflicting interests, and none of his clients seemed disturbed by them. NHL players were represented in the NHLPA by player representatives (one per club), and a half dozen players hand-picked by Eagleson to hold the offices of president and vice presidents of the union. This group of officers was known as the Executive. To us in the league office, it appeared that the Executive and the player reps were absolutely in awe of Eagleson. They respected, trusted, and feared him at the same time. By nature a boisterous and enthusiastic person, he was also capable of unsettlingly crude and uncouth behavior—especially when reaming out a player rep who dared to question his judgment at an NHLPA meeting. In those days, such challenges were almost nonexistent. Eagleson exercised virtually dictatorial control over the NHLPA.

Collective bargaining negotiations were conducted twice a year by what was known as the Owner-Player Council. On the owners' side of the table, the clubs were represented by a committee of owners, general managers, and league officers (on which I served) known as the Owner-Player Executive Committee (OPEC). President John A. Ziegler Jr. and Board of Governors Chairman William W. Wirtz cochaired this frozen OPEC.

Just like the NHLPA, OPEC was also controlled by one man. And Ziegler was that man. His tactics in dealing with his constituents were nothing like Eagleson's—Ziegler wouldn't even think of bullying, embarrassing, or threatening anyone. At OPEC meetings, he was forever calm and polite, giving everyone on the committee a chance to be heard. But he knew going in what he wanted the NHL's position to be, and, with very rare exception, was able to lead the committee members to a consensus in support of it. He seemed to know in advance what the players would probably agree to in the negotiations, and the price the NHL clubs would have to pay to get it. Was he clairvoyant? No. His insights usually arrived courtesy of his cozy relationship with Eagleson. They were, and probably still are, genuinely the best of friends. This friendship was very real—not just a convenient means of "using" the other person to gain a professional or business advantage, and their relationship flourished despite their having radically different person-alities. Eagleson was loud, flamboyant, uncouth, all bluff and bluster—a wild street fighter. Ziegler was calm, genteel and self-effacing—the conservative gentleman in every sense. The old saying "opposites attract" was true here. In addition to being personally attracted to each other, they shared a common interest in their love of NHL hockey.

They also had a mutual fascination with international hockey and the good life, and annually enjoyed joint sojourns overseas while attending the world championships in grand style. To call them the Odd Couple, however, would not be completely accurate. There was a third person in the middle of their tight little circle—Bill Wirtz, the megamillionaire owner of the Chicago Blackhawks. Wirtz was a few years older than Eagleson and Ziegler, but could party with the best of them. An extremely genial and gracious individual, Wirtz had the constitution—

and sometimes the temperament—of a *Tyrannosaurus rex*. He is physically one of the strongest men I have ever known, and no one is even a close second when it comes to handling alcoholic consumption: He can drink anyone under the table. The course of hockey in North America may have been set—and reset—during many a late night–early morning revel aboard the magnificent Wirtz yacht, not surprisingly called the *Blackhawk*. So, it does not take a great stretch of imagination to believe that, when Eagleson, Ziegler, and Wirtz led their respective troops into collective bargaining negotiations, the results may have been preordained by the "Odd Trio."

The staging of Owner-Player Council negotiations was rather routine. A large room would be used in the hotel where they were meeting. Tables and chairs would be set up so that player reps sat on one side of the room, with Eagleson in their forefront, facing the NHL's OPEC, whose members sat at a long table, with Ziegler and Wirtz always occupying center position. There would also be a breakout room, where the OPEC members could caucus in private to consider proposals which had been advanced by Eagleson.

When the term of a multiyear collective bargaining agreement (CBA) was expiring, the negotiation of a new one required lengthy meetings. But even when a CBA was in place, the Owner-Player Council met twice a year in good faith to consider proposals for fine-tuning it. A spirit of harmony existed, with very little bitterness. The leadership provided by Eagleson, Ziegler, and Wirtz kept everyone's focus on what was best for the game, and a reasonable willingness to give and take was always present. At the conclusion of the meetings, the NHL senior management traditionally hosted a lavish dinner party for the player reps and their wives.

The NHL's OPEC would always have a dinner meeting the night before the opening round of negotiations with the players. At this meeting, Ziegler would discuss the agenda—which consisted of requests by each side for amendments to the CBA. He predicted what the NHLPA's reaction to the NHL's requests would likely be, distinguishing those things OPEC would never achieve from those which might be attained through certain trade-offs. He then led a discussion as to which of the players' requests could be accepted in return for specified concessions. All would then retire for the night and reconvene in the morning, while the players were having their meeting.

After conclusion of the players morning meeting, Ziegler would meet privately with Eagleson. He would then report back to the committee what they both had felt would likely be approved by the players, in return for certain concessions from the owners. He then mapped out the meeting strategy, assigning to different owners the job of speaking on different issues, such as how much money they were losing, or why free agency could never be agreed to. And then they went to the meeting room, where a charade of sorts took place.

Eagleson would first make a number of demands on behalf of the players, including, of course, those Ziegler and he had already agreed would likely, at the end of the day, be granted by the NHL. Next came the various owners, speaking on their assigned topics, letting the players know of the precariousness of the NHL's financial picture and why the players' desire for free agency could never be agreed to. OPEC's demands would then be presented by Ziegler, including, of course, those that Eagleson and he had agreed would likely be granted by the players at the end of the day.

OPEC members would then retire to their breakout room, so that each side could review the other's demands. Under Ziegler's guidance, committee members discussed the players' demands, agreeing with him as to what concessions they would be willing to make in return for getting certain things from the players. While discussion was going on in the breakout room, Eagleson would come to get Ziegler, and the two of them would meet privately in the hallway. Ziegler would then return and report what Eagleson had told him, which was usually that his original predictions were still on course, but that at the next meeting Eagleson would stand firm against granting some of the concessions they both felt would eventually be granted, and Ziegler, on behalf of the owners, would do the same.

Reconvening in the big meeting room, Ziegler would lead off, detailing those areas in which OPEC was willing to show a little movement toward a number of the players' demands, in return for receiving everything the owners were seeking. Eagleson would respond, ridiculing the owners' proposals—it looked good in front of the players for Eagleson to tell the owners off—but indicating the players' willingness to consider a bit of what the NHL was seeking in return for all of their demands being met. Again, OPEC would retire to the breakout room to permit both sides to deliberate further. After a while, there would be a knock on the door. Eagleson was ready for another private powwow with Ziegler. After their meeting, Ziegler would return and advise OPEC of how things were progressing in the players' room. All would once again traipse back to the main meeting room for a repeat of what had transpired previously, except this time each side moved further than before, but protested it could move no more.

Then the process would be repeated. It would be back to the breakout room, an Eagleson-Ziegler private meeting, back to the meeting room, a bit more movement, more breakout room, another Eagleson-Ziegler private meeting, back to the meeting room, additional movement, over and over again until finally the differences between the two sides were whittled down and a final agreement reached, usually reasonably close to Ziegler's original prediction. Owners, players, and players' wives then celebrated at a posh dinner party hosted by the owners. Everyone who was there could attest to how difficult the negotiations had been, and how fruitful had been the hard-fought gains for both sides. To us, it appeared the players never suspected the scenario might have been carefully scripted in advance. As Roman lawyer and satirist Decimus Junius Juvenalis observed in his *Satires* in the year A.D. 125, bread and circuses (*panem et circenses*) kept the Roman citizenry pacified.

Notwithstanding the somewhat duplicitous manner in which the negotiations were staged, the players fared well under Eagleson's leadership. In reaching agreement, up front, on what they believed should be the outcome of the collective bargaining negotiations, Ziegler and Eagleson had too much respect for each other for either of them to seek an unfair edge. Members of the NHL board of governors complained frequently among themselves that Ziegler was too generous to the players, and that Eagleson was taking advantage of his friendship with Ziegler. On the other hand, Eagleson's critics—especially the latter-day ones who surfaced after he was removed from power— expressed the view that he had pandered to Ziegler and Wirtz, to the disadvantage of the players. Be that as it may, the old NHL style of collective bargaining came to an abrupt end in 1990, with the ascension to power of Robert W. Goodenow, Eagleson's successor as NHLPA executive director.

Eagleson had been compelled to resign his office after a 1989 player uprising spearheaded by players' agents Rich Winter and Ron Salcer, with the help of Toronto lawyers John Agro, Bill Dermody, and David Dempster, and hired gun Ed Garvey, a labor lawyer who once had been executive director of the National Football League Players' Association. In 1981, an attempt to oust Eagleson led by Boston Bruins defenseman

Mike Milbury, had failed, but might have been the precursor of the 1989 action. One of the principal counts in their public indictment against Eagleson had been his cozy relationship with Ziegler and Wirtz, which they claimed had resulted in the players being sold out in collective bargaining. The battle between Eagleson and his attackers became so vitriolic, and caused so much turmoil within the players' ranks, that, although the players elected to remove Eagleson from power, they also decided to seek his replacement from a source outside of the Garvey, Winter, Salcer group.

The NHLPA Executive appointed a committee of players and charged it with the responsibility of finding an independent replacement for Eagleson. The committee selected Goodenow, a player's agent and former collegiate hockey player (from Harvard), who was thereafter, in early 1990, initially elected to the post of deputy executive director. Although Eagleson's resignation as executive director would not be effective until January 1992, Goodenow had become the de facto head of the NHLPA. Mindful of the fate that had befallen his predecessor and the criticism that had led up to it, it was clear to Goodenow he would have to develop a new style of collective bargaining. He was formally introduced to the NHL during an August 1990, meeting of the Owner-Player Council held at a Cape Cod resort in Chatham, Massachusetts. Unlike Eagleson, he was introverted, sullen, and humorless.

With the existing collective bargaining agreement due to expire on September 15, 1991, one of the items on the agenda was to schedule collective bargaining meeting dates for the forthcoming year. The members of OPEC all had a variety of business commitments, and it made sense for them to block out fixed dates on their calendar far in advance to insure their availability for deliberations. Eagleson announced that, although he would be available to assist as needed, it would be Goodenow's responsibility to handle the negotiation of the next CBA. With Goodenow's participation, a series of dates was blocked out for collective bargaining negotiations following the close of the 1990–91 season, commencing in June 1991.

About a week after the Cape Cod meetings, Goodenow was one of the speakers at a sports law seminar conducted by Minnesota labor lawyer Ed Garvey. What he said was a portent of things to come in the new age of NHL collective bargaining. He reported that he had recently attended a meeting of the NHLPA and the NHL, at which "they" had agreed to meet many times during the forthcoming year to negotiate a new collective bargaining agreement. "Had they asked me," he added, "I would have told them not to bother, since 98 percent of a collective bargaining agreement is negotiated at the eleventh hour, the day before the old agreement is to expire." Based on the results of the negotiations, or should I say the nonnegotiations, that subsequently ensued on those meeting dates which had been set aside, it was evident Goodenow's philosophy had been clearly expressed at the seminar.

Eagleson, now powerless, maintained his close friendship with Ziegler and Wirtz. He told them what he thought of Goodenow, whom he detested. He referred to Goodenow as Jingle-Nuts, a sobriquet readily adopted by Ziegler and Wirtz, who always used it when talking about Goodenow—behind his back, of course. I did not know why Eagleson had named Goodenow Jingle-Nuts, but it was clearly not meant to be complimentary.

Eagleson had no respect for Goodenow, and resented his presence at the NHLPA. He felt Goodenow was his intellectual inferior, and would stumble and fall badly in his first foray into collective bargaining. He harbored the fantasy that, when Goodenow realized he was in over his head and could not negotiate a new CBA with the NHL, he (Eagleson) would be called in to get it done, like the white knight riding in to save the day. The problem with this surreal daydream was that Eagleson really believed it—and so did Ziegler and Wirtz. They had been told by Eagleson that it would happen—and he had also assured them the players would never strike.

The first collective bargaining meeting was scheduled for June 13, 1991, in Toronto. Ziegler and Wirtz decided this would be a good opportunity to put Goodenow down in front of his constituents, so the players would realize how much they needed Eagleson to get the job done. At Ziegler's direction, Ken Sawyer (the league's vice president of finance) and I prepared an inch-and-a-half thick report to present to Goodenow and the player reps at the upcoming meeting. Our report was eighty-seven pages long and was contained in a silver presentation case entitled "Collective Bargaining Handbook." It was later to be commonly referred to as the Silver Bullet. Ziegler felt the contrast between our preparation—as represented by the report—and the meager effort he anticipated by Goodenow, would help convince the player reps that Goodenow was not the man for the job.

The handbook was divided into four sections: "History of Collective Bargaining," "Benefits," "Statistics," and "Proposals." I drafted the history section, which led off with a chronological history of NHL collective bargaining, starting with the June 1967 formation and recognition of the NHLPA as the exclusive representative of all players employed by NHL clubs, prior to the league's first season after expanding from six to twelve clubs. I pointed out that from 1967 to the execution of their first formal collective bargaining agreement on May 4, 1976, the clubs and the NHLPA had reached agreements through collective bargaining on a number of matters, which were reflected in minutes of owner-player meetings, standard player contracts, and an arbitration agreement relating to those contracts. I then tracked the history of the NHL's written collective bargaining agreements, showing that on May 4, 1976, the NHLPA and the clubs published their first comprehensive, printed CBA, followed by successor agreements dated August 1, 1981; November 1, 1984; and June 1, 1988. Next, I described what was unique about hockey's collective bargaining:

> People who are familiar with the strife, strikes, lawsuits, confrontation, and humiliation experienced by owners and players in the other major league sports stand in awe of the special relationship that has always existed between players and owners in the NHL. What are the factors that have created this unbroken twenty-four-year track record of harmony?
>
> First of all, players and owners meet with each other. That sounds simple but it is unique in major league sports and is the cornerstone of the player-owner relationship. The scene of players and owners sitting around a table, discussing mutual concerns and seeking common solutions is one that can be seen only in hockey. Hockey players are envied by football, baseball and basketball players who have never had the opportunity to meet with owners in face-to-face negotiations.
>
> The approach to collective bargaining is also unique. Unlike the experience in other sports, neither hockey players nor hockey owners have ever delivered public ultimatums or practiced confrontational negotiations. Those tactics are designed to result in one side "winning" and the other side "losing." It is a regular happening in certain other sports. Eschewing the "win-lose" philosophy, hockey players and owners have always practiced "win-win" negotiations. Problems have been solved quietly, through responsible give-and-take. As a result, players, owners, and the game of hockey have all been winners—there have been no losers.

Also unique in hockey has been the partnership of players and owners in international hockey. No other sports owners have ever become partners with their clubs' players in such a significant enterprise. Proceeds from international hockey have materially enhanced the pension rights of NHL players.

Finally, one of the unique hallmarks of hockey's collective bargaining is that it is not—as in other sports—a sometimes thing that takes place only when the CBA is about to expire. Instead, hockey's collective bargaining has been a dynamic, ongoing process that has seen the CBA continuously fine-tuned and amended, regardless of when its term was due to expire, with each party responding to the other's needs and requests in an open spirit of cooperation.

I listed, in detail, all midterm CBA amendments which had been approved at Owner-Player Council meetings, and followed this with an eleven-page dissertation on the philosophy underlying the NHL's "equalization" approach to the ongoing dispute over free agency. The root of that dispute was the desire of each player to be free to sign with a new club at the conclusion of the term of his contract with his old club. In the NHL, under the terms of the collective bargaining agreement, a player became a "free agent" when the term of his contract expired, but if a new club wished to sign him, it would be required to compensate the player's old club for its loss with "equalization" compensation, in the form of draft picks, other players, or a combination. Obviously, the requirement of equalization compensation was a deterrent to clubs signing free agents.

I closed the history section with an appeal headed "The Challenge Ahead":

If, in future collective bargaining negotiations, each side continues to keep in focus and respect the vital interests of the other, and continues to make a good faith effort to seek nonconfrontational solutions to each other's problems, then the industry should continue to flourish, and the interests of players, club owners, and the game of hockey will continue to be well-served.

In the "Benefits" section, Sawyer described all insurance and other benefit programs NHL players received, showing with a full color bar graph how, for a ten-year player, the NHL pension was the most generous in all major league sports.

In the "Statistics" section, using a series of color charts and graphs, Sawyer illustrated how the escalation in player salaries had been outstripping the growth in NHL revenues. He showed that over the past six years player compensation had increased 130 percent while hockey revenues had increased only 78 percent. As a percentage of club revenues, player compensation had risen from 49 percent in 1985–86, to 63 percent in 1991–92. He projected that in five years, if player compensation and team revenues continued to rise at the rate of increase of the previous six years, player compensation would be 78 percent of revenues, but that if they were to rise at the rate they had risen in 1991–92, player compensation would be a shocking 173 percent of revenues.

The twenty-six-page "Proposals" section set forth in detail a long list of proposed revisions to the CBA that our general managers committee had prepared.

The Silver Bullet was very impressive, and had an immediate impact on Goodenow, who had not anticipated the NHL would come out with guns blazing at his first meeting. He had prepared nothing to hand out to OPEC members, and was obviously nonplussed when he and his minions were handed the professional-looking silver handbooks. But the biggest shock was yet to come.

The CBA automatically renewed itself from year-to-year unless, at least 120 days prior to its expiration date of September 15, 1991, one party gave to the other a written notice of termination and a list of proposed CBA revisions. In his first act as the NHLPA's new collective bargaining majordomo, rookie Goodenow had sent Ziegler a timely memorandum giving notice of termination, but had failed to include with it the required list of proposed CBA revisions.

Along with the Silver Bullet, Ziegler handed Goodenow a copy of a letter that had been sent to Eagleson and Bryan Trottier (respectively, the executive director and president of the NHLPA), notifying them it was the position of the NHL clubs that Goodenow's memorandum did not effect termination of the CBA on September 15, 1991, because it had failed to include proposed revisions. This was a technical point, to be sure, but a legally sound one. If correct, it would mean the term of the CBA would be extended by a year, until September 15, 1992.

Goodenow was shaken. He was red-faced, figuratively and literally. The Ziegler-Wirtz plan to embarrass him had worked to perfection. But he did not turn to Eagleson to handle the negotiations, as they had hoped he would. Instead, he used the incident to unify the union's Executive behind him and to make the players more militant in their stance toward the NHL. He refused to meet any further with OPEC unless the league recanted its position on the inadequacy of his termination notice, and then stubbornly refused the league's request that the dispute be submitted to arbitration, despite the CBA's requirement that it be done. The standoff lasted through the month of July, and the September 15, 1991, termination date of the CBA was fast approaching. Rather than face a lengthy court battle over the issue, Ziegler convinced OPEC to throw in the towel. Goodenow had won his first battle. Jingle-Nuts was alive and well, thank you.

The Owner-Player Council did not meet again until the final week of August. In advance of the meeting, on August 14, Goodenow submitted to Ziegler an ambitious fifty-four-page laundry list of proposed CBA revisions, most of which would never be acceptable to the owners, including use of an independent arbitrator (instead of the NHL president) to interpret the league's constitution and bylaws; a requirement that all amendments to the league's constitution and bylaws be negotiated with the NHLPA; payment to the players of 60 percent of the revenues from the first four games of each playoff series; substantially increased pensions and insurance benefits; and a total revision of the league's entry draft and free-agency bylaws. On August 19 Ziegler countered with three controversial new proposals by OPEC:

1. (For clarification purposes):
   Each club shall have the right to pay a player's salary in twenty-four consecutive semimonthly installments, in strict compliance with Section 1 of the Standard Player's Contract, notwithstanding any prior practice by Club or other Clubs of having paid players' salaries on an accelerated basis.
   [Under the way clubs had been paying their players, a player would receive his entire annual salary before the start of the playoffs, even though his contract said he was being paid that salary for playing in preseason, regular season, *and* playoff games. Because of the payment practice, Goodenow had been preaching to the players that they were not being paid for the playoffs (other than playoff award money), hence their new demand for a "player's fund" of 60 percent of playoff revenues. Also, on a more practical basis, the owners felt that if players had not yet been paid their full annual salary, it would serve as a

disincentive to their going on strike during the playoffs. These were the reasons the proposal (termed a "clarification") had been submitted to Goodenow by OPEC.]

2. Clubs offer, as part of a new CBA, to permit players to sell to trading card companies the right to use their photographs in the 1991–92 hockey season, notwithstanding the exclusive rights granted to clubs pursuant to Sections 8 and 20 of the Standard Player's Contract.

[This was the first notice given to Goodenow that trading card revenues would be an issue. The language of the standard player's contract clearly gave clubs the exclusive right to the use of the players' photographs. But the NHLPA, under Eagleson, had usurped that right a few years earlier and sold to trading card companies the right to use pictures of the players on their cards. At the time, the annual revenues produced for the NHLPA from this source was modest—less than $100,000— with an equal amount being paid to the clubs for the right to use club uniforms and logos. Because of his close relationship with Ziegler and Wirtz, and since the revenues were not very substantial, Eagleson had not been challenged when he did this. But things had changed. There had recently been a boom in the trading card business, with 1991–92 revenues anticipated to reach into the millions, and, also, the league was now playing hardball with Goodenow. By offering to permit the players to receive trading card revenues in the 1991–92 season as part of a new CBA, OPEC was serving notice that, without a new CBA, Goodenow would be cut off from trading card dollars.]

3. The playing roster in the 1991–92 season to be reduced from 18 & 2 to 17 & 2.

[This had traditionally been a hot-button issue with the players. The CBA prohibited clubs from reducing the playing roster below seventeen players and two goalkeepers, but for years Eagleson had succeeded, albeit on a year-to-year basis, in getting the owners to agree to a playing roster of 18 and 2. To the owners, reducing the playing roster was a way of saving money—one salary per club. To Eagleson, of course, the issue had been more NHL jobs for his players. But Eagleson was no longer at the bargaining table, so OPEC had proposed moving the roster back to 17 and 2.]

The meeting did not open on a very pleasant note. Goodenow was seated in front of the NHLPA's negotiating committee, which was made up of star players Bryan Trottier (Pittsburgh Penguins center), Ken Baumgartner (New York Islanders defenseman), Mike Gartner (New York Rangers right wing), Steve Yzerman (Detroit Red Wings center), and goaltenders Mike Liut (Washington Capitals), Andy Moog (Boston Bruins), and John Vanbiesbrouck (New York Rangers). Goodenow started by stating flatly he would not negotiate over any of the proposals the league had earlier submitted in the Silver Bullet. He referred to them derisively as take-aways.

"We are not interested in give-and-take," he haughtily informed Ziegler and the members of OPEC, "we are only interested in take!" The players, who seemed to have arrived at the meeting with a new militant attitude, were obviously pleased by his obdurate stance.

Ziegler was the spokesman for OPEC, which consisted of club owners Bill Wirtz (Chicago), Marcel Aubut (Quebec), Michael Ilitch (Detroit), Barry Shenkarow (Winnipeg), Ed Snider (Philadelphia), Bob Swados (Buffalo), club officer Paul Martha (Pittsburgh), general managers Dave Poile (Washington), Bob Pulford (Chicago), Serge Savard (Montreal), Harry Sinden (Boston), and Bill Torrey (New York Islanders). Also on the committee were league vice presidents Jim Gregory, Ken Sawyer, and me.

Ziegler responded to Goodenow's harsh beginning by quietly pointing out that collective bargaining required both sides to consider possible trade-offs in order to come to a new agreement.

"Don't waste your time talking to us about trade-offs," Goodenow retorted, "we are only interested in discussing gains."

Wow! It was clear to all that there would not be a new CBA in place by September 15, 1991, when the old one would expire.

The meeting went nowhere. Goodenow clung to his stance that the only thing he would talk about was gains for the players. OPEC members listened patiently to the recital of his requests, then retired to the breakout room. After once again returning to the meeting room, several owners tried in vain to explain the financial predicament team owners were in, with player salaries having outstripped revenues for a number of clubs. Unlike the Eagleson years, Goodenow, and the players on his committee, were plainly not interested.

The meeting lasted for two days, but nothing was accomplished. It was as Goodenow had predicted a year earlier at the Garvey seminar, when he said he didn't know why meetings had been scheduled, since 98 percent of negotiations would take place the night before the CBA expired. The OPEC members left Toronto after agreeing to meet again during the final week of the CBA's term. They did, but nothing was accomplished then either—both sides were just too far apart on too many issues. So, for the first time in NHL history, a collective bargaining agreement expired without a new one having been negotiated.

Ziegler and Goodenow agreed negotiations would continue during the 1991–92 season, and also that, in the meantime, the season would commence without a CBA in place. Ziegler told Goodenow there would be no lockout of the players, in return for which Goodenow assured Ziegler the players would not strike. But he didn't say never. One week before the playoffs were due to start, he led the players on the first walkout in league history. The strike that started on that fateful day did not last long, but it ended up costing Ziegler his job.

Many issues had been resolved during the months of negotiations that preceded the strike, but it must have become clear to Goodenow that OPEC was not going to budge on his more ambitious demands— including relinquishing control over who interpreted the league's bylaws and constitution—and OPEC was holding firm on its trading cards position, which everyone realized was the final chip they would put on the table to make a deal.

The trading card issue was a critical one for Goodenow, since the millions of dollars in royalties from trading card companies had become the NHLPA's principal source of revenue. Unlike Major League Baseball, where the union distributed the lion's share of the lucrative trading card dollars directly to the players each year, the NHLPA, under Goodenow, apparently kept it all—while continuing to collect dues from the players. (I wonder how Goodenow was able to slip that one by aggressive and litigious player agents like Rich Winter.)

In the naïve and mistaken belief the owners were so hungry for playoff revenue that he could bring them to their knees, Goodenow called a strike on April 1, just seven days before the end of the regular season and start of the playoffs. But the rookie labor leader did not calculate that some of the more hawkish owners in the NHL—including Board Chairman Wirtz—were perfectly willing to scrap the playoffs and then force a showdown by locking out the players at the start of the 1992–93 season.

Goodenow soon realized the extent of his miscalculation when

Ziegler informed him there would be no further negotiations unless and until the players came back to work. Within the NHLPA, a group of restless players was beginning to make noises about mounting a challenge to Goodenow's leadership. The standoff continued, with neither side making a move. Finally, on Tuesday, April 7, Ziegler sent Goodenow a "final offer," in which, as expected, the NHL agreed to give up its position on trading cards, but no concessions were made to Goodenow on any of the other issues he had on the table. In his letter, Ziegler said that the offer had to be accepted within forty-eight hours—by 5:00 P.M. Thursday, April 9—or the season would be declared over and there would be no Stanley Cup Playoffs. Ziegler's forceful slapshot had put the puck squarely in Goodenow's end of the ice.

Responding to the pressure being applied by Ziegler—and by his own unhappy constituents—Goodenow placed a phone call to Ziegler on Thursday afternoon, telling him he was prepared to end the strike and agree to a new CBA on the terms of the NHL's final offer, plus a few minor face-saving provisions which he described. Ziegler made a conference call to the board of governors, and related what he had been told by Goodenow. The board authorized Ziegler to make a deal on the terms as outlined, but insisted that, before meeting with Goodenow, Ziegler was to get a fax from him confirming what he had said on the phone. Ziegler called Goodenow and agreed to meet with him the next morning in Ziegler's New York office. He asked for the fax, but Goodenow did not send it.

Later that night, Ziegler received a phone call from Wirtz, who had two other owners on the line with him, Quebec's Marcel Aubut and Winnipeg's Barry Shenkarow. Wirtz asked that Ziegler bring them up-to-date on what had transpired with Goodenow. When he heard Ziegler was planning to meet with Goodenow the next morning without having received the fax, he hit the roof. "You were not authorized to meet with him without getting that fax!" he screamed. Shenkarow and Aubut echoed Wirtz's message.

Ziegler reacted in kind. "Who do you think you're talking to?" he yelled angrily, "I am the president of the National Hockey League, not some secretary!" That did it. Let me explain why.

For the better part of a year, a small group of club owners unhappy with Ziegler's leadership had been trying to muster support among their colleagues to oust Ziegler as president. Led by outspoken John McMullen (New Jersey), Jerry Jacobs (Boston), and Richard Gordon

(Hartford), their numbers had been slowly increasing. Bruce McNall (Los Angeles), Arthur Griffiths (Vancouver), and Peter Pocklington (Edmonton) were among a group of fence-sitters who had privately expressed support for firing Ziegler but did not want to be out front. The dissidents felt Ziegler had not been aggressive enough in dealing with the steady escalation of player salaries, which was leading most clubs to operate at a deficit. The average salary of players had risen to $450,000, and the owners' operating losses were averaging about a million dollars a club. While the anti-Ziegler movement had been growing, its members were not able to unseat him because of one person—Bill Wirtz. Ziegler was being protected and sheltered by the rock-steady support of his friend, who had considerable influence on the board of governors. But that all ended with Ziegler's ill-fated Wirtz-Aubut-Shenkarow phone conversation on the eve of his meeting with Goodenow. When he ignored the board's directive to get Goodenow's terms in a fax before agreeing to meet with him, and further compounded his sin by showing what Wirtz interpreted as arrogance during their phone call, Ziegler lost the support of his friend. After Ziegler had left their conference call, Wirtz told Aubut and Shenkarow he believed it was time Ziegler was replaced, and all three agreed to join the ranks of the anti-Ziegler owners. The next day, Goodenow arrived at the NHL's New York office, along with two members of his negotiating committee, Bryan Trottier and Mike Gartner. Ziegler met with them all day long in his private office, accompanied only by Tony Herman, the NHL's outside labor lawyer from the prestigious Washington law firm of Covington and Burling. Although I was the league's vice president and general counsel, and my office was within thirty-five feet of Ziegler's, I was not invited to participate.

After a full day and night of marathon negotiations, during which Ziegler continually kept the governors abreast of developments through conference calls, the terms of a new CBA were agreed to by Ziegler and Goodenow, and approved by the board of governors. Goodenow ended up getting more minor concessions from Ziegler than he had agreed, in the prior evening's phone call, would be acceptable. But to Ziegler, what was important was ending the strike, and he had done it. At 12:15 A.M. on Saturday morning, April 11, the agreement was finalized and the strike officially ended, just ten days after it had started. The balance of the slate of the regular season's games were played between April 12 and 16, followed by the full Stanley Cup Playoffs.

I had worked under Ziegler for fifteen years, and in my opinion, this was his finest hour. He had laid his butt on the line to save the National Hockey League from the eternal embarrassment of a season-ending strike and the loss of continuity of the Stanley Cup Playoffs. Compare Ziegler's heroic and decisive action with that of Major League Baseball's leaders, who allowed the cancellation of the 1994 World Series. How tragically ironic that it ended up costing him his job. Deserted by Wirtz, his once-steadfast ally, Ziegler was forced to resign his presidency in June 1992.

But what of Jingle-Nuts? How did he fare in the aftermath of the strike? Very well, apparently, at least in regard to job security. He had established himself as the unchallenged leader of the players' union, even though his performance had been considerably less than flawless.

The new collective bargaining agreement was for a term of one year, with an expiration date of September 15, 1993. By the time it expired, Goodenow's new adversary was in place—Gary Bettman had taken office on February 1, 1993, as the NHL's first-ever commissioner. The board of governors had decided in June 1992 to get in step with the other major sports leagues by hiring a commissioner as the league's CEO. The office of president was phased out after the new commissioner took office.

Throughout 1993, Goodenow and Bettman spent a good deal of time alternately befriending and sparring with each other. When the CBA expired, they were nowhere near reaching agreement on a new deal, and they permitted the 1993–94 season to be played to its conclusion without one, while abiding by the terms of the expired agreement. The players were doing fine under it. The average salary had increased to $600,000 and was rising at a much higher rate than club revenues. Club owners were unhappy; most were suffering operating losses. League-wide, these averaged $2 million a club. They wanted a salary cap, or something else that would help put the brakes on the unrelenting escalation of player salaries. Bettman tried to get Goodenow to agree to address the issue, but Goodenow continued to stonewall him. A showdown was looming before the start of the 1994–95 season. Bettman was prepared for it, but Goodenow was not, and Bettman took him to the cleaners.

The hawks on the board of governors had persuaded their fellow owners to initiate a lockout of the players. They believed depriving players of their salaries was the only way they would ever get the union to grant them relief. But they were faced with a giant legal dilemma. The league's lawyers had confidentially alerted Bettman to a major problem that could be caused by a lockout.

In most industries, the only contract employees have is their collective bargaining agreement, and, if it has expired—or if there is none—employees are free to strike and employers are free to engage in a lockout. But in sports, and more specifically, in the NHL, players have two contracts, the CBA and also their individual standard player's contracts. There was nothing in the NHL's standard player's contract that provided its validity was contingent on there being a CBA in effect. Quite to the contrary, there was a provision —paragraph 18.[d]—that specifically stated its provisions would be effective independent of whether or not there was a CBA.

The standard player's contract provided that a club was required to pay the player his salary and, if the club failed to do so, the player could give the club a notice of default, and then, if the club did not make the salary payment within three weeks of receiving notice of default, he would have the right to declare himself a total free agent, not subject to equalization compensation. There was nothing in the contract that gave a club the right to lock out the player and not pay him his salary.

The league's lawyers had advised that in the event of a lockout, if the players gave their clubs a notice of default that was not cured within three weeks, there was a substantial risk the courts might support the players' election to declare themselves free agents. It was a risk club owners could not afford to take. Bettman decided to bluff Goodenow and see where it would lead. When training camp ended, Bettman announced he was deferring the starting date of the season. He carefully side-stepped the lockout issue, claiming it was not a lockout, but merely a delay in the start of the season.

Goodenow never figured out why Bettman was scrupulously avoiding calling it a lockout. He also never advised the players to serve a notice of default on their clubs—a major goof by Goodenow. Had the default notices been served, Bettman was prepared with a backup plan. He would try for three weeks to negotiate a new CBA with Goodenow, and then save face by announcing that, since he was satisfied with the progress of the talks, the season would start. He knew clubs would never risk losing their star players to free agency by ignoring the default notices, so the players would be paid within the three-week deadline.

And then, of course, if their salaries were being paid, a lockout would put no pressure on the players.

If Goodenow had grasped what was going on and directed the serving of default notices, the players would have been paid their entire salaries for the 1994–95 season, and Goodenow would have been dealing from strength in negotiating a new collective bargaining agreement with Bettman. Instead, due to the extended lockout, the teams played only forty-eight games of the eighty-four-game schedule; players lost 43 percent of their season's salaries; and a weak and desperate Goodenow was compelled to make major concessions in the new CBA in order to salvage what was left of the 1994–95 season. In negotiating the new CBA, Bettman slyly made sure the standard player's contract was amended so that, in the future, players would no longer have a means of preventing a lockout. Goodenow never understood. Poor Jingle-Nuts!— Bettman took his pants.

Eagleson's methods may have been subject to challenge, but not his results. He got the players salary arbitration (there is none in the NFL or NBA), no-cut contracts, the best health insurance ever devised (including full, nondeductible coverage for their live-in girlfriends), the best pensions for ten-year players in all sports, and substantial career-ending disability insurance and life insurance. The steady escalation of players' salaries begun in the Eagleson years has continued unabated, thanks to the salary arbitration and free-agency rules Eagleson negotiated.

And what has Goodenow, with all his belligerency, attained for his constituents? Some fine-tuning of free-agency rules, a short-lived strike in 1992 that embarrassed the National Hockey League, and a preventable lengthy lockout in 1994–95 that cost each player 43 percent of that year's salary and resulted in the union's conceding a number of significant take-aways to the owners. When all is said and done, the players fared much better under the Eagle than they have to date under Jingle-Nuts.

6

The Noon Balloon to Saskatoon

Having seen the game of hockey hopscotch played in the NHL the past few years—Minnesota North Stars to Dallas in 1994; Quebec Nordiques to Denver in 1995; Winnipeg Jets to Phoenix in 1996; Hartford Whalers to Raleigh, North Carolina in 1997—you would never know that, during most of the league's eighty-year existence, one of the toughest things to accomplish in all of major league sports was to relocate an NHL franchise.

The league was fifty years old when it expanded from six to twelve teams in 1967. One of the new franchises, the California Seals, with an arena in Oakland in the San Francisco Bay Area, got off to a rocky financial start. The franchise was owned by a limited partnership with multiple owners, headed by Barry Van Gerbig. After experiencing huge operating losses in each of the first three seasons, Van Gerbig, in 1970, requested approval from the NHL board of governors to move the team to Vancouver, British Columbia. This would have been a first, since no NHL franchise had ever been relocated. The board turned him down.

Unable or unwilling to continue shouldering the losses, Van Gerbig and his partners sold the franchise to Charlie Finley and then sued the NHL member clubs under the antitrust laws for having denied their request to move. The U.S. District Court ruled in favor of the clubs, supporting the NHL's position that franchises had to stay in place. But in 1973, after he had suffered three consecutive years of operating losses, Finley also requested approval to move the Seals. His proposed destination was Indianapolis.

The league's lawyers cautioned against denying his request, concerned that U.S. courts might view the turndown as anticompetitive in the U.S. marketplace, since, unlike the prior attempt to move to Canada, this intended relocation was into the Midwest, a bastion of other NHL clubs. Finley's request to move was denied, but, rather than call his bluff and face the uncertainty of an antitrust action he might bring, the league offered to buy the franchise from him. After negotiating a price that gave him a handsome profit, Finley sold the Seals to Members Limited Partnership (MLP), a newly created entity owned by the other member clubs.

MLP operated the franchise in Oakland for a year and nine months, while the board of governors sought to find a new buyer in the San Francisco Bay Area. During that period, MLP suffered operating losses in the millions, causing the restless NHL owners to pressure the board to dissolve the franchise unless a buyer could be found. An exhaustive search produced only one, Mel Swig, who agreed to purchase the franchise on condition that he be given the right to relocate it in the future should he find that operating it in the Bay Area was not financially viable. Having lost $10 million under MLP's operation of the Seals and having no other available options, the board agreed to sell to Swig on his terms, giving him the right to relocate in the future. However, his relocation option was limited to a site in North America not within the territorial limits of another NHL or World Hockey Association franchise. (The NHL was wary of engendering an antitrust lawsuit by the WHA.)

One year later, in 1976, after experiencing further losses in Oakland, and with his hope of building a new arena in the Urba Buena Redevelopment area in downtown San Francisco dashed by the failure of Mayor Joseph Alioto to win reelection, Swig relocated the Seals (renamed the Barons) to Cleveland. It was the first franchise relocation in NHL history. It was to be joined by a second.

In 1974, the NHL had expanded by adding two new teams, the Washington Capitals and Kansas City Scouts. The owner of the Scouts, Ed Thompson, was very thinly capitalized. After suffering big operating losses in each of his first two seasons, he requested board approval for sale of the Scouts to Jack Vickers, a buyer from Denver, Colorado, whose offer was conditioned upon an immediate relocation of the franchise to his hometown. When efforts to find a responsible local buyer proved fruitless, and convinced Thompson was on the verge of bankruptcy, the board concluded there was no avenue available to keep the Scouts in Kansas City. Denver was accepted as an NHL site, and transfer of the Scouts to Vickers was approved in 1976, the same time the Seals were being moved to Cleveland. Unfortunately, this was not to be the last move for the itinerant Kansas City franchise.

After two years of his own losses, Vickers tired of being a hockey owner, and in 1978 sold the Rockies (née Scouts) to Arthur Imperatore, a trucking magnate from northern New Jersey who had visions of moving the team to the Jersey Meadowlands. But the league's policy against franchise relocation had reasserted itself, and Imperatore was getting nowhere with other NHL owners in his quiet lobbying for the move. After two and a half years of losses, Imperatore—who, unlike Coors Beer, grew weary of trying to "tap the Rockies"—sold the team to Peter Gilbert, a cable TV mogul from Buffalo, New York. Armand Pohan, Imperatore's stepson, said that having Gilbert appear in the midst of the 1980–81 season and offer to take the Rockies albatross off their hands was akin to Pohan's having a religious experience. Gilbert readily agreed to keep the team in Denver, and crowed to the governors when the sale was approved that it was the happiest day of his life.

Alas, in 1982, after he had experienced one and a half years of steady losses, at the tail end of which, depleted of funds, he needed a league loan to complete the season, a desperate Gilbert requested board approval to relocate the Rockies to the Meadowlands in New Jersey. In accord with NHL precedent, as well as in response to Senator Gary Hart and other elected political leaders in Colorado who beseeched the league to keep the Rockies in Denver, the board made exhaustive efforts to find a responsible buyer or some other way to keep the Denver franchise alive. These efforts bore no fruit and, upon the governors' approval of the Meadowlands as an NHL site and John McMullen as the new owner, the New Jersey Devils (née Rockies, nay Scouts) were born.

Prior to that, in 1980, there had been one other franchise relocation. The Atlanta Flames had come into existence as an expansion franchise in 1972, the same year in which the World Hockey Association was founded. Because of the new league's competition, players' salaries shot up dramatically. The Flames seemed to get off to a good start in attracting fans, but the cost of player salaries in the new WHA era kept the fledgling franchise awash in red ink. After experiencing heavy losses in each of the Flames first four and a half seasons, the corporate owner of the franchise did not have sufficient financial resources to continue in business. Having expended futile efforts to find a new local owner, the principal owner, Tom Cousins (who had even offered in vain to give the franchise away to anyone who would commit to operate the team in

Atlanta), sought to obtain a substantial bank loan to keep the team afloat, pledging the franchise as collateral. The bank agreed to make the loan on condition that, if there were a default and foreclosure, the foreclosing noteholder would have the right to relocate the franchise. Convinced the Cousins corporation could not continue to operate without the loan and that the only alternative was immediate dissolution of the franchise, the NHL board of governors approved the granting of a conditional and limited future right to relocate, subject to the same site restrictions that had applied to the Seals.

Three and a half years later, in 1980, upon default on the loan, foreclosure and other conditions having occurred, the NHL was offered the opportunity to buy the franchise by paying off the loan. The league declined, after which, with the bank's approval, Cousins relocated the team to Calgary, and sold it there to local owners.

Thus, after sixty years of franchise stability, NHL watchers had witnessed four moves in six years (in addition to the dissolution of the Cleveland Barons, which was merged into the Minnesota North Stars in 1978 after two years of heavy financial losses). Although these had been brought about in each case because the owners were facing bankruptcy, there was at least one deep-pocket corporate owner who decided to take advantage of the trend—not because it was going broke, but because it coldly saw an opportunity to convert an annual operating loss into a capital gain. That corporation was the Ralston Purina Co., which owned the St. Louis Blues.

There had been a change of command at Ralston Purina. The former CEO, Hal Dean, was a hockey fan and had been a strong supporter of the Blues, which he felt was an important asset for the city. Even though the team lost money each year, Dean saw it as a corporate civic duty to keep the team in St. Louis. Besides, the losses were infinitesimal in the overall balance sheet of highly profitable Ralston Purina. But in 1983, Dean's successor, William Stiritz, had been elected as the new CEO. He was a hard-nosed cost-cutter, committed to getting rid of every non-profitable operation of Ralston Purina.

Stiritz immediately trained his sights on the Blues. He did not share Dean's belief that keeping the Blues in St. Louis was a worthy civic contribution by the company. He saw only that divesting itself of the Blues would add about $3 million a year to Ralston Purina's bottom line. If, in doing that, he showed his board of directors that he was a more company-oriented CEO than Dean had been, so much the better.

So Stiritz quietly set about to seek a buyer for the team. Because the Blues' financial statements showed an annual operating loss of close to $3 million, he found no takers in St. Louis.

What he did find was Bill Hunter, an enthusiastic promoter from western Canada who had been an owner in the early days of the now-defunct World Hockey Association. Hunter had somehow gotten wind of Stiritz's interest in selling the team—most likely through his acquaintance with Blues President and General Manager Emile Francis, who conducted the team's training camp each year in Regina, Saskatchewan.

Hunter convinced two Saskatchewan businessmen—Peter Batoni and Les Dube—to finance a $13 million offer to Ralston Purina for the Blues, on condition that the team be moved to Saskatoon. Hunter had convinced himself, as well as Batoni and Dube, that the Saskatoon Blues would be such a hit with the fans that advance sales of season tickets, plus sale of the television rights to Molson Breweries, would provide all the working capital needed to operate the franchise. He was also supremely confident that the provincial government of Saskatchewan would build the team a new arena.

On January 10, 1983, Blues Governor John P. Baird dropped the bombshell on Ziegler, advising him of the proposed sale to the Hunter group. He followed that up with a confirming TWX (the 1980's predecessor of the fax) on January 18, and on January 21 sent Ziegler a letter stating:

> Today Ralston Purina Board of Directors formally authorized management to proceed towards selling the St. Louis Blues NHL franchise. Enclosed please find a copy of our press release on the subject. Although a request was made in person January 10 and again by TWX on January 18, St. Louis Blues Hockey Club hereby formally requests again that the sale of the St. Louis Blues Hockey franchise to Batoni-Hunter Enterprises Limited and the transfer of the franchise to Saskatoon, Saskatchewan, for the 1983—84 season be placed on the agenda of the Board of Governors meeting to be held February 7—8, 1983. We are prepared to make a presentation to the Advisory Committee and to the full Board of Governors.

Stiritz felt he had the league over a barrel, and that it would not dare turn down the powerful and mighty Ralston Purina Co. Not only had the league already broken with its long tradition of prohibiting teams from relocating their franchise cities, but, in California, there had been a recent groundbreaking lawsuit won by Al Davis, the owner of the National Football League's Oakland Raiders, which, it appeared, augured well for Ralston Purina.

Davis had asked for approval to move his franchise to Los Angeles, which was home to the Los Angeles Rams. The NFL denied his request. Davis and the Los Angeles Coliseum then brought suit in the U.S. District Court against all other NFL clubs, alleging a conspiracy in violation of U.S. antitrust laws, claiming the league's turndown had been for anticompetitive reasons, to prevent the Raiders from competing with the Rams in the Los Angeles marketplace.

The NFL clubs were clobbered in the lawsuit. The jury awarded over $11 million to Davis and $5 million to the Coliseum. Since it was an antitrust suit, the award was trebled, bringing it close to $50 million. On top of that, the defendants were ordered to pay attorney's fees for the two plaintiffs, which amounted to an additional $10 million. Add to that what the NFL had to pay its own lawyers (probably in the vicinity of $7 million), and you can see how devastating the result had been.

As it turned out, the Los Angeles Coliseum was paid its award, but Davis was not. The NFL's appeal resulted in a Circuit Court ruling that the league was entitled to set off, against Davis's award, the difference between the value of his old franchise territory (Oakland) and his new territory (Los Angeles). Of course, Davis's original presentation to the jury had puffed and inflated the value of the Los Angeles territory as compared to Oakland's in order to get his initial award. This came back to haunt him when the Circuit Court ruled that, although he had the right to relocate his franchise, since he had chosen to move it to a more valuable territory, the increase in value was attributable to the goodwill of the NFL, not to anything he had done, and so he would be obliged to pay that difference to the league for the benefit of all NFL clubs. Davis ultimately settled the lawsuit for a fraction of what the jury had awarded him.

But these later developments—the NFL's appeal, the Circuit Court ruling, the Davis settlement—were not known at the time Ralston Purina made its move. Stiritz assumed, correctly, that the NHL would be intimidated by the prospect of what had become known as an Al Davis lawsuit. He also assumed, incorrectly, that because of that, the NHL would just roll over and die, allowing Ralston Purina to sell the Blues to the Hunter group, who would then move the team to Saskatoon.

On February 8, 1983, the board of governors convened for their All-Star Game meeting at the Long Island Marriott Hotel in Uniondale, Long Island. Prominent on the agenda was the Blues' request for approval of the sale to Batoni-Hunter, and the relocation of the team to Saskatoon.

Baird showed up with egg on his face. The Hunter group had come up short of money and had been unable to secure the financing needed to guarantee payment of its $13 million to Ralston Purina. Baird asked that the matter be removed from the agenda for this meeting, and said he would contact President Ziegler in the future when all details of the sale had been worked out. The shaky financial status of the Hunter group would not be forgotten by the governors. It would loom large several months later, when they next considered the sale. If the Hunter group was so financially strapped that it couldn't raise the $13 million needed to buy the team, where would the money come from to pay the operating costs in Saskatoon?

A couple of months later, Baird was back. The Hunter group had raised the purchase money and the Blues were seeking a special board of governors meeting to approve their deal. Ziegler scheduled it.

On May 18, 1983, a special meeting of the board of governors was convened, in executive session (two representatives per club), at the Helmsley Palace Hotel in New York City to consider Ralston Purina's renewed request for approval of the proposed sale and move of the Blues. As a prelude to that meeting, President Ziegler had assigned to the league's Advisory Committee (a select group of influential governors) the task of reviewing all the factors involved in the two transfer requests (transfer of ownership to the Hunter group and transfer of the team to Saskatoon). Ralston Purina was represented by two of its corporate executives, John Baird and "Doc" Cornwall.

Ziegler opened the session by laying out some ground rules. Citing a little known resolution the board had approved seven years earlier, he said that, notwithstanding the NHL constitution's language prohibiting relocation of a franchise, the proposed transfer of the Blues to Saskatoon could be effected by a 75 percent vote of approval. He then reminded the governors that, pursuant to the 1979 expansion plan, the four new teams (Edmonton, Hartford, Quebec, and Winnipeg) had been precluded from voting on transfers or expansion until such time as they paid in full the deferred portion of their franchise fees, but that such voting restriction no longer applied to Winnipeg. (Jets owner Barry

Shenkarow had agreed to move to the Smythe Division as part of the Rockies' move from Denver to the Meadowlands, in return for cash and forgiveness of his expansion fee obligation.)

Accordingly, with Edmonton, Hartford, and Quebec ineligible to vote (but entitled to participate in the discussions), Ziegler said there were eighteen member clubs present and entitled to vote on Ralston Purina's proposal, and if all eighteen voted, fourteen affirmative votes would be needed for approval. At Ziegler's request, Baird and Cornwall left the room so the other governors could have a discussion with the league's lawyers. Harry Shniderman, a senior partner in Covington and Burling (of Washington, D.C.), one of the nation's leading antitrust law firms, then answered a number of questions as to what the likely outcome would be if the board denied Ralston Purina's request and the league were sued under the antitrust laws. It was a scary discussion. The potential of a loss, coupled with an award of treble damages, would cripple the NHL, putting a number of its weaker teams into bankruptcy. Shniderman provided very little comfort. He could make no promises of success, but there was always the chance Ralston Purina was bluffing, and, anyway, how could the NHL deal with the certain jolt to its major league image were it to replace St. Louis with Saskatoon?

Baird and Cornwall returned to the room. Baird told the governors Ralston Purina did not intend to operate the club in the 1983–84 season and that all the Blues' staff with the exception of three administrative people had been released, including general manager Emile Francis, who had now been hired by the Hartford Whalers. He said the board of directors of Ralston Purina had approved the sale, and they were now out of the hockey business. The Saskatchewan representatives were then invited in to make their presentation to the governors. Led by Bill Hunter, the putative president of the Saskatoon Blues, the rather sizable delegation consisted of:

Mr. and Mrs. Les Dube, principal owners
Cliff Wright, Mayor of Saskatoon
Garth W. Sandstrom, Canadian attorney
Tim Embray, Saskatchewan's legislative secretary
Bob Gibbs, Air Canada executive
Ralph Weber, another Air Canada executive
John Selinger, member of the new club's board of directors
William Mitchell, another director on the new club's board

Paul Schoenhals, Saskatchewan government representative
Peter Batoni, general contractor (hoping to build new arena)
Paul D'Agata, a vice president of the Batoni Company
Boyd Robertson, a Royal Bank of Canada (Regina) vice president

Robertson addressed the critical area of financing, explaining, with the use of charts and a slide projector, the financial arrangements for purchasing the franchise from Ralston Purina and constructing a new hockey arena. It would be dependent upon the success of a contemplated $15 million public offering, a $3 million TV rights fee from Molson Breweries, and a conditional $15 million loan from Molson. Hunter and Dube would receive a 25 percent interest in the stock of the company in consideration of their contribution in putting the venture together, but they were putting up no working capital.

Schoenhals, representing the Saskatchewan government, told of the strong interest of the provincial government in the transfer of the franchise, and asserted his belief that it would be willing to provide a guarantee of the mortgage needed to finance construction of a new arena. Les Dube, the person primarily responsible for initially financing the $13 million purchase price through his real estate holdings, then discussed his financial net worth and his commitment to financially support the project.

The presentations were followed by a number of questions put by the governors and league officers. The questions were primarily directed to what would happen if the public offering failed (as a recent effort in Edmonton had done); to what extent the principals were investing in equity of the enterprise; what would happen if the Molson loan commitment were terminated—as Dube had admitted Molson was entitled to do if the new building were not completed by the unrealistic deadline of December 31, 1983; and to what extent the various required financial commitments would encumber or reduce Dube's equities in real estate, which constituted the major portion of his net worth.

Dube acknowledged that none of the principals was putting any money into the venture as equity. The financial picture which had been presented left many governors concerned they were being sold a bill of goods based on smoke and mirrors. There was no doubt as to the sincerity and enthusiasm of the people of Saskatchewan, but the project seemed to be a highly speculative one designed more to enrich the promoters than to insure the stability of an NHL franchise.

After the Saskatchewan delegation left the room, Ziegler told the governors that the Advisory Committee had made a lengthy examination of all relevant facts, had met the day before with the Ralston Purina and Saskatchewan representatives, and had completed a written report of its findings just prior to the start of the board of governors meeting that day. Copies of the report were distributed to the governors, and Ziegler recessed the meeting for an hour and fifteen minutes to give them time to read the report. It was quite lengthy and dealt with a number of issues, particularly the obvious inadequate equity and capitalization of the proposed new owners. For example, Hunter's personal financial statement alleged he had a net worth of $500,000. But the fine print showed his purported assets consisted solely of a term life insurance policy (no cash value) in the face amount of $500,000. Of course, this meant that he was only worth $500,000 dead—but not alive.

The governors stayed in the meeting room during the recess, carefully reading the report. After Ziegler reconvened the meeting there was further discussion, and then the Ralston Purina proposal was put to a vote by secret ballot, with St. Louis participating. It was defeated by a vote of 3 in favor and 15 opposed.

Baird and Cornwall, stunned by the finality of the NHL's rebuff of Ralston Purina, returned to St. Louis to report the day's events to Stiritz. Bill Hunter and the Saskatchewan group returned home with their dreams of NHL glory gone. I wondered whether Les Dube and his wife were not somewhat relieved by the NHL's vote, having heard the opinions of the governors that they could be wiped out of all they owned should the franchise meet with failure.

It did not take very long for Ralston Purina to fire the next shot. It announced immediately that it was abandoning the franchise, and then, on May 24, 1983, filed suit in St. Louis against the NHL and all its member clubs, charging the defendants with violating antitrust laws. The suit sought punitive and treble damages in the amount of $60 million.

Covington and Burling's "NHL team," Harry Shniderman, Herb Dym, and Bing Leverich, swung into action and prepared the NHL's defense. They demanded a jury trial, so our fate would be in the hands of St. Louis people who might appreciate that the NHL was on the side of their city. In addition to denying the charges by Ralston Purina, our legal strategists had decided to put the company at risk in the lawsuit in order that, somewhere down the line, the case might be settled. So a counterclaim was filed against Ralston Purina, seeking millions in punitive damages for breach of its obligation of good faith and fair dealing as a member of the joint venture that was the National Hockey League.

Our lawyers were surprised Ralston Purina had sued us in St. Louis. After all, the NHL was the hero in the scenario, trying to preserve an asset for St. Louis, while the company was the bad guy seeking to strip the community of its hockey team. They speculated that Ralston Purina's brain trust, knowing the company had been a longtime power in the political world of St. Louis, had probably felt the chance was good the case would come before one of their many friends in the judiciary.

If that was what they were thinking, they made a bad choice. The case was assigned to a very independent, maverick-type judge, William L. Hungate. "Billy White Shoes" (the nickname we gave him because he wore white shoes with his black judicial robes) had a strong reputation for integrity, and our check on his background showed no connection whatsoever with the "establishment" of St. Louis.

It took two years for the case to come to trial. In the meantime, shortly after the suit had been filed, the board of governors revoked Ralston Purina's franchise, seized its hockey assets and sold them, along with a new franchise to operate an NHL hockey club in St. Louis, to Harry Ornest for $12 million, in response to a bid that he had submitted. The money paid by Ornest for the franchise ($3 million in cash, $9 million in notes) was offered to Ralston Purina to settle the case, but Stiritz turned it down.

Ziegler did not distribute the $3 million in cash to the member clubs, but instead ordered it sequestered in a separate account, to be maintained by the league as a settlement fund, should Ralston Purina change its position. But its position did not change, and, on June 10, 1985, on a steaming hot and sultry day, the trial commenced in a St. Louis courtroom.

When I heard Herb Dym's opening statement to the jury, I knew we were going to win. He carefully and methodically described the events leading up to Ralston Purina's announcement that it was going to ship the big-league hockey franchise that was part of the pride of St. Louis out of town. He spoke of the courage of the National Hockey League in standing up to the fearsome power of Ralston Purina, and the bad faith of the company, which was ruthlessly trying to run the hockey franchise out of town. And then he uttered the phrase which I knew would not only grab the next day's headlines, but, more importantly, would connect with the sentiments of the St. Louis jury: "The National Hockey League did not want to be known as the league that took the noon balloon to Saskatoon." I could see it in the face of the jurors. We were going to win—and the trial was just starting.

During the first week, Herb Dym scored point after point with the jury, eliciting testimony from an array of witnesses from the business community of St. Louis contrary to the picture Ralston Purina had tried to portray, that the company had made no serious good faith effort to keep the team in St. Louis. It was becoming very clear to the jury that Ralston Purina's only concern had been to grab the $13 million from the Hunter organization.

On the morning of June 27, 1985 (the eighth day of testimony), as Stiritz was waiting in an anteroom to be called to the witness stand, he threw in the towel and directed his lawyers to accept the offer of settlement we had continually extended. All they got was what the NHL had received from Harry Ornest for the St. Louis Blues—the $3 million in cash, the interest it had earned in the sequestered account, and the current discounted value of the $9 million notes—not a penny more. Our team of lawyers, Covington and Burling partners Harry Shniderman, Herb Dym, and Bing Leverich, along with Steve Rosenbaum and several other dedicated associates, had done a sensational job for the NHL. Ziegler, Wirtz, all of us at the league, were overjoyed, and we held a celebratory victory dinner for them at a posh hotel in Washington. I wrote this poem for the occasion, which I read at the party to the utter enjoyment of the C and B folk:

HARRY, HERB, AND BING

We're here tonight to thank the firm of Covington and B
    for representing us in courtrooms so successfully.
It's comforting, when sued are we, to give the phone a ring,
    and know we'll have the instant help of Harry, Herb, and Bing.

Of course, at times, we must admit, we shudder at the thought
    of time sheets spewing numbers for the services we've bought,
and question why our governors, for every little thing,
    must pay enormous hourly rates for Harry, Herb, *and* Bing.

Whenever we call Harry with some litigation noise,
  why must he always say to us: "I'll run it by the boys?"
Sometimes we feel like we're the "mark," as in the film *The Sting*,
  who's playing in a poker game with Harry, Herb, and Bing.

Two heads are better, so they say, so three are better still.
  And yet, it's hard to justify such costly overkill.
Is lawyer virtuosity a nonexistent thing?
  Could we not get the same advice from Harry, Herb, *or* Bing?

Why should there be a three-legg'd stool 'pon which we're made to stand
  to gain our legal wisdom from the best firm in the land?
A lone toreador kills bulls in every Spanish ring.
  They'd never give the ears and tail to Harry, Herb, and Bing.

That's it, then, it's decided. From here on we go with one.
  A simple choice will now be made—that's all that must be done.
But, who to choose? And who to lose? It's not an easy thing.
  We'd better talk it over first—with Harry, Herb, and Bing.

Ralston Purina's failed effort was not the NHL's final confrontation with a wealthy owner seeking to relocate a franchise and likely to go to court if league approval were denied. There was to be one more, one that would be particularly heart-wrenching for me. Much to my discomfort, I would find myself, as NHL general counsel, pitted against Gordon Gund, a close friend, in a potentially explosive legal confrontation.

Gund was one of the most respected members of the board of governors. He had for years given of himself unsparingly for the good of the league, serving selflessly on the Advisory Committee and Owner-Player Executive Committee, and as the stalwart chairman of the Finance Committee. He had many admirers in the league, and I was certainly one of them.

In 1990, after losing tens of millions of dollars operating the Minnesota North Stars, Gordon and his brother George had come to the conclusion it was hopeless to continue in Minneapolis. They had quietly set their sights on moving the team to the San Francisco Bay area, where George resided. But it appeared their plans would be thwarted by the league's expansion gold rush.

Thoughts about expanding had been expressed with increasing

frequency by a number of governors, leading President Ziegler to put expansion on the agenda of the semiannual meeting of the board scheduled for the Breakers hotel in Palm Beach, Florida, on December 7, 1989. On that Pearl Harbor Day, Gund was to experience a sense of betrayal by his partners on the board of governors. At the meeting, a spirited discussion culminated in approval of a plan of expansion, despite Gund's impassioned plea for restraint until such time as all existing clubs had achieved financial health. (The discussion is described earlier in chapter 4.)

The plan's timetable called for expansion applications to be distributed to potential applicants by May 30, 1990. Among the governors it was common knowledge that Howard Baldwin, who had spent a year stumping for support for hockey in the Silicon Valley, was planning to apply for an expansion team for San Jose, which was situated within thirty miles of San Francisco Bay.

The Gunds' backs were to the wall. Were a formal application filed for a $50 million expansion franchise in San Jose, the chances of getting approval to move the North Stars to San Francisco would be nil. Gordon and George had very little choice. They would have to stake their claim to the San Francisco Bay Area before expansion applications were received. They left the meeting and headed straight for their lawyers' offices. They had to make their move, and had very little time to do it.

After conclusion of the Ralston Purina litigation, on advice of the Covington and Burling lawyers, the board of governors had approved a new bylaw—number 36—setting forth strict criteria to be followed by a franchise owner seeking to relocate its team. One of the new requirements was that a request for approval had to be filed with the league no later than February 1 of the year of the proposed move.

To preserve their legal position, the Gunds' lawyers felt it was essential to comply with bylaw 36. This meant getting a formal application to move the North Stars to the San Francisco Bay Area completed and filed with the league by January 31, 1990, scarcely more than a month away. A lot of work had to be done within that month. Years of past financial losses and projections of future losses had to be carefully documented, unsuccessful efforts to sell the North Stars to local Minnesota buyers had to be established—and they had to have the appearance of good-faith efforts—and legal strategy in the event of a league turndown had to be carefully drawn up.

Working round the clock with their lawyers, accountants, and staff, the Gunds met the deadline and, at the eleventh hour—on January 31, 1990—the Northstar Hockey Partnership (the name of the Gunds' ownership entity) filed a formal application with the league to move the North Stars to Oakland for the start of the 1990–91 season. An NHL franchise has the exclusive right to the playing of hockey within a fifty-mile radius of its home city, and Oakland is approximately thirty-two miles from San Jose, and just across the bay from San Francisco. A franchise located in any of those cities would have the exclusive territorial rights to all three. (Later, on March 19, Gordon Gund would amend the transfer application to indicate the targeted franchise city was to be South San Francisco, not Oakland.)

With an eye toward the May 30 date for issuing expansion applications and eager to get their transfer approved before Baldwin formally applied for a San Jose franchise, the Gunds asked that Ziegler schedule a special meeting on April 9, 1990, for the board of governors to take action on their application.

Ziegler immediately appointed the "Minnesota Committee," a select group of governors and league officers, assigning it the responsibility of investigating the merits of the proposed transfer and directing that it present a report on the results of its investigation to the board of governors. He also scheduled a special meeting of the board to consider the Gunds' proposal, to be held on April 9, as the Gunds had requested.

The Gunds were facing an uphill battle for several reasons. For one thing, Gordon, as a member of the Advisory Committee, had led the fight within the league to turn down the Ralston Purina proposal. In its lengthy report to the governors on the effort to relocate the Blues, the Advisory Committee had made some pronouncements which were now coming back to haunt Gordon, including: "Every governor knows that (1) no NHL franchise is awarded with a guarantee that it will not lose money; (2) some hockey clubs have been more prudently managed than others; and (3) even with prudent management, a number of members have experienced significant losses in the operation of their hockey clubs."

After reviewing the history of the St. Louis franchise, the Advisory Committee had concluded that, in its judgment, "the demonstrated potential of the St. Louis market, as well as the paid attendance and gross revenue experienced by the Blues in the past, affords a reasonable prospect of sufficient revenue to provide the basis for viability of a prudently managed NHL franchise in St. Louis." Of course, the same could be said for Minneapolis.

Another problem facing Gordon was that, as chairman of the Finance Committee, he had insisted in 1982 that John McMullen not be permitted to move the Colorado Rockies to the Meadowlands unless the league were paid a transfer fee of $10 million, which was deemed to be the value of the Meadowlands as a site for an expansion franchise. It was a rational but new concept that Gund had introduced. This was the first time in NHL history a transfer fee had been demanded. Although a compromise was reached, with McMullen paying a reduced transfer fee of only $5.1 million, the precedent had been set, and an angry McMullen would never let Gund forget how bitterly he resented having to pay it. The stakes were much higher now, with the San Francisco Bay Area deemed to have an expansion value of $50 million. Even if the governors were to approve the Gunds' request to move, Gordon's Meadowlands philosophy might likely result in a league demand that a $50 million transfer fee be paid.

On top of all of that, there was another problem. Ziegler had staked his, and the league's, reputation on the gamble that there would be at least one applicant for an expansion franchise at the new, lofty, $50 million price tag. If the Gunds were permitted to move the North Stars to the Bay Area, where Ziegler had been counting on Baldwin to apply for an expansion team, there might be no applicants, resulting in a gigantic public pratfall for Ziegler and the NHL.

Gordon knew instinctively the cards would likely be stacked against him, but may have hoped that, in view of his long and distinguished service on the board of governors, his partners would afford him favored treatment. If he did harbor such hopes, they were surely jolted by what transpired at a special meeting of the board on March 19, 1990, at the Drake Hotel in Chicago.

As he opened the meeting, Ziegler called upon Gordon to bring everyone up to date on what efforts had been made to find a local buyer for the North Stars in Minnesota. Word had gotten around that a local group headed by Harvey McKay might be interested in purchasing the team. Gordon said he had received no offers, but also said he would not consider any offer less than the $50 million the NHL was seeking for an expansion franchise. This did not please the governors, and several suggested Gordon was being unrealistic and not really making a good-faith effort to find a local buyer by asking so much for his money-losing franchise. The following dialogue then ensued:

NORMAN GREEN (CALGARY): Isn't it impossible for someone to make an offer to purchase the franchise if the final date for approval to move is April 9?

GORDON GUND: The bylaw says February 1 is the deadline for applying. We've met that deadline. What a buyer needs to know can be given to him within twenty-four hours. Harvey McKay's plan is to come in with an eleventh-hour offer and seek to delay, delay, delay—that's his strategy.

We have maintained it's in the best interest of the league to offer the franchise for no less than $50 million, rather than to force us to sell for less than the expansion price. The NBA protected the value of existing franchises. Since they announced their expansion value, all other franchises became more valuable. You're going to hurt the value of your own franchise if you force us to sell ours for less than $50 million.

Another thing to keep in mind is that a buyer who comes in and buys it for less than $50 million might come in after a year or two and demand to move to L.A., or to an area that's been awarded an expansion franchise. Under the antitrust laws, you won't have a chance in hell to stop them from doing so.

Minnesota does not want the present franchise. The only way you'll get Minnesota to want it is to let us leave, then maybe two years later, they'll want an expansion franchise.

ZIEGLER: Let me make it clear that our antitrust counsel has *not* said we cannot prevent a club from moving to an existing NHL territory or to an expansion territory. Everyone who owns a franchise in the NHL has only the right to operate in his franchise area. If Norman Green, for example, wished to move the Calgary Flames, he could not do so without the approval of the board of governors. Absent such approval, his only alternatives would be to continue to operate in the franchise city or discontinue the operation.

MARCEL AUBUT (QUEBEC): Let's say on April 9 we vote, and Gordon has not sold his franchise, and the transfer is not approved.

ZIEGLER: The options for the Gunds would be as set forth in the constitution and bylaws. Remember what happened with Ralston Purina. The request to transfer was not approved,

Ralston refused to operate the franchise, the league took control of the assets, sold them, and issued a new franchise to Harry Ornest. [Then he directed a remark directly to Gund.] What if your partners said to you they were not that concerned about whether the North Stars being sold for less than $50 million would lower the value of their franchises? [Gordon did not respond.]

PAUL MARTHA (PITTSBURGH): Gordon, Pittsburgh felt that a $50 million value for an expansion franchise made sense, *provided* there was a new opportunity presented, with building, market, etc. that would support a $50 million price.

GUND: If we're forced to sell for less than $50 million rather than be allowed to move, how are you in Pittsburgh going to get the leverage to get concessions from your city fathers?

MARTHA: I agree you have to be able to mount a threat, but that doesn't relate to the value.

JACK KRUMPE (NEW YORK ISLANDERS): I want to make it clear, Gordon, that no one here is forcing you to sell for any specific price. That's your decision.

BOB SWADOS (BUFFALO): The league's policy—for which we fought Ralston Purina—is to tell municipalities that if you make the necessary concessions to attract an NHL franchise, there will be stability and staying power.

GUND: Well, I think it's time for the league to consider changing its policy.

It was becoming clear to Gund that Ziegler and the governors were not looking favorably upon his desire to move the team to Oakland and it was becoming equally clear to Ziegler and the governors that Gund had no intention of selling the team in Minnesota. Demanding no less than $50 million for a franchise whose annual losses he had certified were in the millions did not even closely resemble a good-faith effort to sell. The battle lines were being drawn.

On March 26, 1990, the Minnesota Committee issued a thirty-three-page report to the board of governors. The opening paragraphs did not contain good news for the Gunds, who had hoped for a quick decision:

...As directed by the President, the Committee has worked assiduously to complete as much of its investigation as possible within a time frame that would permit a report to be prepared and

submitted to the Board in advance of April 9, 1990, the date
scheduled, at the request of the applicant, for Board action on its
application.

The Committee and the applicant have worked with due
diligence to meet this deadline. However, as indicated in this
report, there were areas of the investigation which could not be
completed to the satisfaction of the Committee within the limited
time available.

Having very little choice in the matter, the Gunds agreed to Ziegler's
suggestion that the meeting to consider their request to move be deferred
for a month. Ziegler scheduled the meeting for May 8–9 at the Hyatt
O'Hare Hilton in Chicago. It left the Gunds with ample time to have
their proposal voted on before the May 30 date for distribution of
expansion applications.

Speaking about expansion applications, all was not well in Howard
Baldwin's camp. He had done his homework well in San Jose, generating
genuine enthusiasm for hockey in the business community. He had a
well-heeled partner in Morris Belzberg. But the one thing they had not
anticipated was a price tag of $50 million. The last expansion fee in the
NHL had been $6 million. In 1982 the governors had gone beyond that,
believing an expansion franchise in the Meadowlands would be worth
$10 million. Even the mighty and successful NBA had only charged $32
million for its most recent expansion franchises. Perhaps the NHL might
reach for the NBA price of $32 million. If so, it would be a stretch for
Baldwin and Belzberg, but they could probably handle it. They were ill
prepared, however, for the news that came out of the Breakers in
December, 1989, that the cost would be $50 million.

Ziegler and the NHL may have been banking on Baldwin's applying
for a San Jose franchise, but as the date for distribution of expansion
applications drew near, it was not a sure thing Baldwin could afford to
apply. Of course, the Gunds did not know this.

The closer we got to the May 8 meeting, the more complicated things
became. Gordon Gund was intent on fighting for the San Francisco site,
fully aware the odds did not favor getting board approval for the move.
He was consulting with his antitrust lawyers, the prestigious Cleveland
law firm of Jones, Day, while we were consulting with our antitrust
lawyers at Covington and Burling. A number of governors were
expressing concern to Ziegler that we could end up with another

Ralston Purina–type lawsuit, which, even though we did not lose, still cost the NHL about $2 million in lawyers' fees.

If Gund won approval to move, it could sabotage the entire expansion plan. If he did not, we could be enmeshed in a costly and distasteful lawsuit with one of our most prominent governors. Gordon had succeeded in tying the NHL into a giant knot, not unlike the intricate knot tied by King Gordius of ancient Phrygia, which was cut by Alexander the Great with his sword after hearing an oracle promise that whoever could undo it would be the next ruler of Asia.

As the May 8 meeting date moved ominously into view, Calgary's Norman Green, a boyhood friend of Baldwin's partner Morris Belzberg, suggested a novel two-part approach to solving everyone's problem: What if the Gunds would sell the North Stars to Baldwin and Belzberg for $30 million, which they could afford to pay, and then, as part of the same transaction, the league would award the Gunds an expansion franchise in San Francisco for the full $50 million expansion price? If that could be accomplished, a destructive lawsuit between the Gunds and the league would be avoided; the Gunds would get their San Francisco franchise for a net cost to them of only $20 million (much less than what the league would have demanded as a transfer fee to move the North Stars); the league would be insured against failure of its plan of expansion by having at least one buyer at the $50 million price; and Baldwin and Belzberg would get an NHL franchise without the embarrassment of having to be a no-show at the $50 million ticket window.

Ziegler liked Green's suggestion and so did Baldwin and Belzberg. But the Gunds did not. They had built the North Stars with good young players whom they were expecting to take to San Francisco so their team could be competitive. They had no interest in starting all over with the dregs of talent that would come from an expansion draft. But the idea had some merit, and could serve as a starting point for negotiations between the Gunds and Baldwin. Ziegler encouraged them to negotiate.

On the eve of the May 8 meeting, the Gund and Baldwin forces reached an agreement under which, in simultaneous transactions, the league would award to Baldwin a $50 million expansion franchise for San Francisco, which would start play in the 1991–92 season; Baldwin would trade that franchise to Gund for the Minnesota North Stars and $19 million (which would be paid to the league as part of Baldwin's $50 million expansion fee, with Baldwin paying the other $31 million); the

North Stars would trade to the new San Francisco team—for delivery at the start of the 1991–92 season—all their players and their 1990 and 1991 Entry Draft picks, in return for San Francisco's draft rights in the 1991 expansion draft; and the North Stars would assign to San Francisco their share of the proceeds from the Plan of Sixth Expansion (which, with as many as three expansion teams coming in, could amount to more than $7 million).

The effect of the complex deal would be that the league would be selling a 1991 expansion franchise in San Francisco for $50 million; Baldwin (and Belzberg) would be purchasing the North Stars franchise for $31 million but would have its players for only one year, after which the roster would be filled with lesser players drafted from other teams in the 1991 expansion draft; and the Gunds would be getting a 1991 San Francisco franchise, Minnesota's 1990 and 1991 entry draft picks, and Minnesota's 1990 roster of NHL and minor league players, at a net cost of between $9 and $12 million.

The obvious one-sidedness of the deal was a testament to either the genius of Gordon Gund as a negotiator, the weakness of the Baldwin-Belzberg financial position, or, more likely, a little of each.

When presented with the deal, Ziegler and the governors were furious. They didn't care about the financial terms, but were outraged by the Gunds' player grab. There is an old saying: "Pigs get fat, but hogs get slaughtered." Most felt Gordon Gund was being a hog in pressing his obvious advantage over Baldwin. They made it clear to Gund and Baldwin they would not approve what one governor called the "rape of the North Stars." With their omnipresent lawyers, particularly Irvin Leonard of Jones, Day, the Gunds engaged in some not-so-subtle sabre-rattling. How would the league like to have to defend an antitrust action for refusing to approve a deal that had been agreed upon by two willing and able parties? Several governors urged Ziegler to let the deal go through to avoid a certain lawsuit, but he was resolute in believing the player portion of the transactions was unconscionable, and succeeded in leading the majority of governors to oppose the proposal.

In the final analysis, the Gunds had to decide whether to sue the league or seek a compromise middle position. They opted for the latter, and, with the league's help, a convoluted "cross-pollination" plan of player distribution was agreed to. Under it, San Francisco and Minnesota would have an inter-club draft and player exchange in June 1991, through which an equitable distribution of Minnesota's players would be made to both clubs. Then, in the 1991 expansion draft, Minnesota's players would be exempt and the two clubs, with alternating picks, would each draft ten of the twenty players to be claimed.

That was the complicated process through which seemingly insoluble problems were resolved, and the metamorphosis of the North Stars into the San Jose Sharks was accomplished.

7

The Real Story Behind the WHA Merger

How many times have you seen legends created by the media that had little or no basis in fact? I saw it happen with NHL president John A. Ziegler Jr.

Newspaper reporters who were unhappy with his seeming aloofness—he did not like dealing with them and so avoided them whenever possible—branded Ziegler as the hockey chief executive who did not really like the game of hockey. Nothing was further from the truth. He had played amateur hockey in Michigan, had grown up as a fan of the storied Detroit Red Wings, and loved the game with a passion. I enjoyed talking hockey with him. He was an informed student of the sport's nuances and, around his busy schedule, never missed an opportunity to attend or watch NHL games on television. However, unfortunately for his personal PR, the false negative image created by the media stuck to him, and millions of hockey fans throughout North America disparaged him because of it.

There was another fiction which the press spun about Ziegler, which, rather than detracting from his reputation, added luster and stature to it. Simply stated, John Ziegler was credited with ending the seven-year war between the NHL and the World Hockey Association. Although he received the acclaim and had indeed worked harder than anyone in trying to achieve it, it was not Ziegler who made it happen.

The Brothers Grimm wrote a fairy tale called "The Elves and the Shoemaker" about a poor man who had only enough leather to make one pair of shoes. He was too tired to make the shoes, so he laid the leather out on his workbench and went to bed. While he slept, elves came into his shop and made magnificent shoes out of the leather, which the shoemaker then found in the morning and sold for a high price, giving him the money to buy enough leather for two pair of shoes. This was repeated over many nights, and the elves ended up making the shoemaker and his wife quite wealthy.

That was a fairy tale, but it is similar to the true story of how Ziegler failed in his effort to get board of governors' approval of a plan to absorb four WHA teams into the league; how he then went to bed frustrated and disillusioned; and how, while he slept—just like in the Grimms' fairy tale—certain "NHLves" went to work in the wee hours of the morning to accomplish what he had been unable to do.

Here, for the first time, you will learn the identity of those elves who worked through the night—without Ziegler's knowledge and while he was sound asleep—to do the job for which he was later given credit.

Ziegler was elected chairman of the board of governors in June 1976, and one year later was elected president of the NHL, effective August 1977, succeeding Clarence Campbell, who had held that title for thirty-one years.

When Ziegler became chairman in 1976, the major ongoing problem facing the League was what to do about the World Hockey Association, or, more to the point, how to rid the NHL of the ravages of the NHL–WHA war that had been raging unchecked for four years. The cutthroat competition between the combatants had caused player salaries to escalate steadily, and they were now going through the roof. Club owners in both leagues were losing millions of dollars.

In the early days of the WHA, which started in 1972, the Old Guard owners of the NHL—Bill Wirtz, owner of the Chicago Blackhawks and Bruce Norris, owner of the Detroit Red Wings—had resisted all efforts within the League to seek a negotiated peace. Norris and Wirtz were respected elders in the league, each having served as chairman of the board of governors. But by 1976, after being bloodied by four years of salary war, the thinking of Norris and Wirtz had gone full circle, and their views now paralleled those of Ed Snider, which they had previously scorned.

As early as 1972, Snider had advanced the then radical idea of merging the NHL and the new WHA. He had been in the National Football League when the upstart American Football League was formed, and based on that experience, foresaw the crippling rise in player salaries that war with a rival league would bring.

Ziegler realized the economic well-being of the league depended on finding a way to end the war. One of his first acts as chairman was to appoint a Fact Finding Committee, headed by Ed Snider and Bill Wirtz, whose job would be to hold informal discussions with WHA owners to explore how the war might be brought to a close. Concerned about possible antitrust liability that might arise from such discussions, Snider and Wirtz directed one of the league's outside antitrust counsel, Richard McElroy of the Philadelphia law firm Blank Rome Klaus and Comisky, to first meet with the WHA's counsel, Harold Kohn, and Judge Leon Higginbotham in the judge's chambers. Higginbotham was the U.S. District Court judge who had jurisdiction over the two leagues in the antitrust suit that had been brought against the NHL by the WHA in the eastern district of Pennsylvania. Higginbotham gave his blessing to the parties, permitting them to meet to discuss a possible ending of their war without fear of antitrust liability arising from such discussions.

Snider and Wirtz reported on the Higginbotham meeting to the board of governors at a meeting on March 7, 1977, and said they had scheduled a meeting with WHA representatives with the intention of listening to proposals, if any, that might be made by the upstart league. They added that NHL Players' Association Executive Director Alan Eagleson had been informed of their intention to hold such a meeting.

Ziegler scheduled the Sixtieth Annual Meeting of the NHL board of governors for June 7–9, 1977, at the Queen Elizabeth Hotel in Montreal. Included on the agenda was a report from the Fact Finding Committee. At the meeting, Wirtz reported preliminary discussions had been held with representatives of the WHA, which centered around a possible expansion of the NHL by admitting WHA clubs. He stressed that the Fact Finding Committee had been authorized only to investigate the interest of the WHA and report back to the board of governors, so no negotiations had transpired. The board then approved a motion giving the committee authority to negotiate terms under which the league could expand by bringing in WHA teams, with the proviso that the committee would not have the authority to commit the league to anything.

Anxious to move ahead quickly in the hope of terminating the WHA before the start of the 1977–78 season, Ziegler announced on June 9 that he was not adjourning the annual meeting, but would instead be continuing it two weeks later in Chicago in order to give the committee an opportunity to have further discussions with the WHA. On June 22, 1977, in Chicago, Ziegler reported to the board on the progress that had been made in discussions with the WHA about possible expansion of the NHL to include WHA teams. He said there were six clubs eager to enter the NHL, and that in order to resolve conflicting claims to players (NHL clubs owned rights to players who had "defected" to the WHA), it would be important that the incoming WHA teams agree to be bound by the NHL constitution. He identified as a potential roadblock the NHL's collective bargaining agreement with the NHL Players' Association, which gave the union the right to reopen the agreement's free agent equalization provisions in the event of an NHL-WHA merger. Under those provisions, a player who became a free agent at the expiration of his contract could sign with a new club of his choosing only if the new club compensated the old one for having lost him. Obviously, this deterred free-agent movement and avoided bidding wars for free agents that might otherwise have occurred.

Ziegler and the Fact Finding Committee had taken great care to describe the pending absorption of WHA clubs as an "expansion," rather than a "merger," in order to avoid having to reopen the issue of free-agent equalization to further collective bargaining. He also described a sticky dilemma facing the three Canadian NHL clubs over the effect new teams in Canada might have on Canadian television rights. Montreal, Toronto, and Vancouver had sold exclusive Canadian rights to Molson Breweries, and Molson was concerned about protecting its TV monopoly in Canada. The Fact Finding Committee was then authorized to continue its negotiations.

Ziegler scheduled the next meeting of the board of governors three weeks later, on July 13, 1977, at the Hotel Toronto in Toronto. He was intent on pushing the "expansion" to quick completion. At the meeting, he reported that an application form had been prepared and would be submitted to the WHA representatives, together with instructions that the National Hockey League would consider reviewing applications on an individual basis submitted by a total of six existing members of the World Hockey Association.

Still on a fast track and hell-bent on achieving the WHA expansion before the start of the next season, Ziegler held another meeting of the board several weeks later, on August 9, 1977, at the Waldorf-Astoria Hotel in New York City. He opened it by distributing copies of a document titled "Proposed Conditions and Provisions for National Hockey League Expansion as Proposed by the National Hockey League Fact-Finding Committee," dated July 27, 1977. He then reported, on behalf of the Finance Committee, that applications and financial documents had been received from six member clubs of the WHA: Cincinnati, Edmonton, Houston, New England, Quebec, and Winnipeg. He said each of the applications had been examined and each applicant had been interviewed at a meeting of the Finance Committee at which a majority of the NHL clubs were represented. The applications were summarized orally. It was pointed out that in a number of instances the applicants had not complied with all requirements of the Fact Finding Committee. The governors reviewed economic and marketing data on each applicant city, and several clubs commented on a letter that had been received from the WHA's counsel that proposed substantial departures from the committee's requirements.

Addressing the various issues that had been raised, Bill Jennings (New York Rangers) made a motion to approve the terms of expansion negotiated by the committee, with several revisions to deal with new issues. The motion was seconded by Abe Pollin (Washington), and its terms were then thoroughly discussed by the governors. Then it came time to put Jennings's motion to a vote. A majority of the clubs voted to have a secret written ballot. A 75 percent vote of approval (fourteen of the eighteen clubs) would be needed for it to pass.

The ballots were counted and, shockingly, the negotiated terms of expansion lacked the necessary fourteen affirmative votes. Five clubs had voted no in the secret balloting. The motion—and Ziegler—had been defeated. Ziegler's heart sank. It was a bitter pill to swallow. With all the work he and the others had done over the past twelve months to advance the ball this far, they had been unable to get it over the goal line. Now they would have to live with the war and its salary escalation by-product for at least one more year.

With a heavy heart, Ziegler got down to the business of running the league. According to the terms of his June election to the presidency, his term would commence at the conclusion of the semiannual meeting on August 24–25, 1977, at the Royal York Hotel in Toronto. On Ziegler's recommendation, Clarence Campbell's executive director, Brian O'Neill, was made a league officer when he was appointed executive vice president, effective August 26, 1977.

The next time the board of governors met was on November 16, 1977, at the Ocean Reef Club in Key Largo, Florida. There had been no further activity on the WHA front. On Ziegler's recommendation, I was made a league officer, being appointed vice president and general counsel.

A few months later, in the early part of '1978, I took a phone call from a prominent New York lawyer, Michael Cardozo, seeking a meeting to discuss the interest of his clients—WHA club owners—in obtaining NHL membership. At Ziegler's direction, I held the meeting in my office. In attendance was our outside antitrust counsel, Harry Shniderman, of the Washington law firm Covington and Burling. Cardozo came with two other lawyers; the three of them represented four WHA clubs—Edmonton, New England, Quebec, and Winnipeg. They expressed their clients' interest in becoming members of the NHL. I listened to what they had to say and told them I would get back to them in due course.

About the same time, Ziegler received written inquiries from two WHA clubs, Houston and Winnipeg, regarding their potential for gaining admittance into the NHL. Ziegler also learned that the Houston club had launched an advertising campaign to sell 1978–79 season tickets, conditioned upon Houston's having an NHL franchise by the start of that season.

Ziegler called a special meeting of the board of governors at the O'Hare Hilton Hotel in Chicago on April 14, 1978, to advise the governors of the WHA contacts we had received, and also to have Jack Vickers, the owner of the Colorado Rockies, report on conversations he had had with the owners of the Houston club in the WHA. Vickers said he had met with the Houston people, who had "made no bones about it, they want my franchise in Houston." The governors agreed that, in order to avoid misleading the public, and as a response to the inquiry I had received from the four WHA clubs, Ziegler would issue a press release making it clear the league had no plans to expand to Houston or any other city.

The next WHA contact occurred just prior to the Sixty-First Annual Meeting of the Board of Governors, held at the Queen Elizabeth Hotel in Montreal, June 12–14, 1978, when Bill Wirtz received a phone call from a friend of his, Don Conrad, a vice president of Aetna Insurance Company, the principal owner of the New England Whalers in the WHA.

As the annual meeting opened, Wirtz reported to the board that he had received a call from a friend in the WHA in which certain things were told to him that he felt should be heard firsthand by Ziegler, members of the Advisory Committee, and me (in my role of vice president and general counsel). He did not relate what he had been told,

but said he had tentatively scheduled a meeting with WHA representatives for that night in Montreal, because he felt it might be important to
meet prior to voting on a number of items on the annual meeting's
agenda. The governors then discussed the pros and cons of meeting with
the WHA. Of course, there were those who advocated a resumption of
negotiations, but the WHA "expansion" had failed to get the requisite
majority last July, and no one was indicating he had changed his mind
and would now support it. Nonetheless, the governors did not wish to
embarrass Wirtz, so they decided he and I should attend that night's
meeting. But we were given no authority to negotiate, and our role
would be limited solely to hearing whatever matters might be presented
by the WHA folk.

What followed was one of the wackiest nights I have ever experienced. Wirtz and I arrived at the Manoir Lemoyne Hotel, located just
behind the Montreal Forum, shortly after 7:30 P.M. Since our meeting
was scheduled for 8:00 we decided to kill some time at the bar, which
was just off the hotel lobby. I ordered a coke, Bill ordered a double
Dewar's Scotch on the rocks. I was halfway through my coke when he
ordered his second. He proceeded to down a third, then a fourth. I had
known Wirtz for six years, during which I had seen him drink many a
man under the table. He was just warming up for the session that was to
follow.

At 8:00 sharp, I pushed the doorbell of the fifth floor suite where our
meeting with the WHA group was to take place. Michael Cardozo
answered and ushered Wirtz and me inside the door. We were introduced to the gathered assemblage, which included two other lawyers—
Harvey Benjamin and Robert Caporale—and five WHA owners, Marcel Aubut (Quebec), Howard Baldwin (New England), Peter Pocklington
(Edmonton), and Winnipeg's coowners, Michael Gobuty and Barry
Shenkarow. I am sure they had strategized all afternoon and evening on
what their positions would be in negotiating with us to bring about a
marriage of the NHL and WHA. When a couple marries in the Jewish
religion, the groom traditionally breaks a glass as part of the ceremony.
These WHA suitors would have been better off had they broken every
glass in their makeshift bar before we entered.

No sooner had the introductions been completed when Wirtz made a
beeline for the bar. Picking up a glass and an unopened liter-sized bottle
of Scotch, he made his way to a club chair with his booty and proceeded

(Above) In a fiery 1990 confrontation, the Gund brothers, George (left) and Gordon, convinced the board of governors to let them take half the players on the Minnesota North Stars roster for their new expansion franchise in San Jose. (Bruce Bennett Studios)

(Left) Washington Capitals Alternate Governor Peter O'Malley chaired a midnight meeting on Bill Wirtz's yacht, the *Blackhawk*, in Key Largo in March of 1979, and got the needed vote to absorb four World Hockey Association teams into the NHL. (Peter O'Malley)

John McCauley, NHL director of officiating on "Yellow Sunday." His vain effort to convince the NHL referee and linesmen to end their walkout and officiate the Bruins's 1988 Mother's Day playoff game against the Devils caused a delay of more than an hour in the start of the game. (Bruce Bennett Studios)

(Below) Marcel Aubut, the wily president and CEO of the Quebec Nordiques, masterminded the 1984 breakup of the Molson TV monopoly and engineered the blockbuster 1992 Eric Lindros trade, which led to a Stanley Cup for the Colorado Avalanche in 1996. (Bruce Bennett Studios)

(Opposite) NHL President Stein became alarmed when it appeared two directors of the Hockey Hall of Fame, Scotty Morrison, (left) and Brian O'Neill (right), were planning to elect themselves to the Hall of Fame as builders in 1993. (Bruce Bennett Studios)

(Above) Substitute linesmen Vin Godleski and Jim Sullivan, attired in yellow sweatshirts, timidly attempt to exert authority over Bruins and Devils players on "Yellow Sunday." NHL officials refused to work the game because New Jersey coach Jim Schoenfeld was behind the bench after having humiliated referee Don Koharski with his public "Have another donut" line. (Bruce Bennett Studios)

Hollywood hot-shot Stanley Jaffe, CEO of Paramount when it owned the New York Rangers at the start of the 1993–94 season. His dream of leading New York to the promised land of its first Stanley Cup since 1940 was dashed when he was fired before the start of the 1994 playoffs by Viacom, Inc.'s Sumner Redstone, who had just acquired Paramount. The Rangers went on to win the 1994 Cup, but without Jaffe. (Bruce Bennett Studios)

Vice President Jim Gregory, who had been put in charge of the NHL's hockey operations by President Gil Stein in 1992, was advised by Stein to abstain in the 1993 Hockey Hall of Fame voting. (Bruce Bennett Studios)

NHL Marketing Vice President Steve Ryan alerted President Gil Stein in November 1992 to the effort underway to elect Hall of Fame Board Chairman Scotty Morrison to the Hall as a builder. (Bruce Bennett Studios)

National Hockey League Board of Governors

Harley N. Hotchkiss,
Calgary Flames and
Chairman of the NHL

Jeremy M. Jacobs,
Boston Bruins

David E. LeFevre,
Tampa Bay Lightning

Charles F. Dolan,
New York Rangers

Michael Ilitch,
Detroit Red Wings

Charlie Lyons,
Colorado Avalanche

William W. Wirtz,
Chicago Blackhawks

William A. Torrey,
Florida Panthers

Peter Karmanos Jr.,
Carolina Hurricanes

Peter Pocklington,
Edmonton Oilers

Jerry E. Ritter,
St. Louis Blues

Robert O. Swados,
Buffalo Sabres

Steve A. Stavro,
Toronto Maple Leafs

Edward M. Snider,
Philadelphia Flyers

Ronald L. Corey,
Montreal Canadiens

Roderick M. Bryden,
Ottawa Senators

Dr. John J. McMullen,
New Jersey Devils

George Gund III,
San Jose Sharks

William M. Skehan
New York Islanders

Thomas Hicks,
Dallas Stars

Richard M. Patrick,
Washington Capitals

John E. McCaw Jr.,
Vancouver Canucks

Robert Sanderman,
Los Angeles Kings

Tony Tavares, Mighty
Ducks of Anaheim

Howard L. Baldwin,
Pittsburgh Penguins

Richard T. Burke,
Phoenix Coyotes

Photos of governors: Bruce
Bennett Studios, except:
Ritter photo courtesy *St.
Louis Post-Dispatch*; and
Burke, Corey, Dolan, Hicks,
Jacobs, McCaw, Sanderman,
Skehan, Snider, Stavro, and
Tavares photos courtesy of
the individual governors.

USA's hopes for a 1998 Olympic gold medal in Nagano, Japan, rest on the shoulders of players like Phoenix Coyotes star center Jeremy Roenick. (Bruce Bennett Studios)

to pour himself a drink. After lighting up a cigarette (Wirtz is a chain smoker), and with his cigarette in one hand and his glass containing a rapidly diminishing quantity of Scotch in the other, he began to speak to the group, who had gathered together in a semicircle facing him. I was seated alongside Wirtz, with a full view of his rapt audience.

They leaned forward attentively, the better to absorb the words of wisdom, and, they hoped, encouragement that the senior member of the NHL Board of Governors had brought. But all they heard was Wirtz-babble. Those of us in the NHL who have experienced trying to have a conversation with Wirtz while he is in his late-night, early-morning drinking mode are quite familiar with Wirtz-babble. Alas, these men were not.

Wirtz-babble is a studied technique that Wirtz has developed—not unlike Casey Stengel's famed "Stengelese"—which he uses to become intentionally vague whenever he's had a few drinks. It can best be described as a rapid-fire, nonstop monologue combining double-talk, semicoherent thoughts, cackling, unintelligible muttering, and throaty sounds not unlike a Native American's war chant, delivered amidst intermittent cigarette puffing and Scotch imbibing. It gives the listener the feeling he has heard something significant, even though he can't quite decipher it. It's like trying to nail Jello to the wall.

On this night, it went something like this: "So the World Hockey Association clubs [gulp], heh-heh, [cackle, cackle, puff] wah-wah-wah Alan Eagleson and the players [puff], heh-heh, wah-wah-wah, John Ziegler [gulp, puff, cackle] thinks the indemnification and wah-wah-wah antitrust problems [gulp] it's possible, wah-wah-wah [puff] expansion by 1978 [gulp] wah-wah-wah-wah-wah [cackle, puff-puff]." Every so often, the glimmer of a thought would shine through, leading our hosts to lean forward and listen more closely to what he was muttering, without interrupting his flow by asking, "What did you say?"

I am sure they were frequently tempted to ask that question, but they did not. They seemed to be mesmerized into thinking he was always on the verge of saying something profound, or at least finishing a sentence. But he never did. Instead, he would just light another cigarette, fill his glass with Scotch, start to down it, and resume Wirtz-babble.

I did all I could to keep a straight face and avoid laughing out loud as I watched the intent looks on the faces of these poor, misguided men who had come to this meeting in the hopes of negotiating. They started out nodding in agreement as they thought a message was being imparted by Wirtz, but after a while they looked at him with frozen smiles, as it became apparent they were getting nothing intelligible from him.

Yet, they were courteous and continued to provide Wirtz with an audience—and lots of Scotch. So he continued to smoke, drink, and babble—until five o'clock in the morning! At around 3:00 A.M., after he had consumed the entire bottle of Scotch and had started on a second, he set his necktie on fire while lighting a match. It was quickly snuffed out, but Bill, without missing a beat, continued to chatter. Finally, mercifully, after 5:00 A.M., they managed to get him up from his chair and point him to the door. His gait was close to a stagger, but tall and erect, he accompanied me out of the suite.

It was drizzling when we left the hotel, and there were no taxis in sight. We started walking in what I hoped was the right direction to the Queen Elizabeth Hotel, which was on the other side of town. After walking four or five blocks, we came upon a taxi driver who had just parked his cab for the night and was headed into his residence. I approached him and got him to agree to take us to the Queen E. As he and I returned to the taxi, we found Wirtz seated behind the steering wheel in the driver's seat, staring glassy-eyed at the windshield.

I assisted him out the door, steered him into the back seat behind the driver, and sat down next to him. Looking at Bill's face, I marveled at his composure. He sat straight up, staring into space, for most of the ride to our hotel. But at one point his eyes closed. They remained closed for about a minute. And that was to be the only sleep he would get that night.

We arrived at the hotel shortly before 6:00 A.M., and I accompanied Bill in the elevator up to his floor. I told him to get some rest, and that I would cover for him at the board meeting, which was to start at 8:00 A.M. He said he had a meeting to attend first, and would see me later. I thought to myself he was in no shape to do so, with all the booze he had consumed. But I underestimated him.

I returned to my room, with barely enough time to shave, shower, and show up at the meeting. I planned to tell the governors we had had an extensive exchange which had lasted through the night, and that Wirtz would be there later that morning to give them a report.

I got to the meeting room at 7:55, and at 8:00 on the dot Wirtz came striding in. I couldn't believe my bloodshot eyes. He was stone cold sober, bright-eyed and bushy-tailed, although he was wearing the same clothes he had on the night before, burned tie and all. I do not know how he does it, but I am in awe of Wirtz's rapid recuperative powers.

Soon after the meeting started, Ziegler called on Wirtz to report to the governors on the discussions held the night before with the WHA group. "This ought to be good," I thought to myself, wondering how Wirtz was going to describe our bizarre evening in Cardozo's suite. To my amazement, he gave a detailed description of terms which he said had been presented to us by Cardozo and the others. Of course, they were the same ones that had been proposed in the summer of 1977. He said that, since we had not been authorized to negotiate, he had been unable to pursue the matter further, but recommended that the league continue discussions with the WHA in the hopes of negotiating a deal before the start of the 1978–79 season. The man was masterful.

Ziegler then conducted an informal poll to determine the governors' reaction to the WHA initiative that Wirtz had described, and whether they favored proceeding with further discussions. As a result of the poll, it was concluded there was not enough interest shown by the NHL clubs to warrant continuing discussions. Wirtz volunteered to deliver the message to the WHA representatives, but Ziegler had been in contact with the WHA owners, and still had hopes something could be done. So, after business was concluded on June 14, he announced the meeting was only being adjourned temporarily, and would be continued twelve days later in Detroit.

The annual meeting was reconvened at the Detroit Plaza Hotel on Monday, June 26, 1978, in broadened executive session (two representatives per club, plus an attorney). Ziegler opened the meeting with a report on the status of the New York Islanders, which was about to go into receivership as a result of an ongoing lawsuit. League approval was given for the judge to appoint John Pickett, one of the limited partners in Nassau Sports (owner of the Islanders), as receiver.

Next on the agenda was a report on the status of the Colorado Rockies, which were on the verge of going under, with owner Jack Vickers having said he could no longer afford to play in Denver without substantial financial help from the city. Ziegler said the Rockies had been unsuccessful in negotiations with the City of Denver, and that Vickers had stated, first, that he had told the mayor the city's proposal was totally unacceptable and that the negotiations had been terminated by the Rockies, and second, that the Rockies definitely would not play in Colorado next season.

Ziegler then said a certain group of WHA clubs was prepared to make an offer regarding a plan of expansion; that this scheme could tie in with the Denver problem; that he had been informed that the WHA group had negotiated the rights to buy out certain other WHA clubs, with such buyout agreements terminating on June 28; and that if the NHL adopted a plan of expansion, one of the WHA clubs might buy out the Rockies as part of the expansion.

Vickers then stood up and said he had been exploring his options in Houston (a city with a WHA club), and in the New Jersey Meadowlands. He said he had told the Houston people the odds of the Rockies going to Houston are a "long shot," and that he had a firm deal in the Meadowlands with a party who had already reached agreement with Madison Square Garden for indemnification (for invading the territory of the New York Rangers). "But," he added, "if a WHA proposal were made, I would give it my best shot."

Ziegler then announced he had invited Don Conrad (an officer of Aetna Insurance Company—one of the owners of the New England Whalers) to address the governors regarding a proposal to expand the NHL by the addition of certain WHA clubs. Conrad entered the meeting room accompanied by Michael Cardozo, in whose suite Wirtz and I had spent the night two weeks earlier in Montreal. Cardozo was presented as the attorney for four WHA clubs—New England, Edmonton, Quebec, and Winnipeg. Conrad presented the terms of his proposal, which were as follows:

1. At the NHL's option, either four or five WHA clubs would join the NHL. If it were five, Cincinnati would join the four clubs Cardozo represented.

2. Each entering club would put up $4 million in cash, of which $8 million (if four clubs) or $12 million (if five clubs) would go to the NHL to purchase two (or three) existing NHL franchises, which would in turn be moved to two (or three) of the cities of the entering WHA clubs. The remaining $8 million would go into escrow to be used by the WHA clubs for "cleanup" costs (such as buyout of nonentering WHA clubs, or payment to the WHA Players' Association).

3. The entering clubs would give joint and several indemnification to the NHL and its member clubs for any and all claims arising as a result of the expansion.

4. The entering clubs would keep their present roster of WHA

players. All players on the rosters of the nonentering WHA clubs, plus all players on the rosters of the NHL clubs being purchased and collapsed, would go into a pool from which they would be selected at predetermined claiming prices by all NHL clubs (including the entering WHA clubs).

5. The first $3 million in claiming payments would be added to the $8 million cleanup fund. The balance would be distributed among the remaining NHL clubs, excluding the entering WHA clubs.

6. All unused cleanup money, up to $3 million, would be distributed among the remaining NHL clubs, excluding the entering WHA clubs.

The proposal did not fall upon very receptive ears. Vickers, for one, had no intention of selling his franchise for only $4 million. But it was seen by everyone as a starting point for negotiations.

Ziegler appointed an Expansion Committee (slightly modifying the structure of the old Fact Finding Committee), and directed its members to join him in commencing negotiations with Conrad and his WHA colleagues. Led by Ziegler, the negotiations started that evening (Monday, June 26) and lasted through most of the night. They were continued on Tuesday evening and lasted through most of that night also. The parties were in a race against time, since the Conrad group had gotten releases from the nonentering WHA clubs permitting them to make a deal, but those releases had a deadline of Wednesday, June 28, at 4:00 P.M.

The negotiating teams, by working virtually round the clock, had made significant progress, but it was clear that by the deadline they would not be able to negotiate all the terms of what was turning out to be a very complex undertaking. Ziegler advised Conrad to ask for an extension of the 4:00 P.M. deadline, but Conrad was unable to get it. So, once again, despite his yeoman effort to accomplish an NHL-WHA union, a fatigued Ziegler had to accept the bitter disappointment of yet another defeat. The war would continue through the 1978–79 season, which, thanks to the NHLves, would turn out to be the WHA's final one.

Undaunted by his latest setback, Ziegler rolled up his sleeves and went right back to work on the project. He joined the Expansion Committee with the league's high level Advisory Committee, and directed them to work together to come up with a detailed plan for the WHA expansion. With the assistance of league officers (myself included), the comprehensive Plan of Fifth Expansion was drawn up over the next few months and made ready for presentation to the board of governors.

Ziegler scheduled a special meeting of the board for March 7–8, 1979, at the Ocean Reef Hotel in Key Largo, Florida. In advance of the meeting, he spent long hours on the phone lobbying with governors to gain approval of the plan. A 75 percent affirmative vote was needed to approve expansion, which meant at least thirteen of the seventeen clubs would have to vote yes for it to take place. (The league had contracted to seventeen clubs in June 1978, when the Cleveland Barons were merged into the Minnesota North Stars.)

Two of the seventeen clubs, Boston and Los Angeles, had consistently been resolute in their opposition to bringing in WHA teams. Three others, Montreal, Toronto, and Vancouver, were believed to be also leaning toward a no vote. In order to woo their support, Ziegler had proposed a controversial provision in the plan that stripped the incoming Canadian clubs (Edmonton, Quebec, and Winnipeg) of their Canadian national television rights for five years, awarding them to the three old NHL Canadian clubs (Montreal, Toronto, and Vancouver). Ziegler hoped the acquisition of the rights would appeal to Vancouver, but he was certain it would be enough to get Montreal's support for the plan, since in September 1978, the Canadiens had been purchased by Molson Breweries, the primary owner of all Canadian NHL television broadcast rights.

But, once again, Ziegler had underestimated the opposition. On the second day of the Key Largo meeting, the last thing on the agenda was the Plan of Fifth Expansion. After a half day spent discussing its terms, the plan was moved for passage. A roll call vote was held, and to Ziegler's dismay, five clubs—Boston, Los Angeles, Toronto, Vancouver, and Montreal—voted no. The meeting was adjourned and a disconsolate Ziegler, frustrated and humiliated once again, had a late dinner, imbibed enough wine to help him forget the day's trauma, and went to sleep.

While he slept, a strange and wonderful thing took place. Peter O'Malley, Washington's alternate governor who was subbing for owner Abe Pollin at the meeting, quietly rounded up governors and alternate governors from most of the clubs and led them to Bill Wirtz's luxurious yacht for a midnight meeting. He was convinced he could turn the vote around. Although Wirtz was not able to be present (he was having a late dinner with Detroit's Bruce Norris), he had agreed to make the *Blackhawk* available for the meeting.

O'Malley was a political strategist nonpareil. He had been president of the Young Democrats and a longtime political leader in Prince George's County, Maryland, where he had managed successful campaigns for a number of officeholders. Among the lessons he had learned, and learned well, inside the Beltway of Washington, D.C., was how to count votes and how to twist arms. He decided to concentrate on turning just one of the no votes to a yes. He felt that if he could isolate one of them from the other nay-sayers, and subject that person to a steady barrage of peer pressure, the mission could be accomplished.

Electing to focus his efforts on Vancouver, he asked Canucks owner Frank Griffiths to come to the meeting. Knowing that John Pickett of the New York Islanders sometimes rubbed Griffiths the wrong way, he did not invite Pickett. He also did not invite anyone from the other antiexpansion clubs—Boston, Los Angeles, Toronto, and Montreal. The cast of elves whom he invited to work through the night and help him do the job on Griffiths were Bob Kent (Atlanta), Seymour Knox (Buffalo), Armand Pohan (Colorado), Gordon Gund (Minnesota), Bill Jennings (New York Rangers), Bob Butera (Philadelphia), Paul Martha (Pittsburgh), Emile Francis (St. Louis), and me.

O'Malley chaired the meeting, having everyone start by talking about how important it was for their franchise to accomplish the expansion. He then persistently, but in a gentlemanly way, challenged Griffiths to come up with all the reasons why he was opposed to it. As each objection was voiced, O'Malley led the others to respond with a polite refutation of its merits. The process was slow and took hours, but Griffiths was eventually won over by O'Malley's artfully administered persuasion.

The final issue that had to be resolved was Griffiths's adamant opposition to an unbalanced game schedule, which was an integral plank in the plan of expansion. Griffiths wanted to have the maximum number of home games against big-name eastern teams like Toronto, Montreal, New York, and Boston, and insisted that a balanced schedule be maintained. Under O'Malley's creative and adroit leadership, a win-win compromise was reached, which Griffiths and the other clubs all agreed to support. A balanced schedule would be guaranteed for at least the first two years after expansion, which seemed like a small price to pay for Griffiths's vote. With that accomplished, Griffiths pledged his support for the Plan of Fifth Expansion. Everyone congratulated him, and the meeting broke up. It was five o'clock in the morning.

O'Malley and I headed straight for Ziegler's apartment. We woke him and told him the good news. He had to pinch himself to be sure he was not dreaming. Needless to say, he was elated. The following week, Ziegler scheduled a new meeting to take another vote on the Plan of Fifth Expansion. It was held on March 22, 1979, at the O'Hare Hilton Hotel in Chicago, and continued a week later, on March 30, at the Warwick Hotel in New York, to incorporate several amendments into the plan. In a fitting gesture, Ziegler gave elf leader Peter O'Malley the honor of moving the resolution to adopt the NHL's Plan of Fifth Expansion. It was seconded by Frank Griffiths.

The plan was approved in a roll call vote by a majority of 14 in favor and 3 opposed (Boston, Los Angeles, and Toronto). Montreal had had a change of heart since Key Largo. The fact that a rifle bullet had been shot through the office of Molson Breweries in Winnipeg may have had something to do with that.

This chapter is not intended in any way to diminish John Ziegler, or the heroic battle he fought for years to accomplish the WHA expansion. Heaven knows, it would never have happened without his leadership. Rather, it is intended as a salute to a very unsung hero, Peter O'Malley.

Peter is a self-depreciating person who has accomplished many triumphs in his life in a behind-the-scenes manner. One of his favorite ways of introducing himself is, "Hi, I'm Peter O'Malley, the lesser," to distinguish himself from his famous Los Angeles Dodgers namesake.

In recognition of his March 7, 1978, feat as leader of the NHLves, I would dub him Peter the Great.

8

The Beer War of '84

In July of 1914, the biggest war in the history of mankind (to that date) broke out in Europe, pitting the Allies—chiefly France, Britain, Russia, Italy, and, as of 1917, the United States—against the Central Powers—Germany, Austria-Hungary, and the Ottoman Empire. It lasted four years, during which an estimated ten million people were killed and twice that number wounded. In the United States, journalists dubbed it "the war to end all wars," a misnomer that was changed to World War I when, in 1939, the far more terrible World War II began.

Historians believe the groundwork for World War II was laid in 1919 when the Allies, in the Treaty of Versailles, imposed upon their conquered foes unrealistic and humiliating terms of surrender and defeat. These conditions included forcing on Germany the burden of monumental reparations, placing limits on German armed forces, restoring Alsace and Lorraine to France, giving Prussian Poland and most of West Prussia to Poland, demilitarizing the Rhineland, and placing the mineral-rich Saar region under French administration. In their one legitimate attempt to install a permanent peace, the League of Nations was also created. Nonetheless, it was obvious that the Allies had no interest in practicing the win-win philosophy.

Because the League of Nations concept was politically unpopular in the United States, the U.S. Senate refused to ratify the Treaty of Versailles. Because it was so odious to Germany, it was unilaterally abrogated by Hitler in 1935, as a prelude to World War II.

The reason for this brief excursion into history is that I believe the situation is similar, conceptually, to what took place in the NHL when the seven-year NHL–WHA war ended in 1979. The NHL's version of the Treaty of Versailles—the Plan of Fifth Expansion—contained repugnant provisions that ultimately and inevitably led to the Beer War of '84.

WHA owners, largely vanquished and mostly helpless, had been compelled to swallow the stipulations for peace forced on them by the NHL. To one of those owners, however, the NHL's conditions were especially humiliating. That owner was Carling O'Keefe Breweries, owner of the Quebec Nordiques. As one of the three major beer companies in Canada, Carling O'Keefe competed on a daily basis with Molson and Labatt's Breweries for its share of the market. As it looked ahead to the Nordiques joining the NHL, Carling O'Keefe was excitedly planning the nationwide TV advertising campaign it would showcase during the broadcast of its team's games. But Molson had other ideas.

For years, Molson had enjoyed a hockey monopoly in Canada by purchasing all the TV rights of the three Canadian clubs (Toronto Maple Leafs, Montreal Canadiens and Vancouver Canucks), and the exclusive Canadian broadcast rights of all fourteen U.S. clubs, through what was known in the NHL as the Trans-Border Agreement (TBA). The TBA was a contract between the U.S. clubs and Canadian Sports Network, or CSN, which was the corporate vehicle employed by Molson to produce its renowned *Hockey Night in Canada* broadcasts.

On Saturday nights, *Hockey Night* broadcasts were watched, it seemed, by every man, woman, and child in the nation. The only beer commercials permitted to be shown, of course, were Molson's. *Hockey Night* was the engine that consistently drove Molson's beer sales to a comfortable lead in market share over its Canadian competitors. As the new owner of the Montreal Canadiens and the exclusive Canadian TV rights holder of the Canadiens, Maple Leafs, Canucks, and—through the Trans-Border Agreement—all U.S. clubs, Molson wielded considerable influence in the NHL, and would use it to protect its exclusive position.

The message was delivered to Ziegler early on by Ted Hough, the president of CSN, and it was later confirmed by the other Canadian clubs. With all the money Molson had invested in the league, so the message went, the NHL owed Molson loyalty and should not bring in Canadian WHA clubs, or in any other way interfere with Molson's exclusive broadcast rights in Canada. To prevent that from happening, the three Canadian clubs would staunchly oppose any accommodation with the WHA.

Ziegler did not have to be convinced. He knew Molson had the power of the pocketbook with NHL clubs. He also personally valued loyalty, and appreciated that Molson had paid millions of dollars to NHL clubs over the years to earn its position as Canada's exclusive broadcaster of NHL hockey. He also knew how to count. Thirteen affirmative votes would be needed from the seventeen NHL clubs to approve expansion. With Boston and Los Angeles in open opposition to bringing in WHA teams, a three-vote Canadian blockade would be fatal.

After all Ziegler and the majority of governors had done to end the dreadful war that was bringing the NHL to its knees, the effort was faced with doom because of Canadian television rights; it would just be too frustrating to stand by and let that happen. So Ziegler devised a strategy of pragmatic piracy to garner the Canadian votes. He decided that it would be a mandatory condition of the expansion that, for five years, the three incoming Canadian WHA teams—Edmonton, Quebec, and Winnipeg—would be stripped of all their TV broadcast rights, which would then be awarded to the three NHL teams in Canada— Montreal, Toronto, and Vancouver—with no compensation whatsoever to the new teams.

With full ownership of Canadian network rights, the three old clubs would be required only to grant back to each of the three new ones a limited local right to televise both its own home and away games through a single transmitter in its home city. But even that limited right would exist only if the game were not being shown over Molson's national network. For example, Molson could choose to preempt the Nordiques' right to show their own game in Quebec by selecting that game for a *Hockey Night in Canada* showing. In that case, the only beer commercials which would be seen by the good citizens of Quebec would be Molson's. After the first five years, the old clubs would have the option to renew their ownership of the broadcast rights, but that would be upon terms to be negotiated.

The Quebec club was represented in the negotiations by its very able president, thirty-year-old Marcel Aubut. He was traumatized when Ziegler presented the Canadian TV grab as a nonnegotiable condition. He wanted to walk out then and there, but could not get the support of his WHA colleagues because they had all been offered large sums by Molson for their local TV rights. Also, they felt it was now or never if they were ever going to get into the NHL. Aubut had no alternative but to agree to the patently unfair demand.

The two most meaningful sources of revenue for an NHL club are ticket sales and sale of broadcast rights. You can well understand that the forceful taking of its valuable TV rights, and, to make matters worse, handing them over to its arch business rival, was seen by Carling O'Keefe as something akin to rape. It was especially degrading and hurtful to Aubut because he is French Canadian, with a heightened sensitivity to being treated as a second-class citizen by the English power elite of the NHL.

Although forced to accept the galling terms in order to gain admittance to the NHL, Aubut would never forget the feeling of violation he had experienced. He would have to live with it for five years—*c'est la guerre*—but then it would be his turn to call the shots, and he would be ready with a plan of his own.

The irony of the situation was that although Ziegler had created and imposed the oppressive condition in the belief it would buy him the votes of Montreal, Toronto, and Vancouver (or at least one of them) which he desperately needed to gain approval for expansion, it did not. In March 1979, when the vote on expansion was taken, all three banded together with Boston and Los Angeles to vote it down. Ziegler felt he had been betrayed and poorly used by Molson, for whom he had loyally gone to bat. If not for the subsequent midnight meeting on the *Blackhawk*, where Peter O'Malley turned Vancouver's vote around (see chapter 7), there would have been no expansion.

But there was expansion after all, and the ruthless pilfering of the new clubs' TV rights left a legacy of bitterness that, five years later, would result in the Beer War of '84.

Although the three old Canadian clubs had been given an "option to renew" their ownership of the new clubs' TV rights after the initial five years, that option was worthless, since it would exist only upon terms "to be negotiated," and there were no terms on which Aubut would agree to let Molson continue to own the Nordiques' television rights. But merely gaining control of his club's TV rights was not enough for Aubut. He had smarted for five years under the thumb of Molson and now would settle for nothing less than dismantling Molson's long-standing monopoly and creating a competing second network in Canada under the control of Carling O'Keefe. Marcel Aubut is a true visionary. He loves challenges, and he always thinks big. Having developed an ingenious plan for accomplishing his ambitious agenda, he set about to implement it as the 1983–84 season was getting under way.

Molson's control over the broadcast of NHL games in Canada had been achieved through long-term agreements with Montreal, Toronto, and Vancouver, and from the Trans-Border Agreement, which gave Molson the exclusive right to broadcast, in Canada, the home games of all U.S. clubs. After the 1979 expansion, Molson solidified its position by signing long-term rights contracts with Edmonton and Winnipeg. Quebec turned down Molson's offer to buy its rights.

In the broadcast industry it was common knowledge that the linchpin of the Molson monopoly was its exclusive right to broadcast the Stanley Cup Playoffs in Canada, which Molson had obtained through its various rights contracts. In all major league sports, you cannot sell a game-of-the-week package to sponsors unless you include the championship game—or at least some playoff games. Although Molson, starting with the 1984–85 season, would no longer own the Nordiques' games, it would continue in the catbird seat by holding onto its other rights. It was improbable that a weak expansion team like Quebec would reach the Stanley Cup Finals in the foreseeable future, and even if it did, Molson could still deliver the games in each round of the playoffs, including half the games in the finals. Molson had long-term exclusive rights agreements with Edmonton, Montreal, Toronto, Vancouver, and Winnipeg. But the Trans-Border Agreement was a different story. It had only a two-year term, and was expiring at the end of the 1983–84 season.

Aubut saw this as the Achilles' heel of the Molson monopoly. Without the Trans-Border Agreement, Molson could not guarantee delivery of the Stanley Cup Finals to its advertisers in the event they were between two U.S. clubs. Half the battle would be to prevent Molson from getting a renewal of the Trans-Border Agreement for the 1984–85 season. The next step would be to create a second Canadian network. Aubut had a plan to do it all.

Since Molson owned the exclusive Canadian broadcast rights of five Canadian clubs, the first step in Aubut's bold plan was to have Carling O'Keefe purchase the exclusive Canadian broadcast rights of five U.S. clubs. That would effectively kill any chance of a new Molson Trans-Border Agreement for 1984–85, since the Canadian rights of five U.S. clubs would be owned by Carling O'Keefe. It would also give Aubut leverage to use against Molson when he got to stage two of his plan, the setting-up of a competing second network in Canada. He could then offer to trade to Molson the right to televise the games of his five U.S. clubs on Molson's Canadian network in exchange for Molson granting to Carling O'Keefe the right to televise the games of Molson's five Canadian clubs on Carling O'Keefe's Candian network. He selected as his five target clubs the New York Islanders, Philadelphia Flyers, Chicago Blackhawks, Minnesota North Stars, and Hartford Whalers. When Chicago's Bill Wirtz declined his offer, he substituted the Los Angeles Kings.

What next followed was the cloak-and-dagger portion of Aubut's mission. He was suspicious of the closeness of Ziegler and Molson, remembering full well that Ziegler had given Quebec's TV rights in the Plan of Fifth Expansion to Molson. Feeling it was essential to keep what he was doing under wraps until he had achieved his objective of signing five clubs, he contacted the club owners and set up confidential meetings with them. He then "got on his horse and traveled the circuit," meeting with each of them either at their homes or at other remote and clandestine locations.

Molson had been purchasing Canadian rights from U.S. clubs through the Trans-Border Agreement, which in 1983–84 paid each U. S. club $150,000. Aubut offered to double that sum and ended up agreeing to pay each of the five U.S. clubs $300,000 in 1984–85, and escalating that amount by 10 percent a year for a term of five years.

The first to sign was John Pickett, owner of the New York Islanders, on the morning of September 8, 1983. After getting Pickett's signature, Aubut headed down the New Jersey Turnpike to Philadelphia and, that same evening, got Jay Snider of the Flyers to sign on the dotted line. Minnesota was next, then Hartford, and then Los Angeles.

While Aubut was in the process of meeting with these clubs, President Ziegler got wind of what was taking place. He learned of Aubut's activity when Pickett called to ask if there were any league prohibitions against a U.S. club selling its exclusive Canadian broadcast rights. The Islanders owner revealed that he had been approached by Aubut. Ziegler hit the roof. He was furious. He thought Aubut was planning to cherry-pick the clubs with a shot at getting to the Stanley Cup Finals, buy their Canadian TV rights, and thereby deny to all other U.S. clubs the trans-border pool of Molson money they had previously been sharing. Of course, Ziegler did not realize the entirety of Aubut's plan, which would eventually create a financial windfall for all fourteen U.S. clubs far in excess of what Molson had been paying. He also did not know that Aubut had met secretly with the board of governors chairman, Bill Wirtz, and had outlined the entire plan to him. Although declining to have Chicago sign with Carling O'Keefe because of his position as chairman of the board, Wirtz had approved what Aubut was doing and encouraged him to see his plan through to completion.

As chairman of the board of governors, Wirtz was concerned about the rising costs of player salaries and the limited revenue sources available to the clubs to meet them. If Aubut were to succeed in his plan, there would be competition for NHL TV rights between two major players in Canada, and the revenues were sure to rise. He shared Aubut's belief that the operation should be kept secret until it was accomplished, and agreed to say nothing about it to Ziegler.

On September 10, 1983, Ziegler fired off this TWX to Aubut, demanding that he stop trying to buy Canadian rights of U.S. clubs:

Dear Marcel:

I have been advised that the Nordiques are seeking to acquire certain U.S. clubs' future broadcast rights in Canada. Based on what I have been advised, this is not permitted. In fact, if this solicitation continues it may result in liability on the part of the league, Nordiques, and any participating member clubs.

Therefore, I must insist that the Nordiques cease this solicitation at once. Further, please furnish to this office as soon as possible, copies of any and all agreements that may have been entered into relating to this matter.

Regards,
John A. Ziegler Jr.
President
National Hockey League

On the same date, Ziegler also sent this TWX to all clubs:

Gentlemen:

I have been advised that the Quebec Nordiques are soliciting certain U.S. member clubs in an effort to acquire future broadcast rights in Canada. This activity does not—repeat—does NOT have league approval.

No U.S. member club should make any commitment with respect to the future broadcast rights in Canada. To do so may very well expose the league and such member club or clubs to liability. Any clubs that participate in assisting the Nordiques in this enterprise from this date forward assume full responsibility to answer for all damages that may be imposed and for compensation to the other member clubs for the losses that may be incurred by them.

Regards,
John A. Ziegler Jr.
President
National Hockey League

But Ziegler's messages were to no avail. Wisely, and confidently, Aubut simply ignored them, certain that Carling O'Keefe had the same right to buy TV rights as Molson did, that what he was doing was not in violation of the league's constitution or bylaws, and—equally important—that it had the approval of Wirtz. Despite Ziegler's TWX, Minnesota, Hartford, and Los Angeles signed with Aubut when he agreed to insert a clause that the contracts would be null and void if their signing was a violation of league regulations.

After obtaining the exclusive Canadian TV rights of the five U.S. clubs, Aubut moved to phase two of his plan. On behalf of Carling O'Keefe, he offered the league a five-year contract at $5 million per year, starting with the 1984–85 season, for the *nonexclusive* Canadian broadcast rights to all regular season games played in the U.S., and all Stanley Cup Playoff games (the rights to which were owned by the league). With exclusive rights, only the rights holder could broadcast NHL games throughout Canada. Nonexclusive rights meant there could be more than one broadcaster. No one had ever before sought to buy nonexclusive rights; they always wanted exclusivity. By doing so, Aubut not only showed he was innovative, he also demonstrated genius.

In offering to buy the rights on a nonexclusive basis, Aubut was giving the league the opportunity to sell Canadian broadcast rights to both Carling O'Keefe and Molson, but, importantly, he was also circumventing Molson's right of first refusal, which would have come into play had Carling O'Keefe's offer been for exclusive rights.

Ziegler, still unhappy with Aubut, appointed a committee of governors from the U.S. clubs to consider the offer that had been received from Carling O'Keefe, and to negotiate, as well, with Molson. Bill Wirtz headed the committee. Its members included Jack Krumpe (New York Rangers), John Pickett (New York Islanders), Gordon Gund (Minnesota North Stars), and Jay Snider (Philadelphia Flyers), and I was assigned to serve as counsel.

On the morning of January 30, 1984, at the Loew's Glenpointe Hotel in Teaneck, New Jersey, during the All-Star Game break, the committee scheduled two meetings. The first was at 9:00 A.M. with Aubut and other representatives of Carling O'Keefe; the second was to be with the Molson representatives, and was scheduled to begin at 11:00 A.M. At Wirtz's suggestion, Ziegler opted not to attend either meeting so he could remain above the fray that would likely develop between the breweries.

At 10:30, the committee sent word out to the Molson people that the Carling O'Keefe meeting was running longer than expected, and that they should go to their hotel room to await word as to when to come down. But Aubut was pressing to make a deal before the close of the meeting. Carling O'Keefe's offer had been $5 million a year for five years of nonexclusive Canadian TV rights to U.S. regular season games and all Stanley Cup Playoff games, starting with the 1984–85 season. Aubut had a hunch that when Molson met with the committee it would top his offer in dollars while insisting on keeping exclusive rights. Based upon past experience, he feared the league might go for it. So he asked the committee what it would take to make a deal then and there, before they left the room. The committee responded they would do so if Aubut would up the ante to $7 million for the first year, with a 10 percent increase each subsequent year. Aubut agreed, conditioned upon immediate closing of the deal. He put it as a take-it-or-leave-it offer: The increased offer would be withdrawn if not accepted and signed, then and there. The committee accepted. A letter agreement was handwritten and signed in the room before the meeting ended, and we all toasted the deal with a glass of champagne.

At 1:00 P.M. the Molson group was ushered into the room. Ted Hough, speaking for Molson, distributed a typewritten handout and began discussing its contents, which was a lengthy, historical discussion as to why it was essential for Molson to have exclusive NHL rights in Canada. Wirtz cut him short and told him there was no chance for exclusive rights, since the league had already entered into a contract with Carling O'Keefe, granting it nonexclusive rights to Canadian broadcast of all U.S. games and all playoff games. He said the committee was offering Molson the same nonexclusive rights that had been sold to Carling O'Keefe.

Wirtz's announcement stunned the Molson delegation. At first they did not fully comprehend what they had heard, thinking Wirtz was merely reciting an offer Carling O'Keefe had made. Hough resumed talking about Molson's need for exclusive rights. But Wirtz stopped him again, and repeated that the only thing the committee wanted to hear was whether Molson would be interested in matching Carling O'Keefe's numbers to get equal nonexclusive rights. Hough and the other Molson people could barely contain their anger at what they felt had been an act of bad faith. How could the committee have made a deal with their competitor while they were cooling their heels outside the meeting room, awaiting their turn to negotiate?

After retiring from the room to caucus, Hough returned with the others and said they were not prepared at this time to respond. He said they would have to return to Canada and review their position before replying. He asked for a copy of the contract that had been signed with Carling O'Keefe so they could review the specific terms offered them. After conferring with me, Wirtz said a written summary of the key points of the deal would be prepared and sent to Molson in due course, and I did so on behalf of the committee on the Monday following All-Star Weekend. Ziegler was subsequently advised by Molson's CEO, Morgan McCammon, that our proposal was being considered.

But then, on Wednesday, April 8, 1984, I received a phone call from Robert F. Dobbin, a partner in the prominent New York law firm of Shearman and Sterling. He said S&S had been retained by CSN, and that, after reviewing the documents, they had concluded the Carling O'Keefe contract was null and void because it violated CSN's right to renew the Trans-Border Agreement. He said he would like to meet with me in my office to elaborate on his position.

I ran it by Ziegler. It was clear CSN had decided to play hardball instead of just signing on with the league for nonexclusive rights. We both assumed the request for a meeting was to demand that we rescind the Carling O'Keefe contract, and if we did not do so, CSN would then sue the league.

Ziegler was concerned about being sued by Shearman and Sterling in New York. This was a big and powerful law firm that might have connections and influence with New York judges. He felt the league would fare much better if the dispute would be litigated in Chicago, where Bill Wirtz was reputed to be politically powerful, with many friends and contacts among the judiciary. In order to get this done, we would need time to obtain lawyers in Chicago, and they would need time to draw up and file the legal papers. It therefore became imperative to stall for time, and to get Molson's New York lawyers to hold up on filing their suit. If we could file in Chicago before CSN did in New York, the Chicago court would have jurisdiction. (When lawsuits are filed on the same matter in two different courts, the court where the first suit is filed will almost always take jurisdiction over the case.) It was going to be a race to the courthouse door, but one which we could win only if CSN's lawyers did not know a race was on.

Ziegler suggested I set up a meeting with their lawyers for the following morning (Thursday), and that at the meeting I show interest in their position and ask for time to review it with the president and board of governors, promising to get back to them with an answer by the beginning of the following week. He then picked up the phone and called one of the top litigation lawyers in Chicago, W. Donald McSweeney, of the prominent law firm Schiff Hardin and Waite. We spoke to McSweeney and two of his associates, William M. Hannay and Barry S. Alberts, laying out the lawsuit we wanted them to prepare and file in Chicago as soon as the courthouse opened on the following Monday morning. It would be a suit seeking a declaratory judgment. The essence of our position was that CSN was going to sue us if we honored the Carling O'Keefe contract, and Carling O'Keefe would sue us if we did not. Since the question of the validity of the Carling O'Keefe contract turned on whether the expiring Trans-Border Agreement required the league to give CSN a renewal of its rights, we would ask the court to decide that issue by giving a legal and binding interpretation of the Trans-Border Agreement. It was the Trans-Border Agreement that gave CSN the exclusive Canadian broadcast rights for all NHL games.

McSweeney, Hannay, and Alberts went to work immediately, laboring day and night over the weekend to have the suit ready for filing first thing Monday morning. In the meantime I did exactly as Ziegler had directed, setting up a meeting with Molson's lawyers, Dobbin and Robert J. Hauser, for Thursday morning in my office. At the meeting, they told me why they felt the Trans-Border Agreement gave CSN an option to renew their exclusive rights package, which precluded the league from contracting with Carling O'Keefe. Instead of disputing their position (I believed the TBA gave CSN only a right of first refusal if someone else made an offer for exclusive rights, *not* an option to renew), I allowed that there might be validity to it, and asked that they give the league until the following week to review it and get back to them. As we had anticipated, they agreed to give us until the beginning of the next week to respond.

On Monday morning, April 13, 1984, at 10:00, when the Circuit Court of Cook County opened its doors, McSweeney filed our complaint seeking a declaratory judgment. Meanwhile, Ziegler and I were sweating it out because of the different time zones—when the Chicago courthouse opened at 10 A.M., it would be 11 A.M. in New York. What if CSN's lawyers had already filed their suit in New York, at 10 A.M., which was only 9 A.M. in Chicago? Fortunately, they did not. We had won the race. The case would be tried in Chicago.

The legal jockeying for position began almost immediately. In addition to the two Shearman and Sterling partners, CSN retained, from the giant Chicago law firm of Jenner and Block, a new battery of lawyers, Jerold S. Solovy, Howard R. Barron, Gail A. Niemann, and Michael B. Brohman. They moved to dismiss the suit on grounds the Illinois court lacked personal jurisdiction over their client. Although its crews had come to Chicago two years earlier to televise a series of playoff games back to Canada, CSN had done no other business in Illinois. Its contacts there were arguably minimal and not sufficient to place CSN within the jurisdiction of Illinois state courts. It was an issue which could go either way.

But, to challenge a court's jurisdiction, you must do so before a judge of that court, and we were hopeful Bill Wirtz's power in Chicago would swing the decision our way. I will never know whether Wirtz's influence played a part in it, but the decision went in our favor. On May 3, 1984, Judge Arthur L. Dunne denied the motion to dismiss, and directed the parties to proceed with the trial in his court.

CSN next asked for a change of venue from Judge Dunne's court, in effect asking that Judge Dunne recuse himself from the case. In legal parlance, a judge's recusal means he has voluntarily taken himself out of a case, thus requiring that a new judge be assigned. Under Chicago's state court rules, each party has a one-time-only right at the outset of a case to obtain the recusal of the judge to whom the case has been assigned. We argued against it, since a step in the case had already taken place—the motion to dismiss for lack of jurisdiction. But Judge Dunne granted the request and recused himself. A new judge was assigned— Judge Irving R. Norman—but that did not affect the key jurisdiction issue, which had already been decided in our favor.

CSN's lawyers then filed a motion to dismiss the case on the grounds of *forum non conveniens*, claiming it would be an undue hardship for CSN to try the case in Chicago, and asking that it be transferred to

Canada. On June 29, 1984, Judge Norman denied the motion. Then CSN filed its answer to our complaint, along with counterclaims seeking money damages and an injunction prohibiting the NHL from complying with the Carling O'Keefe contract pending conclusion of the trial. Judge Norman denied the motion for the injunction. This was critical. It meant the league could go forward with the Carling O'Keefe contract and all that would be left to CSN in the case would be the hope of a monetary award for damages.

McSweeney was confident we would win on the merits. The basic issue in dispute was rather simple. The Trans-Border Agreement gave CSN the exclusive right to broadcast U.S. games in Canada. It also gave CSN a right of first refusal, which meant that, at the end of the term of the TBA, if the NHL got an offer for a new TBA (with the same exclusive rights) from a third party, CSN would have the right to match that offer and get the new TBA for itself.

But that only applied to an offer for *exclusive* rights. It provided assurance to CSN that it would not be locked out by the NHL's award of exclusive rights to someone else. Since Carling O'Keefe's contract was only for *nonexclusive* rights, the right of first refusal obviously would not apply. If it did, CSN would only have a right to match Carling O'Keefe's contract to buy nonexclusive rights, an offer we had already extended to CSN.

CSN argued that its right of first refusal was really meant to be a right to renew the TBA, and since the NHL was therefore obliged to give it a new exclusive TBA for the 1984–85 season, the NHL had no right to sign a contract with Carling O'Keefe. CSN's theory had no support from the wording of the TBA, which spoke only about a right of first refusal, *not* a right to renew. So CSN's courtroom strategy became to attempt to prove, through testimony, that when the TBA was negotiated with the NHL, it was really a right to renew that had been agreed to and that the language of the TBA was ambiguous.

The TBA had been negotiated by two men. Ted Hough had represented CSN, and I had represented the NHL. So, when the trial began, on October 1, 1984, CSN's lawyers called me to the witness stand and grilled me unendingly for three consecutive days.

In my years as a litigation lawyer I had done that to many witnesses, but had never tasted it on the receiving end. It was awful. I had never experienced such pressure. I knew that if I forgot some little detail, or got confused into making a mistake by the barrage of questions being fired at me, I could blow the entire case. There was a certain sense of cosmic justice in what I was going through: It seemed like just punishment for the sins of my prior professional life.

On the morning of my second day on the stand, I was suddenly seized by an acute pain in my stomach. It felt as though I had been punched in the solar plexus. I doubled over and broke into a cold sweat. A brief recess did not help me feel better, and I testified the rest of the day while in the most extreme pain and discomfort. I could not eat anything for lunch, and found it close to impossible to concentrate on the questions or my answers.

It was then that I learned what a supportive and caring friend I had in Bill Wirtz, who had been present in the courtroom. He contacted one of the leading doctors in Chicago and got a prescription filled for medicine to treat my stomach spasms, then personally escorted me to my hotel room and ordered me some tea. He stayed with me throughout the evening, attending to my every need. By the following morning, I felt better and was able to finish my testimony with no further pain. I will always be grateful to Bill for the extraordinary care he provided to me during that time.

The trial came to a close on October 24, 1984, and we awaited, with confidence, the judge's ruling on the interpretation of the TBA. While he had it under advisement, however, Molson came to the league and agreed to settle everything by entering into the nonexclusive contract we had previously offered, on the same terms as Carling O'Keefe's.

Thus was born a new era in Canada of two national TV networks showing NHL games. Molson continued to broadcast its *Hockey Night in Canada* games over the two government-owned national networks, the CBC (in English) and Radio Canada (in French), while Carling O'Keefe showed its games over privately owned national networks, CTV (in English) and TVA (in French). Also conceived was an important new concept in the NHL, the sharing of league generated revenue by all clubs on an equal basis, which was a necessary step for the survival of small-market teams. Instead of fourteen U.S. clubs getting $150,000 a year from the Trans-Border Agreement and a small additional amount from U.S. cable, the clubs agreed—starting in 1984—that all NHL teams would share equally in the Molson and Carling O'Keefe Canadian network rights payments and all U. S. national network rights payments. As a result of this new sharing concept, each club in the league received over $750,000 in 1984, a payment which grew substantially every year thereafter.

In addition to the Chicago case, Molson also agreed to settle another one it had instigated in Canada, in which five Canadian clubs (all but Quebec) had sued the league, challenging the League's right to permit U.S. games to be shown in their franchise territories without their approval, and also challenging the league's right to control the TV broadcasts of the Stanley Cup Playoffs. The settlement of all the 1984 litigation arose out of the recommendations of the "Can-Am" Committee, which had been appointed by President Ziegler to deal with the issue of television rights north and south of the border after commencement of the Chicago case.

The two Canadian networks did not last very long, however, nor did Carling O'Keefe. With its market share of beer sales showing no increase, Carling O'Keefe decided after three years to discontinue its costly network, and told Ziegler it would like to get out of its annual commitment to pay TV rights fees to the league. Molson eagerly offered to step in, agreeing to double its rights fee to once again have exclusive broadcast rights in Canada. Since the third Canadian brewery, Labatt's, showed no interest in broadcasting NHL games, the league made the deal with Molson.

Now everyone was happy. Carling O'Keefe had rid itself of millions of dollars of annual expenses, Molson once again had its monopoly, and each NHL club was receiving a million dollars a year in league generated revenue (that figure has since risen to $3 million).

Two years later, Carling O'Keefe Breweries was acquired by Molson.

So, looking back upon the maelstrom initiated by Aubut in 1984, was everything for naught, as are so many wars, or did this one accomplish something? Clearly the positive effects of the war were tangible and lasting, uniting the league as never before and making it stronger through the concept of all clubs equally sharing millions of dollars in Canadian and U.S. TV revenues. This was a watershed step in the growth of the National Hockey League, and was the permanent legacy of Marcel Aubut and the Beer War of '84.

9

The Mother's Day Massacre

Where in the world is Carmen San Diego? Sunday, May 8, 1988, was Mother's Day. In most homes in North America, children were paying homage to Mommy, serving her breakfast in bed, while Daddy was busy relieving her of household chores and preparing to take the family out to a restaurant for dinner. I had hoped this would be the scenario in my home when I got up that morning. It wasn't to be.

Let me start at the beginning. The New Jersey Devils were the Cinderella team of the 1988 playoffs. Their new head coach, Jim Schoenfeld, had only just been named to the job on January 26, but after he took the reins the Devils finished strong, going 17–12–1. They stunned the hockey world by making the playoffs with the final shot taken in the 1987–88 regular season—in a game they had to win to make the playoffs. All other league contests had been completed when the Devils outlasted the Blackhawks in Chicago and miraculously squeaked into the playoffs with a goal by John MacLean at the 2:21 mark of overtime. With his team trailing 3–2, MacLean had tied the game with a goal at 11:57 of the third period.

Though decided underdogs, the Devils had gone on to upset the New York Islanders in six games in the division semifinals and had taken the division finals with a game seven win over the Capitals in Washington. But now they would have to face the heavily favored Bruins for the conference championship.

On Monday night, May 2, Boston comfortably won its home opener by a score of 5–3. Two nights later, though, the gritty Devils struck back, winning a grueling battle when Doug Brown scored New Jersey's third goal at 17:46 into overtime. The scene of combat then shifted to the Meadowlands, where the Bruins trounced the Devils, 6–1, on Friday night, May 6. Infuriated by some of the calls (and noncalls), by referee Don Koharski, Schoenfeld—a former talented, but often hot-tempered defenseman—lost his cool. As the final seconds of the game ticked off, Schoenfeld moved from behind his players' bench to the opening in the boards and glass used by the officials to exit the ice. Stationing himself squarely in the path of Koharski as the referee and his two linesmen, Gord Broseker and Ray Scapinello, were leaving the ice, a steamed Schoenfeld greeted him with expletives, denouncing the "horse-shit" game he had called.

Koharski made no response. Quickly brushing by the red-faced coach, he headed for the officials' dressing room along the narrow black rubber mat which lay atop the concrete floor, allowing safe passage for people on skates. But his failure to respond seemed to infuriate Schoenfeld, who by now had worked himself up to the point where he was pretty much out of control. With Devils' assistant coach Doug McKay trying in vain to restrain him, Schoenfeld followed closely on Koharski's heels, passed him, and again planted himself directly in his path. Appearing intent on escalating his verbal onslaught into a physical confrontation, the enraged Schoenfeld loudly accused Koharski of having stepped on his foot with his skate: "You fucking walked right into me. I'm standing there and you stepped on my fucking foot."

Once again Koharski walked past him on what now had become a rather crowded rubber mat, while McKay tried to pull Schoenfeld out of the way. A much bigger man, Schoenfeld resisted McKay's restraint, and in the process McKay was shoved. He inadvertently nudged Scapinello who, equally inadvertently, bumped into Koharski from behind, pushing him off the rubber mat onto the concrete, where his skates skidded, causing him to fall. Believing Schoenfeld had physically assaulted him, Koharski got up and yelled, "That's it! You're gone now! You're gone! You're out of here! You won't coach again!" He then continued on his way to the dressing room.

Schoenfeld, who by then was being pulled away by Scapinello, McKay, and several others, retorted by yelling above the crowd in a loud and derisive voice, "You fucking fell and you know it! Go ahead, you fat pig, have another donut!" It turned out to be one of the truly memorable lines in sports history.

In the pressure of playoff hockey, this was not the first time a coach and referee had exchanged unpleasantries after a game. But this time the entire confrontation had been captured by network television cameramen and shown to every hockey fan in North America. After the game, Koharski telephoned NHL executive vice president Brian O'Neill and reported Schoenfeld's abuse. The incident was replayed over and over again on all news broadcasts that night and the next day, and quickly became a cause célèbre throughout the sports world.

Koharski, whose figure was admittedly not at its trimmest, instantly became the butt of jokes by every comedian and TV talk show host. "Have another donut!" was the battle cry of everyone seeking to have fun at his expense. It was a humiliating experience, made even worse by his belief that he had also been the victim of a physical attack by Schoenfeld.

In solidarity with Koharski, all NHL referees and linesmen were outraged. Dave Newell, president of their union, the NHL Officials Association, tried to reach President Ziegler on Friday night and Saturday to voice their protest. But Ziegler was nowhere to be found. Calls to the NHL's offices in New York, Montreal, and Toronto, and to Ziegler's residences in New York and Ortonville, Michigan, proved fruitless. His secretary did not know his whereabouts, nor did his fiancée, nor did Board of Governors Chairman Bill Wirtz, nor did any of the league's vice presidents.

Late Friday night, unable to find Ziegler, Newell reached O'Neill, to whom Ziegler had delegated the responsibility for disciplining hockey players (but not coaches). Newell demanded of O'Neill that the league do something to discipline Schoenfeld before the next game in the series, which was scheduled to be played at the Meadowlands on Sunday night, May 8.

On Saturday, O'Neill spoke by phone to Schoenfeld and league officers Jim Gregory (vice president of hockey operations) and John McCauley (director of officiating). Schoenfeld admitted making the now infamous derogatory donut statement, but insisted the confrontation had been only verbal, and that he had neither pushed Koharski nor done anything else which caused the referee to slip on the concrete. Gregory and McCauley, who had seen the videotapes and talked to other witnesses, could offer no support for Koharski's allegation that he had been physically abused.

O'Neill tried in vain to reach Ziegler. No one knew where he was. Faced with a potential rebellion by the league's officiating staff, O'Neill took it upon himself to do something about it. At 12:30 P.M. on Sunday, May 8, still unable to reach Ziegler, O'Neill notified Devils General

Manager Lou Lamoriello that he had suspended Schoenfeld for at least one game because of his verbal abuse of Koharski, and that his investigation was continuing to determine if there had been physical abuse, for which there might be a further suspension. And he said that because of the suspension, Schoenfeld would not be permitted behind the Devils' bench for Sunday's game four of the conference championship series.

The phone rang at 5:00 P.M., while my wife and I were preparing to leave our suburban Philadelphia home to go to dinner. It was Lamoriello, calling to advise me that lawyers for the Devils were on their way to the residence of a judge in northern New Jersey, James F. Madden, to seek a temporary restraining order against the league to prevent us from implementing the suspension of Schoenfeld, decreed by O'Neill. He said the judge would be conducting a hearing in his home in about a half hour, and he was calling me as a courtesy to advise the league of their action. I said it would take several hours for me to get there, and asked if he would agree to postpone the hearing until later that evening. He refused, but gave me Judge Madden's home phone number.

I called the judge and made the same request. Again it was denied. In our conversation, he first said he knew nothing about the case, and had merely agreed to make himself available for a hearing. But when I said this was a very important matter that could affect the Stanley Cup Playoffs, and the league's position should be heard, he responded, "How could O'Neill have suspended the coach without even giving him a hearing?" It was obvious the Devils had found a judge sympathetic to their cause, and I assumed it was a foregone conclusion he would sign the restraining order, even though he said he would call me during his hearing to let me present the league's position.

In vain I tried to reach Ziegler, learning—as had Newell and O'Neill—that no one knew his whereabouts. One of the people I called in trying to find Ziegler was Board of Governors Chairman Bill Wirtz, who was at home. I filled him in on what was going on. He did not know where Ziegler was, but said he would try to find him. He also asked that I call him as soon as I learned what the judge had done. I told him I would get word to the game officials to let them know what was afoot, and that we might be under a court order to permit Schoenfeld to be behind the bench.

I reached Gregory at his hotel room in Edmonton, where he had gone to supervise the officiating in the Campbell Conference championship series between the Oilers and Red Wings. He said McCauley was the supervisor on the scene in New Jersey and that he had already left his hotel for the Brendan Byrne Arena in the Meadowlands. But he was expecting to hear from McCauley shortly and said he would tell him to call me. I gave him the number of my second phone so I could keep my primary line open to receive the call from the judge.

I called Wirtz, who had still been unable to locate Ziegler. He asked that when I heard from McCauley I add him to the conversation through my phone's conference feature. Within minutes McCauley called from a pay telephone at the arena and I hooked him up to a conference call with Wirtz. McCauley said he had been told by Newell that the officials would refuse to work the game if Schoenfeld were behind the bench. Wirtz asked if he thought they were bluffing. McCauley said, "No. I believe they're dead serious."

"Wow!" I thought to myself, "every hockey fan in North America is planning to watch this game tonight. What a fiasco it will be if we have to call it off because we have no one to officiate. Damn those Devils!"

Wirtz directed McCauley to immediately find non-NHL substitute officials and have them ready to fill in should the NHL officials walk. Wirtz said the most important thing of all was that the game be played, and that it start on time—with or without NHL officials. McCauley said he was sure he would be able to line up substitute officials, and that he would get right on it. I told him I would get back to him and directed him to post two people at the pay phone who could find him when I called.

Within a half hour Judge Madden called. Devils' attorneys John A. Conte and Patrick Gilmartin were at his home, along with Lamoriello. He said he felt Schoenfeld had been denied due process because he had been suspended without a hearing. I argued that there had been no need for a hearing since Schoenfeld had admitted to O'Neill on the telephone that he had made the derogatory statements to Koharski, which had been the sole basis for his one-game suspension. I also told him the league might be faced with a terrible crisis because of the stand the game officials were taking. The judge listened to what I had to say, then, at about 7:00 P.M., said he was signing the temporary restraining order prohibiting the league from enforcing its suspension of Schoenfeld, and that he had scheduled a court hearing on Tuesday morning, May 10, to decide whether a permanent injunction would be issued.

I got Wirtz on my conference line. We called the New Jersey pay phone number and asked McCauley's aide to call him to the phone immediately. It took him about ten minutes to get there. I told McCauley of the judge's order and that we would have to permit Schoenfeld to coach the game. McCauley said he still believed the assigned officials, referee Dave Newell and linesmen Gord Broseker and Ray Scapinello, would refuse to work the game, although he would try to convince them to do so. Wirtz asked if he had the backup officials ready. He said he did, having arranged for amateur referees to work the game; they were on standby alert. Wirtz repeated what he had said earlier: "The most important thing is that the game start on time." As it would turn out, however, McCauley was more committed to playing shuttle diplomat than he was to following Wirtz's direction.

McCauley then left to attend to his business, and Wirtz and I continued to talk about a number of things, including what disciplinary steps should be imposed on the officials (he wanted to come down hard on them); where Ziegler might be (we had no clue); how important it was that the game be played; and that it must start on time.

As game time approached, Wirtz and I were on the phone with each other watching our television screens. We were horrified and could not believe our eyes, and ears, when the television announcers said there had been an unexpected delay in getting the game started. An announcement had also been made in the arena that the 7:45 starting time had been delayed. The players had returned to their dressing rooms.

We frantically put in a call to the pay phone monitor and told him to get McCauley to the phone immediately. He found him in the officials' dressing room, conferring with the NHL officials, still trying to convince them to work the game. By the time he got on the line with us, it was 8:10. Wirtz was fuming. He read the riot act to McCauley and ordered him to get the substitute officials on the ice immediately and start the game. But once again, McCauley went back to the NHL officials to try to get them to take the ice.

The spectators were starting to get restless, chanting "We want hockey! We want hockey!" Wirtz and I watched helplessly as the minutes ticked by. Wirtz was outraged that McCauley's failure to follow his strict directions was giving the league a huge black eye. But the worst was yet to come.

At 8:45 the players returned, and we were shocked to see the new officials who timidly skated onto the ice. They appeared to be in their fifties, or older, and were visibly not in top physical condition, like NHL referees and linesmen. McCauley's choice for substitute referee was Paul McInnis, a fifty-two-year-old Devils' goal judge who managed a skating rink in Yonkers, New York. The linesmen were fifty-one-year-old Vin Godleski, the Devils' timekeeper, who was sales manager for a satellite dish company, and Jim Sullivan, a fifty-year-old retired police officer who served as timekeeper for the New York Islanders. Sullivan had been scheduled to be the official timekeeper for this night's game.

As they circled the rink, they were wobbly on their skates. The two linesmen collided while making the turn around a goal net.

Instead of wearing officials' black-and-white striped shirts, the two linesmen were attired in plain yellow practice jerseys. Wirtz cursed McCauley. What the hell had he been doing all evening? Although he had assured us he had the substitute officials ready to go, he apparently never quite believed the NHL officials would carry through on their threat, and consequently was woefully unprepared. Now the NHL would be the laughingstock of North America. After giving the players time to warm up, the game got underway at 8:50, more than an hour late.

McCauley, a former referee, spoke to both coaches before the game and cautioned them to have their players behave themselves and not let the game get out of control. He then stationed himself at the time-keeper's table and did a pretty good job of giving the sub-refs confidence by his presence. At every stoppage of play, they would skate over to him and confer.

The game was played with no major catastrophes, thank goodness. When the second period started, Godleski and Sullivan were wearing striped shirts. The Devils were victorious, 3–1, tying the series at 2–2 as the venue shifted to Boston for game five.

As expected, the media roasted the NHL over the incident, and seemed particularly incensed that Ziegler had not been available to deal with the crisis. Ziegler showed up in Boston on Tuesday, May 10, and held a press conference before a particularly hostile group of reporters. They demanded to know where he had been. He said it was none of their business, which, needless to say, endeared him to all. Smooth. As for the New Jersey lawsuit, on Monday, May 9, Ziegler revoked the suspension order O'Neill had issued, thus rendering the entire matter moot. The New Jersey court had no choice but to dismiss the case on Tuesday morning. Then, on Tuesday afternoon, in Boston, Ziegler gave Schoenfeld a full-scale hearing on the Koharski "donut" incident, after which he suspended Schoenfeld for game five.

The officials had now been appeased and were prepared to return to work. Despite Wirtz's urging him to discipline them, Ziegler declined to do so for fear they might walk out again with the Stanley Cup Finals on the horizon. Without their coach behind the bench, the Devils were annihilated by the Bruins, 7–1, in game five, but they returned the favor back at the Meadowlands, beating Boston 6–3, to force a seventh game. The Devils' late-season surge finally came to a close in Boston Garden, however, with a 6–2 loss to the Bruins.

I wish I could tell you where Ziegler had been during the Mother's Day Massacre, but I can't. Ziegler was my boss. I was not in a position to ask him, and he didn't volunteer to tell me.

Almost a decade has passed since that fateful Mother's Day, which some in hockey have called Yellow Sunday. As happens sooner or later to most coaches, Jim Schoenfeld was fired by the Devils early in the 1989–90 season. In the middle of the 1993–94 season, he was hired as head coach by Washington, and then was fired by the Caps after the 1996–1997 season, only to then be hired as head coach of the Phoenix Coyotes. Don Koharski became serious about training and eating right, and slimmed down noticeably. He is now considered to be one of the best referees in the NHL. The substitute officials, Paul McInnis, Vin Godleski, and Jim Sullivan, never reffed another NHL game, but their place in hockey history is secure forever.

10

A View From the Top

On Monday, June 22, 1992, in Montreal, in the midst of its annual meeting, the NHL board of governors created an uproar in the world of hockey when it replaced the league's longtime leadership structure without prior notice. The office of chairman of the board, occupied for fourteen consecutive years by the dean of governors, Chicago Blackhawks owner Bill Wirtz, was turned over to Los Angeles Kings owner Bruce McNall. John Ziegler, fifteen years the league's president and CEO, was suddenly gone. In his place, I had been elected to serve as the league's new chief executive. As president, I was confronted with the "buck stops here" responsibility known only to the man at the top, and the exhilarating challenge of creating my own agenda and moving it forward. What follows, in no particular order, are some of the memorable events of my one-year stint as the fifth and last president of the National Hockey League.

The Eric Lindros trade flap was a saga in progress when I took office. On Saturday, June 20, 1992, the morning of the entry draft, President Ziegler had been advised by Marcel Aubut, president of the Quebec Nordiques, that his club had traded the rights to superstar-in-waiting Lindros to the New York Rangers. This was immediately challenged by Philadelphia Flyers President Jay Snider, who told Ziegler Quebec could not make that trade to New York because it had already traded Lindros's rights to Philadelphia.

Lindros was a nineteen-year-old center from London, Ontario, who had been a Junior All-Star with Oshawa in the Ontario Hockey League, and had starred for the Canadian National Team in the 1991 Canada Cup Tournament and the 1992 Olympics. Among hockey experts the consensus was that Lindros would be the successor to Wayne Gretzky and Mario Lemieux as the NHL's primary superstar. Gretzky had been called the Great One. Lemieux had been called the Magnificent One. Lindros was being called the Next One.

While the entry draft was proceeding on the main floor of the Montreal Forum, Ziegler held a meeting in a back room with Aubut, Snider, Rangers General Manager Neil Smith, and me.

The parties expressed their positions clearly. Snider claimed Philadelphia had concluded a trade with Quebec earlier that morning, trading a package of players, draft picks, and cash for the rights to Lindros. Aubut acknowledged such a trade had been discussed that morning, but said it had not been consummated and, instead, Quebec had subsequently traded Lindros's rights to New York for a similar package. Smith could shed no light on what had earlier transpired between Quebec and Philadelphia, but confirmed Aubut's account of the trade the Rangers believed they had made with Quebec.

Some Flyers people, including minority owners Sylvan and Fran Tobin, suspect to this day that they may have been victims of skullduggery by Aubut. I do not share that view. French-Canadian Marcel occasionally misses the meaning of a word or two in English, and I believe that may possibly explain the unusual dilemma in which he found himself as a result of the Lindros trade talks.

Although Quebec was intricately involved, the conflict Ziegler had to deal with was one between the Rangers and Flyers over the rights to Lindros. Under the NHL's constitution, it was the duty of the president to arbitrate such disputes, but, at the request of any party, an independent outside arbitrator would be used instead of the president.

Because of the stature of Lindros—the most heralded amateur hockey player in the world—Ziegler was concerned about the potentially divisive effect of having the dispute arbitrated within the league, and suggested that the parties consider using an outside arbitrator. They readily agreed. Ziegler recommended Toronto lawyer Larry Bertuzzi as the arbitrator and, after making some phone calls to check on his reputation, all the parties agreed to the appointment.

One thing Ziegler insisted upon was quick resolution of the dispute. A phone call to Bertuzzi resulted in his agreement to drop everything and start right away. He was on the next flight to Montreal, and had his first meeting with the parties the next day, Sunday morning, June 21.

On Monday, June 22, I was elected president. While Bertuzzi was conducting his hearings, I was busy planning my travel schedule, having decided to start my presidency with a tour of NHL cities. Eager to complete my tour by August, I had set an ambitious work schedule of Sunday through Wednesday for the tour, Thursday and Friday in the office, and Saturday as a day of rest at home.

Although scrupulously avoiding discussion of the merits of the case, I remained in touch with Bertuzzi and followed his progress so as to know when he would be concluding his work. Interest in the Lindros case was extremely high, and there was no doubt the announcement of Bertuzzi's decision would be a mammoth media event.

On Friday night, June 26, less than a week after beginning his assignment, Bertuzzi told me he had completed his hearings and would write his decision over the weekend. I did not ask which team had won. With my known Flyers background (I was a Philadelphian, a Flyers fan, and had worked for the Flyers in the seventies), I was particularly sensitive to the importance of keeping hands off. We decided to allow an extra day, Monday, in case Larry needed it to complete his writing, and agreed we would make plans to have him announce his decision to the teams and the media on Tuesday, June 30.

Gary Meagher, the league's director of public relations, arranged all the details, setting up two conference phone calls for Tuesday. The first would link the Nordiques, Flyers, Rangers, Bertuzzi, and me. I would be in Chicago, on my tour. Bertuzzi would be in his law office in Toronto. The second call would immediately follow, making Bertuzzi and me available to the media in North America for a telephone press conference. Meagher issued a press release on Monday, notifying the media how to get hooked up to the conference call. The response was overwhelming. An all-time record number of applicants, 125, signed up to participate.

A consummate professional, Meagher promptly developed logistics for the precedent-setting electronic press conference. He would lead off by explaining ground rules. When it came time for questions, he would be the gatekeeper, giving first preference to media representatives from Quebec, New York, and Philadelphia, and then to the media at large. I would then make a brief introductory statement, and Bertuzzi would read his decision. After that, we would throw it open to reporters' questions.

On Tuesday morning, Meagher and I were stationed in the conference room of the Wirtz Corporation's offices in Chicago, which Bill Wirtz had made available for us to use as our Chicago headquarters. The

conference call with Bertuzzi and the three hockey clubs began at 10:00
A.M., Eastern time. After the conference operator called the roll of the
parties on the line, I opened with the following statement:

> Good morning, gentlemen. This is Gil Stein. The league is
> grateful to Larry Bertuzzi for the hard work he has done in
> performing this most difficult assignment in record time. Had this
> dispute gone to court, it would have taken months to get it
> resolved. We are all about to hear for the first time the decision he
> has reached. I have no idea who will be the winner, but I do know
> only one team can win and the other must lose.
>
> An unprecedented number of media representatives are waiting
> to hear the decision as soon as this call ends. The entire hockey
> world will be watching. I remind you that you are all sportsmen,
> and urge that you accept this decision in the same spirit of
> sportsmanship that our players display with their traditional
> handshakes at the conclusion of the Stanley Cup Playoffs.
>
> I now introduce arbitrator Larry Bertuzzi.

Bertuzzi then read his lengthy decision. You all know how it came
out. The Flyers won—they got Eric Lindros. But the way he had written
his decision, the announcement of the winner did not come until the
end.

As soon as he had finished, Meagher was on the phone to the
conference operator to get the media press conference underway. While
he was doing that, the phone rang in the adjoining office. It was for me.
Stanley Jaffe, the governor of the New York Rangers, was calling.

"Hello," I said.

"I'm fucking furious!" Jaffe yelled.

I put my hand over the receiver's mouthpiece, rolled my eyes
heavenward, and uttered aloud, to no one in particular, "Sportsmen!"

"I know you're upset, Stanley," I said.

"I'm not upset! I'm fucking furious!" he screamed.

"You talked to that arbitrator, didn't you?" he demanded accusingly.

"Yes, I did," I said.

"So thats what happened!"

"No, that's not what happened!" I said, getting my back up. "I never
talked to him about the case, only about when his decision would be
ready."

"I find that hard to believe," he responded.

"Well, you'd better believe it, because it's true," I said. "I know you're unhappy, Stanley, but you had better be careful what you say. Don't push your luck too far."

He got the message. The conversation ended. So much for sportsmanship.

After my election as president, the number-one priority on my quickly developed agenda was to get NHL games broadcast on U.S. network television.

In the wake of the NHL's first expansion in 1967, the league had sold U.S. rights for a game-of-the-week package to CBS for less than $2 million a year—total! Three years later, the rights were bought by NBC for slightly more. The national ratings were consistently weak, however, coming in a poor third behind ABC's *Wide World of Sports* anthology and CBS's NBA telecasts. In fact, the ratings were, so poor that by 1974 no U.S. network was interested in broadcasting NHL hockey. Interestingly, at around the same time the National Basketball Association, the NHL's rival for network television dollars, had sold its network rights for a game-of-the-week package to CBS for under $2 million a year.

Fast forward to 1992. The NHL was still limping along, having sold its U.S. network rights in the 1991–92 season to cable carrier Sports-Channel for $5 million. By contrast, the NBA was receiving $230 million a year from NBC and cable's TNT. Unlike the NHL, the NBA for the past twenty years had made building its U.S. network television revenues its top priority.

I felt we had to start playing catch-up—better late than never. The discrepancy in local revenues between our small-market and big-market teams was getting so great that the small-market teams would soon be unable to compete in the marketplace for star free agents. A significant leap in shared league generated revenues from U.S. network rights could be the key to the ultimate survival of the league.

The major networks had shown no interest in hockey because of its traditionally low ratings, but no one had ever made an effort to determine why the ratings were so crummy and what could be done to boost them. Oh, sure, there were theories galore. The leading ones usually voiced: It's too difficult to follow the puck on TV (how many times have you heard that one?); and, hockey's too violent, people don't like the fighting (another favorite of theorists).

Forget those old wives' tales. There was one reason, and only one, why we could not deliver ratings—there simply weren't enough hockey

fans in the U.S. Ask yourself this question: Have any hockey fans that
you know ever said to you they won't watch hockey on television
because they can't follow the puck? With all due respect to the Fox
Network, and the blue circle–red streak electronic puck they started
using recently, I am sure your answer is no.

The same is true for fighting. Hockey fans are about evenly divided
on the issue. Some fans like the fighting, some do not. But no fan stops
watching hockey because of it. It is only the nonfans, who would not
watch hockey anyway, who delight in suggesting reasons why people
don't tune in. In fact, my own personal experience taught me all I needed
to know about nonhockey fans, because I had been one of them.

I grew up in a Philadelphia without NHL hockey. (Remember, in the
1950s this was not strange; only four U.S. cities were lucky enough to
have major league hockey.) I was a committed sports fan, but the sports
I knew and followed were the big three—football, baseball, and
basketball. I had never seen a hockey game and did not see this as a
missed experience in need of correction. If, while scanning *Sports
Illustrated*, I came to a hockey story, I would just turn the pages without
reading it. I had no interest. The same was true for stories about
bowling, soccer, or harness racing, for that matter. Likewise, if I were
spinning the TV dial and came upon a hockey game, I would move on to
the next channel.

In the early fifties, while attending Boston University Law School, I
rarely missed a Celtics basketball game—I loved NBA basketball. As a
fan of the rival Philadelphia Warriors, I scouted the Celtics for Warriors
owner and coach Eddie Gottlieb.

Several times a year, seeking to promote NBA basketball in Boston
(the Celtics were far from a sellout in their early years), Walter Brown
(who owned Boston Garden, the Celtics, the Bruins, and the American
Hockey League Braves) scheduled hockey-basketball doubleheaders at
the Garden. The Celtics and Braves played their regularly scheduled
games on the same night—two games for one price. The doubleheaders
were popular and usually sold out.

The evening would begin with the Celtics game. It would be played
on a basketball floor laid on top of the ice surface, separated from the
ice by only a thin layer of black rubber mats. The mats did not cover the
entire ice surface, but only a portion of it extending about ten feet past
the perimeter of the basketball floor. When the game ended, Garden
workers would come out to remove the basketball floor and the rubber

mats, and then the hockey teams would skate out to start their game. While the conversion to an ice surface was taking place, I would leave and go home. Yes, even for free, I had no interest in watching hockey.

So, you see, I know what's in the heads of nonhockey fans, because that's how it was for me—until 1967, the year the Flyers were born. I was a friend of Flyers owner Ed Snider and of Irv Kosloff, who owned the Philadelphia 76ers basketball team in the NBA. Both clubs played in the brand-new local arena, the Spectrum, and I was invited by each owner to sit with him in the "super box" at his club's games. I had never before seen a hockey game. I believed NBA basketball was the best and most exciting sport in the world, and the 76ers were a championship team, starring Wilt Chamberlain.

With the opening of the 1967–68 season, I began a new ritual. Following work, I went to 76ers games on Wednesdays and Flyers games on Thursdays. After three or four weeks of watching both sports from the same vantage point in the arena, I began to experience a feeling of boredom at the basketball games. I couldn't believe it—in comparison to hockey, basketball had begun to seem slow to me. Amazing. I was hooked on hockey. I soon stopped going to the basketball games and couldn't get enough of hockey—whether live, on TV, or on radio.

My experience taught me valuable lessons. I learned you can't just put NHL hockey on TV and expect nonhockey fans to watch. I also learned the only way to get people to watch NHL hockey on television is to first make them fans, and the best way to make them fans is to put an NHL team in their city, and then, provided the club does a good job of promoting and finds a way to get people to come to games, hockey will do the rest. Over time, the fan base will grow, and once people became hockey fans, they will remain devoted to the sport for life. If we did that in enough cities in the U.S., the TV ratings would follow.

So I realized what had to be done. If we were ever going to increase our ratings, the NHL would have to expand into the major television markets of the United States. California had a larger population than Canada, yet we had only two franchises there. Each of the other major sports had four. There were no NHL franchises in other large TV markets like Miami, Dallas, Houston, Phoenix, Denver, and Atlanta. Hockey was among the best-kept secrets in the United States, and expansion into these markets would be crucial to get the kind of ratings that would appeal to major networks. Thus, as president, expansion became the key to my agenda.

But there was another opportunity to build ratings, which I had also learned about from personal experience and observation. And that was the unique world stage that is presented once every four years by the Olympics. From the opening parade of nations to the closing ceremonies, it seems just about everyone in the U.S. is addicted to the Olympics. People who would never think of watching events such as bicycle racing, water polo, downhill skiing—or hockey!—at any other time will do so avidly if they are televised as part of Olympic competition. They would even watch dancing bears if it were an Olympic event.

For years, whenever the Winter Olympics were discussed at board of governors meetings, the emphasis would be upon what we needed to do to prevent the Canadian and U.S. Olympic governing bodies from taking our star hockey players for their teams. Whenever that came up, Philadelphia Flyers owner Ed Snider would say, "Instead of working on keeping our players out of the Olympics, we should be figuring out how to get them *into* the Olympics." But few listened.

With the 1994 Winter Olympics on the horizon, I decided to propose a bold new idea to the board of governors and the hockey world. What if we were to declare an Olympic holiday in our 1993–94 schedule, and block out a two-to-three-week period in February 1994, when we would schedule no NHL games? Furthermore, we would make our players available to their countries' Olympic teams. We would still play our full eighty-four-game schedule by starting the season a week earlier and ending it a week or two later than usual. Instead of the comparatively second-rate quality of hockey usually displayed in the Olympics, the huge number of committed Olympic watchers would be treated to a sight they had never previously seen—the NHL's stars displaying their dazzling virtuoso skills while competing on the world stage for Olympic medals.

Unlike the NBA's "Dream Team" Olympic participation, the winner of the gold would not be preordained. Strong teams from Canada, the United States, Russia, the Czech Republic, Slovakia, Sweden, and Finland would do battle for Olympic supremacy, providing the most exciting, high-quality hockey competition the world had ever seen. With a reasonable amount of luck, our strong U.S. entry (led by John Vaniesbrouck, Mike Richter, Brian Leetch, Jeremy Roenick, Chris Chelios, Kevin Stevens, Pat LaFontaine, and others) should reach the medal round and have a shot at the gold. Nothing turns the American TV audience on like the sight of the Stars and Stripes being waved furiously by hockey fans at an Olympic match with a gold medal on the line.

What if the U.S. team won it all? It would not be like 1980, when the U.S. hockey team won the 1980 Olympic gold medal. The hockey players became instant heroes, but the acclaim was short-lived because those new heroes, like goaltender Jim Craig and team captain Mike Eruzione, were not talented enough to play in the NHL, so they were never to be seen again as hockey stars. No. This time it would be different. Our Olympic stars would be fully on display in NHL games as soon as the Olympics ended, and—with a new TV contract that provided maximum exposure for the NHL—a wide audience in the U.S. could continue to see their new heroes in action. The more I thought about the impact the Olympics could have in giving us a jump start in building TV ratings in the U.S., the more excited I became. I saw it as a step we had to take.

Cable TV giant ESPN was planning to introduce a second cable sports network in 1993, and was eager to start with NHL hockey as one of its exclusive products. As a start-up network, ESPN-2 would be seen in only a fraction of the seventy million households its big brother reached. We needed better exposure than that, but the situation created an opportunity for negotiation.

My grand plan for building U.S. TV ratings for hockey, utilizing expansion and the Olympic opportunity, called for the following:

1. 1992–93: Obtain maximum exposure of NHL games through ESPN cablecasts and through over-the-air broadcast of one Stanley Cup playoff game a week on one of the big three networks, ABC, CBS or NBC.

2. 1993–94: The same as 1992–93, with the opportunity to gauge the effect of the Olympics by comparing post-Olympic ratings on ESPN and the major network with those of the prior year. With luck, it would show a demonstrable jump in ratings.

3. 1994–95, 1995–96, 1996–97: Continue to improve ratings through expansion into major U.S. television markets, and, prior to the 1997–98 season, negotiate a new long-term TV contract with the major U.S. network that owns U.S. broadcast rights to the 1998 Winter Olympics.

I appointed a committee of TV-savvy governors and alternate governors—Jack Krumpe (Islanders), Stan Jaffe and Bob Gutkowski (Rangers), and Joe Cohen (Flyers)—to negotiate with ESPN's president and CEO, Steven Bornstein. Gutkowski, previously a longtime colleague of Bornstein at ESPN, became our lead negotiator.

We spelled out what we needed. We would agree to give ESPN-2 the rights to NHL hockey games on three conditions: First, ESPN would have to show an NHL game-of-the-week on its primary network. Second, ESPN would have to arrange to broadcast at least five Stanley Cup playoff games each year over one of the three major U.S. networks—ABC, CBS, or NBC. (We assumed it would be ABC, which was one of ESPN's sister corporations, both being owned by Capital Cities.) Third, we were seeking a minimum of $30 million a year.

After some arm wrestling, Bornstein agreed to the first two conditions, but asked for a six-year agreement at $25 million a year. In view of the timetable that I foresaw, I would not agree to go beyond five years. The committee and Bornstein finally agreed to make a five-year, $125 million deal that was broken down into two contracts. The first contract would cover just the 1992–93 season, and would pay the league $30 million. The second would be extended for the four succeeding years, with equal annual payments totaling $95 million. All looked good, but once again legal difficulties took center stage.

SportsChannel, then the incumbent NHL cablecaster, claimed its 1991–92 contract gave it a right of first refusal on a contract for 1992–93 rights. Although we disputed its position, we offered to let SportsChannel match the ESPN one-year contract for the 1992–93 season. ESPN could live with that, since ESPN-2 was not scheduled to get off the ground until 1993–94.

After some discussion, SportsChannel chose not to accept our offer. Instead, they took us to court at the eleventh hour, when the season was about to begin and when ESPN had to be out on the street seeking sponsors for our games, suing to enjoin the NHL from proceeding with either of the two ESPN contracts.

Thanks to some speedy and brilliant lawyering by our outside counsel, Stephen A. Marshall of the New York law firm Rubin Baum Levin Constant and Friedman, we won the lawsuit, and, most important, we won it quickly. The request for injunction was denied within a week of its having been filed. After making monetary adjustments in our TV contracts to compensate for the NHL's requirement of local blackouts, we began our new relationship with ESPN, the number-one sports network in America. The committee had done an outstanding job. After years of virtually no national exposure, we were back in the big time, with ESPN and ABC showing NHL games. It was a giant leap forward for the league—and for my ratings-building agenda.

But the exultation I allowed myself to feel was short-lived. My dream of having our players compete in the 1994 Winter Olympics was next on the agenda. It would not be accomplished so easily.

In advance of the August 25, 1992, board of governors meeting in St. Petersburg, I presented to the advisory committee (a select group of governors who reviewed the agenda of each board meeting in advance) my plan for getting our players into the 1994 Winter Olympics in Lillehammer, Norway. To implement it, I asked for approval of the following resolution:

> Be It Resolved that the president is authorized to take such action as is necessary to effect the participation of NHL players in the 1994 Winter Olympics provided there is no resultant diminution in the number of NHL games in which such players will be available to play.
>
> It is contemplated the 1993–94 NHL schedule will start approximately one week earlier than usual and end approximately two weeks later than usual in the 1993–94 season to permit a three-week hiatus during Olympic play.

I was heartened by the advisory committee's enthusiastic support of the plan and its unanimous agreement to recommend approval of the resolution to the board. But when it was moved at the subsequent board meeting, New York Rangers governor Stanley Jaffe questioned the wisdom of approving the plan at that time, and convinced a number of governors to postpone a decision until a study of the feasibility of our participation in the Olympics was conducted. I was directed to conduct the study and report back to the board at its December 1992, meeting. Although it seemed like a prudent and reasonable way to proceed, the postponement of the decision turned out to be a the project's death sentence.

I later found out what was behind Jaffe's opposition. Stanley Cup-less since 1940, the Rangers were enjoying the best record in the league and playing their best hockey at the time of the 1992 strike—which took place virtually on the eve of the playoffs. Although the strike was relatively short-lived, the layoff was long enough to disrupt the Rangers and throw them off their game. The New York blueshirts were never able to regain their earlier dominant play, and were thus a surprisingly early elimination from the Stanley Cup Playoffs. Jaffe was firmly convinced the strike's layoff had cost New York the 1992 Stanley Cup, and feared an Olympic break might do the same in 1994.

As things turned out, the New York Rangers—without an Olympic interruption—did win the Cup in 1994, but, alas, it was not to be Stanley's cup, for he had been fired before the playoffs when his company, Paramount Communications, Inc., was acquired by Sumner Redstone's Viacom, Inc. Ah, well.

As soon as the August 1992 board of governors meeting ended, chairman Bruce McNall and I appointed an Olympic Participation Committee to conduct the feasibility study. Bruce and I were members and cochairmen, along with eight governors or alternate governors, and five league officers. In concert with USA Hockey and Hockey Canada, the Olympic bodies of the two countries, we organized two separate working groups, the U.S. Olympic Participation Task Force and the Canadian Olympic Participation Task Force, to look simultaneously into all the details that would be involved for the NHL to participate in the 1994 Olympics.

The Hockey Canada Task Force met in Toronto on October 15 and November 18, 1992. The USA Hockey Task Force met in Chicago on October 22 and November 10. Since use of NHL players was what the project was all about, Bob Goodenow, the executive director of the NHL Players Association, actively participated in the meetings to gather information and furnish input. The full committee held three meetings to identify and address the component issues and variables inherent in the project. We met in New York on October 27 and November 21, and in Palm Beach on December 8.

On December 2, 1992, in advance of the upcoming board of governors meeting, the committee issued a confidential forty-seven-page feasibility report to all governors and alternate governors. The stage was set to bring it before the board for action, but it never got there. There was an anti-Olympic movement within the board being led by Jaffe and Wirtz. I have already chronicled the reason for Jaffe's objection. I believe Wirtz's reason was more tangible—it had to do with dollars.

Several years earlier, the board had made a commitment to Hockey Canada and USA Hockey to provide, in the Olympic year, a series of exhibition games between NHL clubs and each country's team to help prepare them for Olympic play. Part of the deal was that the NHL would make financial contributions to Hockey Canada ($500,000) and USA Hockey ($750,000) to support the Olympic programs of these organizations. Each NHL team was obliged to include the Olympic game in its home schedule, and, gifted with fiscal foresight, Wirtz had shrewdly gotten the board of governors to rule that each club would be required to include that game in its season ticket plan. If left to trying to sell that exhibition game to fans on its merits, most clubs would be lucky to sell five thousand tickets, but by making it a mandatory buy as part of the season ticket plan, virtual sellouts would be assured for the NHL clubs that had strong season ticket bases.

One such club was Wirtz's Chicago Blackhawks. Although gate receipts were required to be shared 50-50 with the NHL Players Association, concession revenues were not. The Olympic teams exhibition games were big money-makers for teams like Chicago. If we were to supply NHL players for the Canadian and U.S. Olympic teams, however, there would be no exhibition games, and that revenue would be lost. Was that enough of a reason for Wirtz to oppose my Olympic plan? Nah, not "Dollar Bill!"

The semiannual meeting of the board was held at the Breakers hotel in Palm Beach. It was to be a three-day meeting, running from December 10–12, 1992. On the first day, we surprised the hockey and business world by granting expansion franchises in Miami (to Wayne Huizenga) and in Anaheim (to the Walt Disney Co.). The next morning, Gary Bettman was elected commissioner. As there was a new commissioner in place, the board decided not to vote on the Olympic proposal until he had had a chance to study it and make his recommendation. That was the last anyone heard of the project. It was an opportunity lost.

Although my dream of seeing NHL players in the 1994 Lillehammer Olympics was not realized, the league eventually saw the merits of Olympic play and adopted my blueprint for getting it done. Commissioner Bettman announced in 1996 that the league would have an Olympic break in its 1997–98 schedule and NHL players would compete for medals in the XVIII Olympic Winter Games in Nagano, Japan, in February 1998.

While my first priority as president was getting the NHL back on network television through increased TV exposure, expansion, and the Olympics, this was not my only goal. As a hockey fan turned president, I decided to use the influence of my office to bring about some changes in the playing rules that I thought would improve the game.

Nothing annoyed me more than seeing a skilled offensive player frustrated by having his stick held by an opponent, and this had become epidemic in the league. A player would make a dazzling rush into the offensive zone, then find his effort neutralized by some journeyman hacker grabbing his stick and holding onto it while skating alongside him. I hated seeing it, and so did all hockey fans. I felt it was as ridiculous a sight as it would be in baseball to see the catcher grab the batter's bat and hold it while the pitcher throws a strike. The referees could penalize this hacker's trick with a holding penalty, but somehow they never did. It had become an acceptable and unpenalized practice. I decided to do something about it to make the game better for our fans, so I proposed a new rule for the general managers committee to consider. It would amend Rule 59, the existing holding rule, by adding a subsection "b," which provided:

A minor penalty shall be imposed on any player who closes his hand around the stick of an opponent so as to hold such stick.

With the general managers' recommendation, the new rule was approved by the board of governors at its August meeting and became effective at the start of the 1992–93 season.

Another rule I was determined to amend was Rule 27(d), which had eliminated exciting four-on-four hockey. In their heyday, the Edmonton Oilers had been a dynamite team when playing four players against four after coincidental minor penalties had been called. With players like Wayne Gretzky, Mark Messier, Paul Coffey, and Glenn Anderson, and more open ice for them to make their plays, four-on-four became a virtual Oiler power play.

The other clubs could not outplay the Oilers, but they could outvote them, so Rule 27(d) was rammed through to take away Edmonton's edge. It provided that, after coincidental minors, teams would substitute for the penalized players and play five against five. Edmonton was not the only loser when Rule 27(d) was passed. The NHL also lost, because some excitement had been taken out of the game. The fans, of course, were the biggest losers.

I believed it was time to restore four-on-four play, and asked the general managers for their help in pushing for a repeal of Rule 27(d). With their support of my recommendation, the board of governors amended the rule at the August meeting, and four-on-four hockey was returned to the game at the start of the 1992–93 season. Another fan-friendly rule change that resulted from my prodding was the imposition of a minor penalty to a player intentionally taking a dive on the ice to trick the referee into calling a penalty against his opponent.

The issue of fighting also got my attention, and I induced the governors to engage in an extended debate on the subject. The board decided against increasing the penalty for spontaneous fights, but amended the rules to impose a game misconduct penalty for instigation. The high-sticking standard was redefined from shoulder height to chest height in the hope it would help bring sticks down and reduce the incidence of eye and facial injuries.

And then there was the matter of player discipline.

Traditionally, players had been disciplined for excessively violent acts against other players by being suspended for a number of games. This system did not appear to be much of a deterrent, though, and incidents of violence seemed to be on the rise. The reason it did not deter violence was no secret within the league. Although the players were allegedly suspended "without pay," the clubs' practice was to wink at the penalty and quietly pay the player. I felt this unenforced and nondeterrent system cheated the fans, since repeated game suspensions deprived fans of the opportunity to see a team's best twenty players on the ice.

So I proposed, and the board approved, a bylaw amendment that would enforce suspension-without-pay orders by automatically fining a club an amount equal to the pay the player was to lose through his suspension. I believed a club would not want to pay twice, so, if it had to pay a fine, it would be unlikely to also give the player his pay for the suspended period. In addition, the new bylaw gave the president the power to audit a club's books to determine if a suspended player had been paid, and if he had, the club could be fined $500,000.

Those parts of the amendment were not that controversial, but the next part was. Under the new bylaw, a player could be suspended without pay for days on which no games were scheduled, while continuing to play in all games. I'm afraid the hockey world was not quite ready for such a revolutionary idea, and I was roundly criticized for it. The practice was eliminated a year later, after Commissioner Bettman took over.

Forcing a club to refrain from paying a suspended player, however, proved to be an effective deterrent. The first player I had to discipline was Bernie Nicholls. Bernie is a skilled player, not a thug, but he had developed a dangerous habit of taking two-handed swings at other players with his stick. While playing for Edmonton in a game against Boston on September 28, 1992, Nicholls struck the Bruins' Darren Banks in the shoulder with a two-hander. The case came before me for supplementary discipline.

When I conducted the hearing and reviewed his past record, I learned this was the third time Nicholls had struck a player with a swinging two-hander. The first time he did it, March 9, 1988, he was suspended for five games. The second time, February 9, 1991, I expected he would have been given a stiffer sentence, but, to my surprise, I found he had only been suspended three games. For this third offense, I suspended him for seven nongame days and made sure—probably for the first time in his experience—that he lost his pay for the seven days of suspension, which amounted to $10,143. Losing that amount made a profound and lasting impression on Nicholls. In the four seasons since that incident, he has never again faced supplementary discipline for swinging his stick at a player.

When all was said and done, my short tenure as the fifth and last president of the National Hockey League was a pure gift to a hockey fan like me. Imagine being able to effect rule changes to make the thrilling game of hockey even more exciting for fellow fans.

Others took notice of the changes I had made. On December 10, 1992, responding to the press's inquiry as to what had brought about Disney's willingness to associate itself with the NHL, Michael Eisner acknowledged that recent changes made in the game had played a part in his decision: "We are pleased with the new direction, with the reduction of fighting and the increase of action, and skill, and scoring."

I am proud of my other accomplishments as well—opening the league to the media as never before, getting NHL hockey back on ESPN and ABC, bringing Blockbuster's Wayne Huizenga and Disney's Michael Eisner into the league with strong expansion franchises in Miami and Anaheim, creating the impetus for getting NHL players into the Olympics, and showing how that could be done by taking a break in the middle of the season.

When I turned the reins over to Commissioner Bettman on February 1, 1993, I hoped and believed the league was in better shape than it had been when I took the helm eight months earlier.

11

The Truth About the Hall of Fame

In the spring of 1993, I took a beating in the press after being elected to the Hockey Hall of Fame. To summarize quickly, this relatively simple procedure was transformed into a witches' brew of accusations, lies, vengeance, and unbridled backstabbing. Only now am I prepared to reveal the truth about what really happened and why I found myself in the most uncomfortable position of a long career.

THE PRELUDE

The first six months I served as NHL president were the most hectic of my life. I was optimistic about the future of hockey, and immediately upon assuming the presidency in June 1992, I embarked on an extensive North American tour. By mid-August I had visited every National Hockey League city, and at each stop, I met with the local club owner and also conveyed an upbeat message about hockey's future. I talked directly with fans, visited editorial boards of local newspapers and radio and television stations, and conducted full-scale press conferences. As simple as this sounds, nothing like it had ever been done in the NHL.

In addition to inaugurating a new era of accessibility to the media, I was able to listen to and learn, firsthand, the concerns of grass-roots fans about our game, as well as those of owners. It was great fun and, for an unprecedented step in the NHL, seemed to be very well received.

After the tour, I found myself inundated with daily tasks, television negotiations, and long-range planning responsibilities that consumed eighteen-hour workdays six and sometimes seven days a week. It was during this period I learned something strange was going on at the Hockey Hall of Fame.

Everyone knows while the cat's away, the mice will play. What I discovered was that while I was engaged in other league business and, therefore, not focusing upon the activities of the board of directors of the Hockey Hall of Fame, two directors who were serving solely at the pleasure of the NHL president, Ian "Scotty" Morrison and Brian O'Neill, appeared to be scheming to use their influence on the board to elect themselves to the Hall.

The Hockey Hall of Fame (actually named the Hockey Hall of Fame and Museum) was established in Toronto in 1943 to honor people who had made exceptional contributions to the game of hockey. Being elected a member is considered the greatest honor that can be bestowed on an individual involved in the game of hockey. Members are elected annually in different categories. The most important, of course, is players, but members are also elected in three nonplayer categories— builders, referees or linesmen, and media. To date, 207 players, 84 builders, 13 referees and linesmen and 53 media honorees have been inducted.

As I was to learn, according to its corporate bylaws, the Hockey Hall of Fame was supervised by a twelve member board of directors. Although players are elected by a separate player selection committee appointed by the board, builders are elected directly by the Hall of Fame board of directors. It appeared that what Morrison and O'Neill had targeted for themselves was having the board on which they served elect them as builders.

The directors were elected annually to serve a one-year term, based on their having been nominated by various bodies. The president of the National Hockey League chose seven of the twelve directors, and, under the Hall's bylaws, had the right to remove them from the board at any time during their term. Of those seven NHL nominees, five served on the board without compensation. The other two, who were designated by the NHL president to hold the offices of chairman and president of the Hall of Fame, were paid significant six-figure salaries. As for the remaining five board members, all of whom served without compensation, Metro Toronto (short for the Muncipality of Metropolitan Toronto, a regional government comprising the cities of Toronto, North York, Etobicoke, Scarborough, and the borough of East York) nominated two, the board of Exhibition Place nominated two, and the Canadian Amateur Hockey Association (CAHA) nominated one. The board of governors of Exhibition Place is a separate corporation that operates the Canadian National Exhibition fairgrounds on the shores of Lake Ontario, where the old Hockey Hall of Fame and Museum was located. The Canadian Amateur Hockey Association is self-explanatory.

In February 1992, then-NHL president John A. Ziegler Jr. had named Morrison and O'Neill to serve as Hall of Fame directors until March 1993. He also designated Morrison to serve as the Hall's paid chairman. Ziegler's five other selections that year were Walter L. Bush Jr., R. Alan Eagleson, Danny Gallivan, T. N. (Tommy) Ivan, and A. David M. Taylor, with Taylor to be the Hall's paid president. Bush was president of USA Hockey. Eagleson was the very controversial former executive director of the NHL Players Association. As a longtime fixture on the popular *Hockey Night in Canada* broadcasts Gallivan had been one of the best known TV play-by-play announcers in Canada. A member of the Hall of Fame as an NHL coach and general manager, Tommy Ivan had been around the league for over half a century. Taylor was a professional administrator hired from the business community with no prior hockey experience.

In June 1992, I succeeded Ziegler as NHL president, and thereby became responsible for the continued service on the board of his seven appointees. Until I learned what Morrison and O'Neill were up to, I did not realize the power the NHL president had to remove Hall of Fame board members, and had given no thought to replacing them. However, they both knew they were continuing on the board as appointees of the NHL president, and should have sought my approval before involving themselves in something as awkward and potentially explosive as a scheme to employ their insider positions to put themselves into the Hall of Fame. Of course they knew I would not have given my approval, which probably explains why they never asked for it. Hall of Fame directors owe a fiduciary duty to the Hall. They should not use positions on the board to advance their self-interest, especially with regard to something with as high a public profile as electing Hall of Fame members.

I had known Morrison and O'Neill quite well, all of us having served for a number of years as NHL vice presidents under Ziegler. Morrison had worked in Toronto, first as referee in chief, then later solely for the Hall of Fame. O'Neill worked in Montreal, where he supervised the league's hockey operation. I worked in New York as the league's general counsel. In August 1992, as part of a reorganization of the league's executive structure, I had trimmed the number of NHL vice presidents from seven to three. Morrison and O'Neill were among those who lost the title of vice president.

Although removing their titles, I had not reduced their pay. On the contrary, I gave a salary increase to Morrison, whose duties remained the same. For a number of years, Morrison had worked solely as full-time chairman of the Hall of Fame, performing no duties at all for the National Hockey League, so there was no rational basis for him to continue to retain the title of NHL vice president. As for O'Neill, in view of his years of service to the league, I recommended to the NHL's Compensation Committee, and obtained its approval, that O'Neill be given a severance package that would: keep him employed by the NHL in an untitled consultant capacity beyond his normal retirement age of sixty-five (he was sixty-three at the time); keep his salary intact; provide him with a large tax-free severance bonus; and significantly increase his pension. All told, the value of his compensation, increased pension, and other severance benefits came to approximately $750,000. I also offered him the opportunity, which he accepted, to announce publicly that he was retiring from his position as vice president and to write the league's press release that announced it. In addition to providing for his financial well-being, I saw to it that he was given a prestigious office in the league's Montreal headquarters, with secretarial service, where he would be stationed while serving in his new capacity as NHL consultant.

Despite having preserved their financial security, and having enabled O'Neill to maintain his personal dignity by publicly announcing his retirement and retaining an office in NHL headquarters, I continuously received feedback from others in the league about how bitterly Morrison and O'Neill were expressing their resentment at my having removed them as NHL vice presidents. Although they did not know it, their August removal had been fully reviewed and endorsed by the NHL governors during my tour, when I learned there was a widespread belief there were too many vice presidents in the league, and that a number of governors felt O'Neill was arrogant and overpaid, besides being super-fluous in light of the stronger contribution being made by vice president Jim Gregory in overlapping responsibilities. I was informed by some owners that these views had previously been expressed to President Ziegler, and I assume Commissioner Bettman was later told the same thing by the owners, since he showed no interest in returning O'Neill to his former position after my tenure as CEO ended.

The first inkling I had of the apparent Morrison-O'Neill plan to elect themselves to the Hall of Fame came in early November 1992, when I received a copy from Morrison of a November 5 letter he had sent to all members of the Hall of Fame board of directors asking that one or more of them nominate O'Neill to the Hall of Fame in the builder category. Under the board's rules, only a board member could officially nominate someone for election to the Hall of Fame as a builder, so, while refraining from doing this himself, Morrison was asking other board members to do it.

I had received a copy of the letter because at the bottom of it Morrison had shown that copies were being sent to the top officers of the NHL. In addition to showing a copy had been sent ("cc") to me, the president of the league, Morrison also indicated copies had been mailed to Bruce McNall, chairman of the NHL board of governors, and NHL vice presidents Steve Ryan, Ken Sawyer, and Jim Gregory. This was highly unusual.

As Hall of Fame chairman, Morrison had no obligation to send copies of his correspondence to NHL officers. In fact, this was the first time in my fifteen years as NHL vice president and now president that I had ever been sent a copy of a letter being mailed to others by an officer of the Hockey Hall of Fame. I thought about why NHL officers were being shown in the letter as recipients, and concluded Morrison may have been attempting to mislead his fellow board members into believing it was the NHL's wish that O'Neill be elected to the Hall.

Why else would Morrison show our names as "cc"? If he felt obliged, as my appointee, to keep me advised of what he was doing, then why only in this case? And, knowing how sensitive a public issue it could become were Hall of Fame directors to elect one of themselves to the Hall, why would Morrison not have spoken to me about it before actively lobbying his fellow board members on O'Neill's behalf? Had Ziegler still been president, Morrison would never have had the guts to do this.

I called Board of Governors Chairman Bruce McNall and discussed the matter with him. He had not yet received his copy of the letter, and was shocked when I told him about it. He concurred with my conclusion that the likely explanation of why Morrison had sent copies to us was to create the false impression the NHL was seeking to have O'Neill elected to the Hall of Fame.

I checked with the three NHL vice presidents who had also received copies—Steve Ryan, Ken Sawyer, and Jim Gregory. None knew anything about the matter prior to receiving the letter, and each reacted negatively to what Morrison was doing. As league officers who were working to obtain financing for construction of the new Hall of Fame complex, Ryan and Sawyer were particularly concerned that negative publicity stemming from the Hall's board electing one of its own members to the Hall of Fame could prove especially harmful.

I knew Morrison and O'Neill were close friends, and therefore suspected O'Neill was fully aware of Morrison's activity on his behalf. This hunch was confirmed when I read two letters from nonboard members nominating O'Neill, which Morrison enclosed with his letter. One was an October 26, 1992, letter from Bill Hay, president of the Calgary Flames. The other was an October 29, 1992, letter from Glen Sather, president of the Edmonton Oilers. One look at the detailed description of O'Neill's NHL background contained in these letters was enough to indicate he had been involved in drafting them. Common sense told me that only O'Neill, not Sather nor Hay, would know the intricate and intimate details of his NHL career which were included in Sather's letter. For example, Sather wrote: "Mr. O'Neill joined the National Hockey League in 1966 as Director of Administration. Later, he served as Executive Director before being named Executive Vice President on August 25, 1977."

I knew Sather was very intelligent, but he would not have known the exact date, fifteen years earlier, when O'Neill had been promoted to vice president, nor would he have known O'Neill's earlier job titles. The fact that O'Neill had obviously provided biographical data to Sather and Hay to assist them in nominating him was not unusual. How else would they have obtained it? However, it was unusual that these letters were to be used for a purpose that conflicted with O'Neill's fiduciary duty as a member of the Hall of Fame board of directors. The board had the sole power to decide who would be elected to the Hall of Fame as builders, so it was surely unethical for board members to participate to any degree in an effort to elect themselves.

On November 16, I received a copy of another letter that had been written the same day as Morrison's (November 5, 1992). This one was written to Taylor, the Hall of Fame president, nominating Morrison for election to the Hall of Fame as a builder. It had been sent by Mary

Keenan, a longtime secretary in Morrison's league office in Toronto. Was it mere coincidence that two letters sent on the same day sought to elect to the Hall of Fame two members of the Hall's board?

Just as the Sather and Hay letters nominating O'Neill contained information that would only be known to O'Neill, Keenan's letter contained facts about Morrison's background that would probably be known only to Morrison. For example, Keenan, who did not begin working for the league until 1971, would not likely have known twenty-one years later the precise date that Morrison had started at the NHL, which occurred six years prior to her employment. Yet her nomination letter included the following: "Joining the National Hockey League under the guidance of Mr. Clarence Campbell 27 years ago, June 8, 1965, Mr. Morrison currently enjoys the longest tenure with the NHL of any League executive or any League employee."

Unlike Morrison's letter, which had numerous "cc's," Keenan's letter was sent only to Taylor. It came to me by way of NHL vice president Steve Ryan, to whom Taylor had faxed it after becoming alarmed at what he saw going on with Morrison and O'Neill. As with the case of O'Neill, Morrison's apparent involvement in Keenan's effort raised serious ethical questions.

My initial inclination was to have Morrison and O'Neill removed from the Hall of Fame board, but I did not know whether I had the power. Also, to do so would have meant Morrison's losing his job as paid chairman, a move that would surely have led to negative publicity about the manner in which the Hall of Fame was being operated. Mindful of the concern Ryan and Sawyer had expressed about the impact negative news could have on corporate financing, I decided to seek an alternative course of action.

I telephoned Rosanne Rocchi, a Toronto attorney whom I believed to be the reigning expert on Hall of Fame procedures, because I knew she had served for years as counsel to the Hall's board of directors. Briefly describing the sticky situation with which I was confronted, I asked Rocchi to meet me in Toronto several days later. At her request, I agreed that she bring Larry Bertuzzi, one of Rocchi's law partners with whom I was familiar. In June he had been appointed by Ziegler to arbitrate the dispute among the Philadelphia Flyers, New York Rangers, and Quebec Nordiques over Eric Lindros.

We met on Wednesday evening, November 18, 1992, in my room at the Toronto Hilton, and, after discussing what was transpiring, re-viewed the Hall of Fame bylaws and procedures. We also considered the names of possible replacements whom I might nominate in March 1993, when the terms of the existing board members would expire. Rocchi said Taylor had complained to her in the past about board members not being qualified to deal with business and financial matters, and urged me to take that into consideration. I asked Bertuzzi if he would be willing to serve on the board and he said he would. He then volunteered to ask John Turner, former prime minister of Canada and then a senior partner in Bertuzzi's law firm, to serve on the board if I wished. I asked him to do so.

We reviewed the incumbent board members. As for O'Neill, I said that, apart from my concern over his participation in the perceived joint action with Morrison, I would have replaced him on the board in any event with NHL vice-president Jim Gregory, whom I had promoted to O'Neill's former position as the league's vice president in charge of all hockey operations. We then turned to Morrison and Taylor, the two paid Hall of Fame officers. Rocchi liked Morrison, and persuaded me to reconsider my initial inclination to sack him. She said that as the public spokesperson for the Hall of Fame, Morrison had made a good impression on the Toronto community, and that if I were to make him aware of my serious concerns regarding this kind of insider dealing by directors, she was certain he would not do it again. With that assurance, and hoping to avoid negative publicity for the Hall, I said I would reappoint him. As for Taylor, Rocchi praised the professional job he had done as president and recommended that I reappoint him also. Again, I agreed to do so.

Rocchi said Gallivan had previously submitted his resignation, leav-ing Bush, Eagleson, and Ivan as the remaining incumbent NHL nomi-nees. Interestingly, Canadians Bertuzzi and Rocchi recommended that I appoint more Americans to the board, since the Hall of Fame was not intended to be a Canadian-only club. They suggested that, with the Hall of Fame's pending move from drab Exhibition Place to its glamorous new home in downtown Toronto's upscale BCE Place (BCE standing for Bell Canada Enterprises), the board position previously reserved for an Exhibition Place nominee might be permanently allotted instead to USA Hockey, whose nominee would undoubtedly be its American president, Walter Bush. If I then nominated two additional Americans to the board, that would create a Canadian-American ratio of 75 percent to 25 percent, which they felt would be desirable. I agreed to think about finding qualified Americans who would serve.

As for Eagleson and Ivan, I was strongly inclined to drop both. Rumors were rampant that Eagleson was about to be indicted by the U.S. government as a result of a long-running grand jury investigation in Boston. (The rumors turned out to be true). At eighty-two, Ivan was an old-timer whose talents were probably better suited for the Hall's Player Selection Committee than its governing board.

We proceeded to talk specifically about what Morrison and O'Neill had been doing and agreed it could be damaging to the Hall's reputation were the board to begin electing its own members to the Hall of Fame. O'Neill had already been formally nominated, with four board members (Bush, Gallivan, Metro Toronto's Robert G. Bundy, and CAHA's Murray Costello) having responded to Morrison's letter soliciting such nominations. Morrison himself had not yet been formally nominated, but, for all we knew, his nomination might be the next shoe to drop.

We tossed around various suggestions, and concluded the best approach would be to ask the new board to amend its rules to prevent one of its members from being eligible for election to the Hall of Fame by his fellow board members. Rocchi said it was common practice for the board to make last-minute rule changes at meetings in order to effect whatever result they were seeking to achieve at the time, and Bertuzzi agreed to draft a rule change that would address this issue.

Rocchi also felt that, to avoid possible backlash from O'Neill's friends in the media, it was not sufficient to just prevent O'Neill's nomination from being voted on by the board. She suggested that other builder nominations should be made, preferably of people whose qualifications were greater than O'Neill's. I said I would seek the nomination of Frank Griffiths and Seymour Knox, two senior NHL governors whose contributions to the building of hockey would be recognized as having far surpassed O'Neill's. Rocchi advised us that the deadline for nominations would be in March 1993, and no board action to elect anyone to the Hall of Fame could take place until after that. Accordingly, we agreed to meet again during the February 1993 All-Star Game break in Montreal.

In January 1993, a new subplot developed. On January 14, Morrison sent a letter to the members of the Hall of Fame board advising that its annual meeting would be held March 30, 1993. In the letter, he recommended that the board name Bill Hay chairman of the Player

Selection Committee, and said that such recommendation had come about as a result of a meeting he had had with O'Neill and retiring board member Gallivan. Hay, you will recall, had sent the initial letter to Morrison nominating O'Neill. Morrison failed to mention that Hay was ineligible to be elected chairman of the Player Selection Committee, because he was not a member of the Hall of Fame board of directors. The Hall of Fame's rules stated that the board could name as chairman of the Player Selection Committee only someone who was a member of the Hall of Fame board of directors whom the NHL had nominated to the board.

Unlike his solicitation letter on behalf of O'Neill, Morrison did not "cc" me on the Hay letter. He did, however, send a copy to the board's lawyer, Rocchi. Because Hay was ineligible to serve as chairman of the Player Selection Committee unless he were first nominated to the Hall of Fame board by the NHL president, Rocchi sent me the letter so I could consider whether to nominate Hay. Morrison's letter also stated that he, O'Neill, and Gallivan were recommending that the Board appoint Dick Irvin to fill the vacancy on the Player Selection Committee being created by Gallivan's retirement. Morrison's letter concerned me. Since Gallivan, O'Neill, and Morrison were known to be NHL appointees to the board, the letter carried with it the implication that Irvin and Hay were being recommended by the NHL. In fact, neither I, as NHL president, nor Bruce McNall, as chairman of the NHL Board of Governors, nor Gary Bettman (who was to become NHL commissioner) knew anything about what Morrison was recommending. Had Rocchi not sent me a copy of the letter, I might never have known.

As a board appointee, Morrison was expected to exercise his best independent judgment when casting his vote on any and all matters coming before the board. However, it was also expected he would respect the right of other members to exercise their independent judgment. It was not his role as chairman to attempt to influence their vote, and he was certainly out of bounds if he tried to do so in a way that implied he was acting on behalf of the NHL. In advising board members what was "recommended" by three NHL nominees to the board, one of whom was the NHL-nominated chairman, the message being delivered was, at best, a mixed one.

It appeared Morrison was treating the Hall of Fame as his private preserve, avoiding all consultation with his appointing authority and displaying a disturbing lack of concern over how his cronyism might be putting the image of the Hall at risk. I decided it was time to have a chat with Morrison and summoned him to meet with me in New York.

The meeting did not turn out as conciliatory as I would have liked. I started by telling him that I was concerned about a number of things he had done, which I then enumerated. To put it politely, the responses Scotty gave me appeared less than candid. To put it not so politely, I told him I did not appreciate the bullshit. Initially, he became indignant and angry, but after a while he calmed himself.

When I questioned him about his November 5, 1992, letter soliciting a nomination for O'Neill, his first response was to deny that it was a solicitation, claiming it was merely a standard form letter he, as chairman of the Hall of Fame board of directors, would send to its members whenever he received a letter of nomination from a nonboard member. (Remember, only a board member may formally nominate someone for election to the Hall of Fame in the builder category.) But I recalled that in his January 14, 1993, letter he had simply reported that Dr. Douglas G. Kinnear had been nominated by nonboard member Serge Savard (the Montreal Canadiens general manager). In that letter, he did not solicit a board member nomination for Kinnear, as he had done for O'Neill. I pointed that out to him and said I did not buy his story. He could not explain why he had not afforded Kinnear's proffered nomination the same treatment as O'Neill's. It was clear to me that he was not telling the truth, and I told him so.

I also asked why he had sent me and McNall copies of his O'Neill solicitation letter and, before he could reply, told him I thought he had done so to mislead the recipients into believing it was the NHL that was seeking O'Neill's nomination. He vehemently denied that was his motive, but could offer no explanation for the highly unusual number of "cc's."

I then asked about Mary Keenan's letter nominating him. His face turned red and I got the clear impression he was surprised I knew about it. I said that from the content of Keenan's letter it appeared that he had had a hand in drafting it, and asked him if he had given any thought to the damage that could be done by board members voting themselves into the Hall of Fame. He did not deny that he had helped draft Keenan's letter, but said he had decided not to pursue his own nomination, and that he had made that decision prior to our meeting. As to O'Neill's nomination, he made no response.

I brought up his letter recommending that Hay be elected chairman of the Player Selection Committee. Again, my knowing about that startled him. I asked if he were aware that Hay was not eligible to be elected chairman of the Player Selection Committee, as he was not a member of the Hall's board of directors. He admitted knowing that and, to my astonishment, said he felt that if he could get his fellow members to elect Hay committee chairman, I would be forced to appoint Hay as one of the NHL's seven nominees to the board. Morrison's sudden burst of candor truly stunned me. I said I was shocked at what he had just told me and did not appreciate his trying to ambush me into nominating Hay. In reply, he said he would make no further effort to elect Hay committee chairman.

Now, Scotty was not going to let this meeting end without his getting in a few good licks. He was especially ticked off at me for the rather indelicate manner in which I had let him know he was no longer an NHL vice president, a title he had held for a long time. In the hurly-burly of the August, 1992 board of governors meeting, I had caught up with him in an elevator and passed on the news there. I suppose that didn't exactly do it for him. When he complained about it during our New York meeting, I realized I had been inconsiderate, and admitted that the way I had told him was wrong, and apologized.

We wrapped up our meeting with Morrison pledging to take no further action on the matters we had discussed and with my statement that, subject to his future behavior, I was inclined to recommend his reappointment as chairman of the Hall. I am sure he ran back to his buddies Hay and O'Neill with a full report.

On February 4, 1993, in Montreal, during the All-Star Game break, I met again with Bertuzzi and Rocchi. By this time there had been several new developments. I guess the really important one was the election of Gary Bettman as the first NHL commissioner. At its December 1992 meeting, the board of governors had named him to the job, effective February 1, 1993. Although still president, I had agreed to subordinate my role as president and CEO to the new commissioner. Therefore, any decisions to be made on new NHL appointments to the Hall of Fame board would first have to be approved by Bettman.

Also, in early January 1993, prior to Bettman's start as commissioner, several new nominations for election to the Hall as builders had come fluttering through its office doors. At my request, Taylor had nominated Frank Griffiths and Seymour Knox. Murray Costello, the CAHA-nominated member of the Hall's board, had nominated Fred Page, a lifelong activist in Canadian amateur hockey. He had been a player, referee, and executive in Junior A hockey, and served as Canadian Amateur Hockey Association (CAHA) president from 1966 to 1968, and first vice president of the International Ice Hockey Federation from 1969 to 1972. And last, but certainly not least, at Bruce McNall's request Taylor had also nominated me. And, yes, this one hit the proverbial fan real quick. Here's how.

McNall, who owned the Los Angeles Kings, was chosen to be chairman of the NHL Board of Governors in June 1992, the same time I was elected NHL president. He was technically my boss, and we spoke by telephone constantly. In late December 1992, I told him I would like to push the nomination of Griffiths and Knox for election to the Hall of Fame as builders, and asked if he concurred. He said he did, but also said, "You belong in the Hall of Fame more than any of them. You've done so much for hockey over the years, but especially since you became president." Until he said that, the thought of my being elected had never entered my mind. But once he said the magic words, the thought never left my mind. Having worked fifteen years in hockey, I knew what a singular honor it was to be elected to the Hall of Fame, and I was very excited at the prospect that I might be considered. That my children's children might someday visit the Hall of Fame and read about their grandfather was a positively intoxicating vision. But please, believe me when I state that the idea was initiated by Bruce—with no prompting from me at all—not even subliminally.

The next time I spoke to him I said, "Bruce, if you really believe what you said about my belonging in the Hall of Fame, I would appreciate your being the one to sponsor me." I knew that a nomination coming from the NHL's chairman of the board of governors would carry a lot of weight.

"Great!" he said with his usual enthusiasm, "How do I do it?"

I told him a formal nomination had to come from a Hall of Fame board member, and suggested he could make the request by writing to Dave Taylor.

"Will you draft the letter for me?" he asked.

I agreed I would, and promptly did so, sending him a draft. But then I heard nothing further from him about it for a couple of weeks, and refrained from bringing the subject up again. After all, he was my boss, and I did not know whether he really had any intention of pursuing it.

In early January 1993, McNall came to New York to attend a board of governors meeting. He came into my office and showed me a copy of the letter he was sending to Dave Taylor, requesting my nomination. Even though it was basically the letter I had drafted, until I saw it on the Los Angeles Kings letterhead, signed by McNall, I didn't really believe he was going to do it. Taylor then nominated me and later, at Rocchi's suggestion, McNall directed that board members be sent copies of press clippings about what I had accomplished since becoming president.

As I retell it now, a few years later, I realize some may question that McNall initiated and pushed my nomination on his own, without any presssure by me. But that is exactly what happened. Also, since this was occurring simultaneously with my taking Morrison and O'Neill to the woodshed, I have to wonder why a little voice didn't ever say to me, "Gil, certain actions here appear contradictory and this could embarrass you." I think my law school education trapped me: Precedent, ah precedent, how holy it seems. Since my two immediate predecessors, Clarence Campbell and John Ziegler, had been elected to the Hall of Fame while they were sitting presidents, why not me?

At our February 4, 1993, meeting, I discussed a number of things with Rocchi and Bertuzzi, including of course, who would be the 1993 NHL nominees for the Hall of Fame board. In November, the focus had been on whom I might decide to nominate. Now, however, all I could do was make recommendations to Bettman, and he would have the final say.

We reviewed the incumbents. I told them I planned to recommend that Eagleson, O'Neill, and Ivan not be renominated, and that Bush's nomination be left to USA Hockey. I said I would recommend Morrison and Taylor be renominated, and that the other five nominees be Gregory, two new Americans, and, assuming they were willing to serve, Bertuzzi and Turner. Bertuzzi said he had spoken with Turner, and assured me both of them would accept NHL nominations to the board. I had not as yet approached the two Americans I had in mind, so did not identify them to Bertuzzi and Rocchi.

Bertuzzi then presented the rule change he would propose to deal with the O'Neill situation, were he elected to the board. He would ask it to consider amending its rules to provide that its members be ineligible to be elected to the Hall of Fame as builders until three years after they had left the board. Under the rules, a three-year ineligibility period was already applicable to the categories of players, veteran players, and referees.

Before reviewing the Rocchi and Bertuzzi reactions to my recommendations, let me risk introducing a wee digression in order to
provide some necessary perspective for understanding what happened
next. A review of the board's minutes over the past decade had shown its
past practice was often to make last-minute amendments to its rules,
and sometimes even to just act in disregard of them. After all, the NHL
controlled the Hall of Fame and the prevailing attitude was—and
always had been—this is the NHL and we make the rules to meet our
needs.

A few examples: In 1984, the rules provided that a 75 percent vote of
the entire board, not just 75 percent of those present, was required to
elect builders to the Hall of Fame. Yet, at its 1984 meeting, chaired by
Clarence Campbell, the board simply ignored that rule. With only five
of the eleven board members present, a 75 percent vote was not possible.
Yet, with only five votes, Punch Imlach and Jake Milford were deemed
elected to the Hall of Fame as builders. Imlach was the storied coach and
general manager for the Buffalo Sabres and Toronto Maple Leafs who
had led Toronto to four Stanley Cups in the 1960s. Milford was a
popular lifetime toiler in the vineyards of minor league hockey who had
risen to become general manager of both the Los Angeles Kings
(1973–1976) and the Vancouver Canucks (1977–1982).

One of the other rules in effect in 1984 required that a secret ballot be
used to elect builders. This, too, was ignored and, just as was done in
1985 and 1993, a motion to elect Imlach and Milford was approved by
voice vote.

At its 1985 conclave, chaired by Brian O'Neill, the board granted an
ad hoc waiver of its rules by permitting the late filing of a nomination
for Rudy Pilous as a builder. This was done in spite of the fact that the
deadline for nominations had passed and there was no rule granting the
board authority to waive any of its rules. Pilous had put together a
checkered hockey career as coach and manager at the junior and minor
league levels, and in the WHA and NHL, interspersing years of defeat
with a few true highlights, such as coaching the Chicago Blackhawks to
their most recent Stanley Cup, in 1961, and managing the WHA's Avco
Cup champion Winnipeg Jets in 1976 and 1978.

Additional ad hoc actions were taken at the 1985 meeting in
derogation of the rules regarding builder elections. There were only
seven members present at the 1985 meeting, one less than the eight
required to comprise 75 percent, so CAHA's Murray Costello moved

that an amendment to the rules be approved, changing "75 percent of the board" to "75 percent of those present." This change had not been circulated to the directors in advance of the meeting. Costello's motion was approved by those present, and the rules were so amended. Then, ignoring the rule that election of builders was to be by written ballot, Costello and the other members present voted orally to elect John Mariucci as a builder. Mariucci, known as the Godfather of Minnesota Hockey, was the longtime coach at the University of Minnesota, who led the U.S. Olympic team to a silver medal at Cortina in 1956.

Next, a motion was made that a second builder be elected by secret ballot. Costello seconded that motion and it was approved. Instead of ruling that motion out of order because the rules already provided for a secret ballot, Chairman Brian O'Neill permitted the motion to be put to a vote. By doing that, O'Neill and the board showed they believed the rule calling for a secret ballot was only to apply if a specific motion to have a secret ballot was first approved. Pilous, who had been nominated after the deadline in violation of the rules, was then elected, denying admission to the Hall of duly nominated candidates Keith Allen, Hap Emms, and Bill Hanley. Allen was the general manager who had led the Flyers to two Stanley Cups, the first expansion team to win the Cup. Emms and Hanley were successful veteran coaches in the amateur ranks of the powerful Ontario Hockey Association.

At its 1986 meeting, again chaired by Brian O'Neill, the board met to consider a number of builder candidates. Just as had occurred the prior year, Murray Costello offered a last-minute nomination in violation of the rule which imposed a nomination deadline, which had passed ten days earlier. Once again, O'Neill permitted the rules to be waived and, with only six members present, the board accepted Costello's late-filed nomination of Bill Hanley. The board then voted to elect just one builder candidate, and Hanley, who had been nominated after the deadline in violation of the rules, was elected, thus denying admission to the Hall of properly nominated candidates Scotty Bowman, Frank Carlin, Hap Emms, Fred Page, and Billy Reay. Bowman, who has since become the winningest coach in NHL history (and was elected to the Hall of Fame in 1991), had coached the Montreal Canadiens to five Stanley Cups. Carlin, born at the turn of the century, coached the Montreal Royals from 1936 to 1953, and the Flyers' farm team, the Quebec Aces, from 1957 to 1960. Reay had been the coach of the Chicago Blackhawks over many successful seasons.

Everyone followed the rules for a few years, but then, at its 1989 meeting, chaired by Brian O'Neill, with Murray Costello, Scotty Morrison and the usual crew in attendance, the board amended the rules to eliminate the 75 percent voting requirement for builders. Under the new rule, once a simple majority, by oral vote, determined the number of builders to be elected, that number had to be elected, by a 75 percent vote if possible, but if not, then by a simple majority vote. In all categories other than builders, a strict 75 percent vote was still required. (Rocchi told me Bud Poile's election as a builder in 1990 was by simple majority vote.)

There were nine builder nominees in 1989, three of whom, Father David Bauer, Joe Kryzcka, and Fred Page, had been nominated by Murray Costello on behalf of the CAHA. The other nominees were Keith Allen, Scotty Bowman, Frank Carlin, Alan Eagleson, Bud Poile, and Gunther Sabetzki. Bauer had coached the Canadian National Junior Team, but was best known as the inspirational mentor at junior power St. Michael's College, and was a longtime leader of Canada's Olympic and international hockey efforts. Kryzcka, a former president of the CAHA, had been the chairman and chief negotiator of the 1972 Canadian-Russian hockey series. Eagleson was executive director of the NHL Players' Association and a member of the board of Hockey Canada, the body that controlled Canada's Olympic and international hockey program. Poile was a longtime minor league and NHL general manager and a minor league commissioner, a genial fellow who had served as general manager of the NHL Flyers in their inaugural season. Sabetzki was the current president of the International Ice Hockey Federation, the worldwide governing body for hockey.

Costello asked that at least one builder be required to be elected from among the three Canadian Amateur Hockey Association nominees. The board granted his request, voting to elect two builders, but requiring that one be a CAHA nominee. This was classic rule-making, Hall of Fame style.

As he had done in 1985, O'Neill then permitted a motion that the election be by secret ballot, once again demonstrating the board's interpretation of the rules was that, in order to have a secret ballot, a motion to that effect had to first be approved. Two men were then elected to the Hall as builders, Alan Eagleson and CAHA-nominee Rev. David Bauer.

The events that transpired at the 1987 meeting, when Ziegler was elected to the Hall as a builder, are very relevant to my controversial election in 1993. In 1987, a majority of the Hall of Fame board members were Ziegler nominees and, since he was the sitting president of the NHL, they knew that their future tenure on the board (if any) would be solely up to Ziegler. (By contrast, in 1993, although a majority of the board members had nominally been appointed by me, they all knew their appointments had been approved by Bettman, who would be the only one to decide whether they would continue to serve in the future.)

Brian O'Neill, who chaired the 1987 meeting, was employed by Ziegler as an NHL vice president, as was Scotty Morrison, another Hall of Fame director. (In 1993, the only NHL vice president on the Hall of Fame board was Jim Gregory, and he was then employed by Bettman, the new CEO of the NHL, not by me.) In 1987, O'Neill had played a very active role in getting Ziegler elected to the Hall of Fame as a builder. (In 1993, Gregory played no role in getting me elected as a builder, abstaining when the vote was taken.)

How active had O'Neill been in getting Ziegler elected? According to the official minutes, O'Neill personally proposed Ziegler and two others, Keith Allen and Hap Emms, as candidates in the builder category. But then he said he would like to limit that year's election to one candidate, so that "if the one successful candidate were the president of the NHL, it was appropriate that Mr. Ziegler should be inducted alone." Murray Costello expressed concern about electing Ziegler, who was still active in hockey, since that might undermine the credibility of the elections in the perception of the public. But O'Neill stood his ground, supported by Metro Toronto's Robert Bundy, who said a different criterion appiled to the election of builders, as opposed to players who were still active. (Players cannot be elected until three years after they retire.) Bundy pointed to the precedent of Clarence Campbell, who had been elected as a builder while still actively serving as NHL president.

Costello dropped his opposition and, as requested by O'Neill, Bundy moved and Tommy Ivan seconded a motion that only one builder be elected for the 1987 year. It was a foregone conclusion that O'Neill's active effort on behalf of Ziegler would result in his election. A secret ballot was held and—surprise!—it was announced that Ziegler had been the one candidate elected as a builder by the requisite vote.

Without reservation, I believe Ziegler deserves to be in the Hall of

Fame. However, his election unquestionably was aided, if not effected, by the active role played by his employee, Brian O'Neill, in chairing the Hall of Fame board meeting. Based on my knowledge of the relationship between Ziegler and O'Neill, I doubt O'Neill would have dared mount a campaign to elect Ziegler to the Hall without his knowledge. I am not suggesting there was anything amiss about Ziegler's being elected. On the contrary, I believe it was a well-deserved and long-overdue honor. It is just that, in view of the furor raised by certain members of the media regarding my election in 1993, one has to wonder why they never uttered a peep when O'Neill orchestrated Ziegler's election in 1987. Maybe someday they'll explain that to me.

Enough detour. To return to our ongoing drama: After reviewing the minutes, Rocchi suggested we consider whether the rule change Bertuzzi was planning to recommend—to require a waiting period for O'Neill's eligibility—should be broadened to also apply to mine. I asked if there were any precedent for the Hall of Fame board electing one of its own members to the Hall. She said there was none. In view of that, and the clear precedent of the Campbell and Ziegler elections, I felt the two situations were not analogous and rejected the idea of seeking a rule change to require a waiting period for me. In retrospect, it is clear I was being foolishly naïve in ignoring the danger of exempting myself from a waiting period rule. But I had been bitten—and bitten hard—by the Hall of Fame bug.

Influenced by our study of a board accustomed to rule-making on the fly, we launched into a lengthy discussion of other amendments Bertuzzi might recommend to streamline and reinforce the board's rules. On the issue of a secret ballot as opposed to an oral vote, we agreed it would be a good idea for Bertuzzi to propose that the rule be amended to conform to the board's prior practice of voting orally unless a majority voted to have a secret ballot. This was the same procedure followed by the NHL at board of governors meetings.

As for the voting percentage to elect members to the Hall of Fame, we agreed that Bertuzzi would propose a rule amendment to make the approval vote for *all* categories—builder, player, veteran player, and linesman or referee—the same, a simple majority, rather than the existing 75 percent for players, veteran players, and linesmen or referees, but only a simple majority for builders.

We then turned our attention to the Hall of Fame's Player Selection Committee, whose fifteen members were appointed by the Hall's board of directors to fixed terms of either one, two, three, four, or five years. This committee had the important role of deciding which former hockey players would be elected to the Hall of Fame. Rocchi said the terms of four members—Bud Poile, Tommy Ivan, Danny Gallivan and Ed Chynoweth—were expiring in March 1993, and that Gallivan had submitted his resignation. We discussed various alternative appointments, after which I said my thinking was that I would likely recommend to Bettman that the four vacancies be filled by Ivan, Walter Bush, Jim Gregory, and Bob Goodenow.

After that All-Star Game meeting, I thought about Americans who might serve on the Hall of Fame board, and decided on two whom I would recommend to Bettman. Each was an ardent hockey fan, each had a son who played hockey, and each would bring something unique to the board.

Leslie Kaplan was a millionaire Philadelphia businessman whom I had known and respected for many years. He was self-made, having earned his fortune in communications (namely billboards and an advertising agency), and real-estate investments. I knew him to be intelligent and creative, two attributes that would be helpful to the Hall as it entered its new building and would need to deal with fund-raising activities and creative programming for its consumers—the fans of hockey—of which he most certainly was one. His wife Barbara was also brilliant and creative, and had earned a reputation as one of the leading fund-raisers for Cornell University.

My second choice was attorney Lawrence Meyer, a partner in the large, prestigious Washington, D.C., law firm that represented the Washington Capitals. I had known him less than two years, but was impressed with the breadth of his political contacts and personal *Fortune* 500 connections. I felt he would be an ideal person for the board in that, as he became interested in Hall of Fame activity, he might open some badly needed doors for the Hall in corporate America.

I asked each of them whether he would be willing to serve on the board if appointed. They both responded in the affirmative, and I said I would recommend them to Commissioner Bettman for nomination. Soon after Bettman began his term of office, I told him the NHL would have to make nominations to the Hockey Hall of Fame board. Two weeks later I followed that up with a written memorandum giving him my specific recommendations, and we later met to review each of my proposals.

At our meeting we discussed, and he approved, my recommendations that Eagleson, O'Neill, and Ivan not be renominated to the board by the NHL, that Morrison and Taylor be renominated, and that Bertuzzi, Gregory, Kaplan, Meyer, and Turner be the NHL's other nominees. As part of the conversation, we considered that Bertuzzi and Turner were partners in the same law firm, but we were satisfied the stature of both men was sufficient to justify their appointment. Although Bettman did not personally know Kaplan or Meyer, he accepted my recommendation.

With regard to the Player Selection Committee, he approved that the NHL would propose that Ivan be reappointed to a new term, that Gregory be appointed as chairman, and that Bob Goodenow, Al Strachan, and Stan Fischler be appointed to fill the remaining vacancies. Goodenow was the new executive director of the NHL Players' Association, Strachan and Fischler were well-known hockey writers, Strachan in Calgary and Fischler on Long Island, New York.

We then talked about who had been nominated as builders. After I told him Bruce McNall had joined in my recommendation of Frank Griffiths and Seymour Knox, he approved the NHL's support of their nominations. I told him neither McNall nor I felt the NHL should support Brian O'Neill's candidacy, and he concurred.

As for my own nomination, he was aware McNall had recommended it, but said he had been subjected to quite a bit of lobbying by Wirtz against it, and asked if I had given thought to withdrawing for this year. Wirtz had been openly critical of me and McNall when I returned the NHL to the more prestigious ESPN (he wanted the NHL to stay on SportsChannel), and when I tried to put NHL players into the 1994 Olympics. Evidently he had decided I was the enemy.

I said that if I withdrew, I knew we would be reading in the newspapers that Wirtz had beaten McNall in a show of strength. I also felt I had earned the honor—Bettman assured me that was so—and said I was unwilling to withdraw unless he ordered me to do so. He said he would leave the decision up to me. I told him I would think about it, but was not inclined to withdraw. Had Bettman known the furor that would ensue over my election, he would have ordered me to withdraw. Had I known, he would not have had to do that. Then he gave me the okay to implement the board appointments that he had approved.

On Friday, March 12, I was introduced to former Canadian prime minister John Turner for the first time, in his office, by Bertuzzi and

Rocchi. He said he would be willing to serve on the board and, on behalf of the NHL, I expressed our gratitude. On Tuesday of the following week (March 16), I formally advised Scotty Morrison of the NHL's nominees, and a press release was issued announcing the new members of the Hall of Fame board of directors. There was no press reaction whatsoever.

Prior to the press release being issued, I wrote to each of the outgoing board members, advising them they were not being renominated. Eagleson and Ivan responded by letter, thanking me for the notice I had sent them. Ivan also expressed gratitude for the decision to recommend his reappointment to the Player Selection Committee. I heard nothing from O'Neill.

About a week later, I received a phone call from an obviously distressed Jim Gregory. He said he had been subjected to a great deal of pressure from certain NHL people, whom he declined to identify, who were voicing concern (and possibly threats) that if he were to vote in favor of my election as a builder, he would be publicly humiliated and disgraced. He said he had been honored to have been named to the board, but now, as a result of these phone calls, he was unable to sleep at night. We had a long talk about it and I advised him to abstain from voting on my nomination. He was relieved—but I was furious. Who could be doing this, and why? I had no way of knowing, but the list of likely suspects surely featured Morrison, O'Neill, Hay, and Wirtz. I called Bruce McNall and shared my anger at the behind-the-scenes campaign being waged against me, and, indirectly, against him.

In the meantime, Bill Wirtz had been continuing his calls to Gary Bettman to lobby against my election. Bettman told me about them and asked whether I had given any further consideration to withdrawing. I told him about the underhanded campaign of intimidation being waged—citing the Jim Gregory episode—and that it was infuriating me. Again I said I would withdraw if he ordered me to, but he said he would not do that.

THE 1993 ELECTION

The new board met on March 30, 1993. Prior to the meeting, I hosted a breakfast for the seven NHL nominees, Rosanne Rocchi, and Bruce McNall (who was in Toronto for a game his Kings were playing with the Maple Leafs). The meeting was scheduled in response to Scotty Morrison's asking, during a phone conversation with me and Rocchi, for an opportunity to review in advance of the board meeting the somewhat complicated procedural steps he, as chairman, would be expected to perform.

At the breakfast, Rocchi carefully explained the procedural steps to Morrison and the others. I spoke on behalf of the Griffiths and Knox candidacies, and also expressed hope the board would amend its rules to prevent one of its members from being elected to the Hall of Fame until a period of time had passed after he left the board. I said I was asking for their support for Griffiths and Knox, but did not ask anyone to vote for me. McNall then expressed concern over Brian O'Neill's candidacy, and asked the board to consider taking action to amend its rules. He then spoke on behalf of my candidacy, praising my record as president and expressing the hope I would be elected as a builder.

Larry Bertuzzi led a brief discussion on rule changes he would be proposing, and then we all went to the new Hall of Fame Museum for a tour. Afterwards, the Hall of Fame membership meeting was held, at which the new board of directors was elected. After this was over, the new board held its first meeting. Although I did not attend, I later learned what had occurred.

As noticed on the advance agenda and consistent with board practice, a number of amendments to the rules were proposed. There was extensive debate on each proposal, and the NHL nominees did not all agree with each other, either in the debate or in the vote. Consequently, some of the amendments were approved, some were not.

A proposed amendment to create a three-year waiting period before a departing board member could be elected to the Hall of Fame as a builder was unanimously approved after reducing the waiting period to two years. Although this disqualified the candidacy of Brian O'Neill it was supported and approved by Scotty Morrison, a personal friend of O'Neill who had earlier solicited builder nominations for him, and by Walter Bush and Murray Costello, two non-NHL board nominees who had personally nominated O'Neill. Obviously, the new rule had been approved on its merits.

A proposed amendment to permit nominees in all categories to be elected by a simple majority vote was not approved, but a modification limiting the change to the referee/linesman category, in addition to the builder category, was approved. During the discussion, Rosanne Rocchi explained that under the existing rules (since 1989), builders could be elected by simple majority vote, while all other categories required 75 percent. This was confirmed by Morrison.

A rule amendment was proposed for both the board and the Player Selection Committee that would specify voice votes for motions unless a majority voted to have a secret ballot. This amendment was approved for the board, but not for the Player Selection Committee. In voting to appoint members for this committee, the board approved most—but not all—of the NHL's recommendations.

In voting for builders, the board unanimously approved John Turner's motion that four be elected. Once having made that decision, the board was obliged to elect four builders, and since there were only four eligible nominees, all four were elected. With two members absent and Jim Gregory abstaining, the four nominees (Griffiths, Knox, Page, and myself) were, on Turner's motion, unanimously elected by a 9–0 vote. Although the rules provided for a secret ballot if the board so desired, no one requested it. This was not the first time the Hall's board had orally elected builders as a group rather than individually; it had done the same thing in 1984 with Imlach and Milford.

THE AFTERMATH

The day after the meeting, CAHA-nominee Murray Costello resigned from the board, citing undisclosed "personal reasons." There has been speculation that his resignation was a protest, but, if so, against what? Certainly not over the amendment of the rules—given Costello's lengthy personal history of rule amendments during his years on the board. And certainly not a protest against O'Neill's disqualification—Costello voted for that. And certainly not because four builders were elected—Costello voted for that, too. And certainly not because a sitting NHL president was elected to the Hall of Fame—Costello voted for that also, and furthermore, he did not resign in protest when sitting NHL president Ziegler was elected in 1987.

Three days after the March 30 board meeting, a press release was issued announcing who had been elected to the Hall of Fame as builders. Then I received a phone call from *Toronto Star* reporter Bob McKenzie, who questioned me about the propriety of a sitting NHL president being elected to the Hall. In response, I cited the Campbell and Ziegler precedents. The election was duly reported by the press, with no cries of outrage at the news that Stein and the others had been chosen.

Under the headline "New Guys in the Hall," the April 3, 1993, edition of the *Toronto Sun* read:

> Gil Stein, president of the NHL, is now in the NHL Hall of Fame.
>
> Stein, who will step down in June, was elected in the builders' category by the Hall of Fame's board of directors, it was announced yesterday.
>
> Also selected in the builders' category were Seymour Knox III, board chairman of the Buffalo Sabres; Frank Griffith, Vancouver Canucks chairman, and Fred Page, a veteran Canadian hockey executive.

In the April 3 *Toronto Star*, however, McKenzie led his story with the news that CAHA president Murray Costello had resigned from the Hall of Fame board:

> A number of NHL sources said yesterday that Costello's resignation is directly linked to the board's decision to induct NHL president Gil Stein into the Hall in the builders' category and the simultaneous shabby treatment of former NHL vice president Brian O'Neill.

Oops! I knew Bob McKenzie and Brian O'Neill were friends, and now it was apparent from his choice of words that he was angry about how he saw O'Neill being treated. I then recalled how upset McKenzie had been with me when we issued the August 1992 press release announcing O'Neill's retirement (which I had permitted O'Neill to write). McKenzie had taken me to task because the release did not contain a statement by me praising O'Neill for his years of service.

Further on in his April 3 article, he wrote: "Five men were nominated.... They included... O'Neill, who was unceremoniously stripped of his twenty-six-year vice presidency by Stein last June..." and "So, the well-respected O'Neill is on the outside looking in while Stein, a stopgap chief executive officer, is on his way to the highest individual honor the game has to offer."

Clearly, McKenzie had it in for me over O'Neill's being left out, but I wasn't about to call him to disclose the Morrison-O'Neill maneuvering that had led up to it.

The next day, April 4, McKenzie wrote a follow-up story, which contained lies and half-truths someone apparently had fed him. This time he did not call me to check the truth of his "facts" before printing them. It was clear he was still fuming in the belief his friend O'Neill had been screwed, as he wrote:

> ...the 12-member board voted on five nominees in the builders' category. Stein was among the five nominated. So, too, was former board member O'Neill.
> Four of the five got in. Stein was one of them. O'Neill, who was unceremoniously stripped of his job by Stein last June, was once again given the short straw.
> O'Neill never even had a chance. The board, claiming to be acting in the interests of propriety, invoked a new rule. It said no board member could be elected to the Hall and any ex-board member should have to wait two years before he's eligible for entry.
> So, O'Neill, one of the NHL's most respected hockey men in his almost 26 years on the job, had the door slammed sharply in his face. Meanwhile, the man who fired O'Neill not once but twice was elected by the Board he had revamped just two weeks earlier.
> ...And Stein's ascendancy to the Hall at the expense of O'Neill is just plain wrong.
> ...O'Neill's treatment by the league he was so committed to is nothing short of a travesty. How the Hockey Hall of Fame board members can get up and look at themselves in the morning is anybody's guess.

In his fury, McKenzie decried my being elected by a board which he said (incorrectly) I oversaw, yet he noticed nothing amiss in the unprecedented action of his friend Brian O'Neill being nominated to the Hall by the same board while serving on it. What was even more startling was how cavalierly McKenzie dashed the Hall of Fame's long-standing precedent regarding election of a sitting NHL president:

> Of course, Stein doesn't see it that way. He cites precedent. Clarence Campbell was elected by the board he oversaw. So was John Ziegler. Stein is right, but times have changed, especially in the NHL.
> What was all right in the Campbell and Ziegler eras isn't all right now. Not by a longshot.

McKenzie offered no explanation for his imperial decree that what was okay for Campbell and Ziegler was not okay for Stein.

The same day, April 4, a story appeared in the *Montreal Gazette* that claimed I had orchestrated my election. The article had no byline, but appeared to be the work of Red Fisher, a writer whom I knew was O'Neill's close friend. Sparked by these stories, which seemed to have struck the fairness nerve rooted deep in the soul of Canadians, other hockey writers north of the border jumped on the bandwagon. The flame was quickly fanned into a major conflagration that engulfed the North American hockey world. More and more hockey writers joined in the kind of all-too-familiar feeding frenzy that occurs from time to time, and most of them were portraying me as the rankest type of villain, who had stacked the board in order to rig his own election into the Hall of Fame.

The irony of the situation was not lost on me. What had started as an exercise to prevent Scotty Morrison and Brian O'Neill from abusing their board membership by electing themselves to the Hall of Fame had been transformed into a witch hunt against me for allegedly doing the same. I was shocked by the stridency of the rhetoric being published calling for my head. Days and days of press attacks continued. I waited in vain for them to abate. Surely sooner or later the truth would be told. It never was.

There were a number of falsehoods that had been fed to McKenzie. He was told that I had, on my own—without Commissioner Bettman's being informed—removed Eagleson, Ivan and O'Neill from the Hall of Fame board. The truth was that the decision not to reappoint them had received the prior approval of Bettman and NHL Board Chairman McNall. The Hall of Fame board is appointed *annually,* and Eagleson, Ivan, and O'Neill were removed in 1993. Had this been contrary to Bettman's wishes, he could have reappointed them in 1994. He did not.

McKenzie also had been told that, on my own and without Bettman's knowledge, I had appointed five new members (Bertuzzi, Gregory, Kaplan, Meyer, and Turner) whose sole qualification was presumably that they would vote for me. But the truth was that both Bettman and McNall had given their prior approval to all five new appointees, and each was eminently qualified to serve on the board. Despite the fuss raised by certain members of the press over these new appointees, all of them (except for Bertuzzi, who was dropped in 1994 after being engaged by the NHL to assist in player salary arbitrations) were reappointed by Bettman in 1994 and each year since, and one of them, Kaplan, has served continuously as the board's audit committee chairman.

Perhaps the biggest whopper fed to McKenzie was that I had eliminated the 75 percent voting requirement for builders in order to insure my election. The truth was this had been done back in 1989, when the rules had been changed to eliminate the mandatory 75 percent requirement for builders, permitting them to be elected by a simple majority vote. Also, I had no power to unilaterally change the rules even had I wanted to do so; only the board had the exclusive power to do this. No one on the board answered to me and, in fact, all members whom I had appointed knew their appointments had first been approved by Bettman, and that it would be Bettman who would decide whether to reappoint them the following year. By the time of my election to the Hall, any power I ever had was history.

Implicit in the McKenzie and Fisher attacks was the accusation that, through my new appointees to the board, I had secured enough votes to assure my election. The truth was that I (along with the three other builder nominees) was elected to the Hall of Fame by unanimous vote, with Gregory abstaining. There were ten board members present, and with Gregory on the sidelines, five votes were needed for election. Of the nine voting members, only four were my new appointees, and their vote alone would have been insufficient. The votes of Bush (nominee of USA Hockey), Costello (CAHA nominee), Gentile (nominee from Metro Toronto), and Morrison and Taylor (prior board members, and nominees of the NHL), were enough. Those votes, combined with those of the four new NHL appointees, unanimously elected me and the other builder nominees to the Hall of Fame.

Further implicit in the McKenzie and Fisher articles was that the NHL board nominees were under pressure to vote for me because I controlled their appointments. The truth was that all NHL nominees knew it was Bettman, not I, who controlled their appointments and potential reappointments. Of course, the underpinning of the media attack was the inference that I did not deserve to be elected to the Hall of Fame on merit, thus there must have been something nefarious about how it happened. It is not for me to say whether my accomplishments warrant Hall of Fame election as a builder. But I imagine the Hall board members thought so.

Still, allow me to present a short brief on myself. All four prior NHL presidents (I was the fifth in the league's history) had been inducted into the Hall of Fame, and my election had been sponsored and recommended by NHL Board of Governors Chairman McNall. For fifteen years I had served as the NHL's first-ever vice president and general counsel. Prior to that I had spent five years as the Philadelphia Flyers alternate governor. I had been the Flyers executive vice president and chief operating officer during critical formative years in which we laid the base for one of the great franchises in American sport, and I was the founding president of the Maine Mariners, winner in its first two seasons of the American Hockey League's Calder Cup. And, in my truncated term as league president, I had returned the NHL to ESPN and ABC, in Blockbuster's Wayne Huizenga and Disney's Michael Eisner I had brought major corporate ownership into the league, and I had helped create the first truly equitable formula for stocking expansion teams.

In 1992 I had been voted Hockey Man of the Year by the *Detroit News,* was named the fifty-fifth most influential person in all of sports by the *Sporting News* in the same year, and in 1993 had been awarded the Lester Patrick Trophy for contribution to hockey in the United States.

When the press release was issued announcing my election to the Hall of Fame, the news was reported by the media with no raised eyebrows nor any suggestion my nomination had been undeserved. It was only days later, after the lies had been leaked and published, that the press campaign against me commenced. It's always interesting when one tracks down the lies to discover the stories were planted—they rarely arise spontaneously.

Having been portrayed effectively as Canadian hockey's "public enemy no. 1," I felt that I no longer had the standing or credibility to tell my side of the story. Noting that McKenzie had said in his April 4 article that Commissioner Bettman "apparently was unaware of what had happened at the Hall until after it had transpired," I beseeched McNall and Bettman to tell the press that the new appointments to the board had received their prior approval. Neither did. Instead, McNall said nothing, and Bettman announced he was appointing independent counsel to investigate the charges that had been made against me in the press. McNall's silence disappointed me, but I couldn't fault Bettman for declining to get involved. None of this was of his doing, and it wouldn't have happened had I followed his suggestion to withdraw my name from nomination.

Bettman told me the media attacks had become so intense that he felt the only way to quiet them was to appoint independent counsel, and he also asked whether I might wish to announce I would decline induction into the Hall of Fame. I consulted with several NHL governors whom I considered true friends and received mixed opinions on what to do. Jerry Jacobs of Boston felt I should immediately announce I was declining induction. However, Quebec's Marcel Aubut and my old boss from Philly, Ed Snider, each felt that to do so would be tantamount to a guilty plea, and they recommended I await the result of the investigation, which we were all confident would clear me of the charges. I chose to state publicly that I would decline induction to the Hall of Fame if the investigation were to show there had been any impropriety in my election. Privately, though, I told Bettman I would decline no matter what the investigation showed, since the whole affair had become so traumatic for me and my family. Furthermore, I feared that whoever was out there stirring the pot to keep me out of the Hall of Fame would do so again despite my being cleared, and I did not want to risk a repetition of the horror. It just wasn't worth it.

I suggested to Bettman that I meet with the press to give them my side of the story, but he thought it would be a mistake at the time and felt I should say nothing until conclusion of the investigation. I took that as a directive to keep my mouth shut, which I did.

But I was taken aback when I learned Bettman had appointed Arnold Burns as "independent" counsel. Burns was a senior partner in the New York law firm of Proskauer Rose Goetz and Mendelsohn, which represented the NHL. Furthermore, the NHL was one of the firm's more lucrative accounts. In the two-and-a-half months Bettman had been commissioner, Burns's firm had been paid close to $1 million in legal fees from the league. (Since the date of Burns's appointment as "independent counsel," his firm has received additional millions of dollars representing the NHL). I did not know Burns personally, but I regarded the Proskauer firm as one of the best law firms in the country, and still do. But Burns "independent"? Hardly.

Although the NHL's press release announcing Burns's appointment stated he was a partner in the Proskauer firm, it did not mention that the firm represented the NHL. Nor did Burns ever make such disclosure. In his final report, coauthored with Canadian lawyer Yves Fortier, Burns referred to himself as independent counsel, while failing to disclose that his firm had been, and continued to be, heavily employed by the NHL in matters other than the investigation. One of the recommendations of the Burns report was: "To insure that the Hall continues to function independently from the NHL, we suggest that in the future the Hall use counsel and auditors who are not employed by the NHL."

Based upon his own clear definition of what constitutes independence, Burns's portrayal of himself as independent counsel was a complete crock.

The accusations leveled by the press, starting with the McKenzie articles, were what Burns and Fortier, the Canadian lawyer, were charged with investigating. These amounted to: In essence, without Bettman's awareness, did Stein rig his election by "stacking" the board with his own appointees? Did Stein manipulate a rule change so that only a 51 percent vote, instead of 75 percent, would be needed to elect himself? Did Stein do something improper to thwart O'Neill's being elected as a builder?

Burns and Fortier spent close to four months on their investigation. One of the first things they learned was that, contrary to the press reports, Stein had not "stacked" the Hall of Fame board, but instead all appointments had received the prior approval of Bettman and McNall. Yet, despite the press charge that I had made those appointments on my own—with Bettman unaware I was doing so—which was one of the key issues they were charged with investigating, the Burns report made no mention of Bettman's prior approval. The closest it came was the statement that shortly after Bettman's arrival at the league, "Stein presented him with his selection of new directors to the Hall." But the Burns report never stated that those selections were merely recommendations being made to Bettman, and that all appointments were approved by Bettman before being made! With regard to the appointees, the report stated: "In our opinion, all of Stein's appointees to the board are outstanding individuals with impeccable credentials and vast experience which could only enhance the credibility and respect for the new Hall of Fame. Each one of them, in his own right, was worthy of selection to the board."

Another thing Burns and Fortier learned in their long investigation was that I had not violated any statute, law, regulation, bylaw, or rule of the Hall of Fame or the NHL, and they stated so in their report.

When Burns interviewed the members of the Hall of Fame board, each confirmed that I had not asked anyone to vote for me and that they had done so solely through the exercise of their independent judgment. Burns, exercising his "independent" judgment, left that out of his report. Acknowledging I had never sought their vote, Morrison and Taylor said only that they felt they were under pressure to vote for me because of McNall's support of my candidacy.

Burns and Fortier learned from me, Bertuzzi, and Rocchi of our concern over the perceived Morrison-O'Neill plot to use their influence on the board to elect themselves to the Hall of Fame—which provided the basis for all the actions taken—but they covered it up by never even mentioning the Morrison-O'Neill activity in their report. Instead, it merely stated that I had "opined" that the nomination of O'Neill gave the appearance of a conflict of interest, and characterized my opposition to his election as personal in nature, claiming that several unnamed witnesses had expressed the view that O'Neill and I had had "cool relations" while working under Ziegler. It is true O'Neill and I were not the best of friends. But so what?

As for Morrison, my concern about his attempt to have himself elected to the Hall of Fame was conveniently glossed over by Burns. It was never mentioned in the executive summary of the report that Burns distributed to the press. The full report, which was not given to the press, merely noted the existence of the Mary Keenan letter nominating Morrison, and said that "as soon as" Morrison learned of Keenan's "unsolicited" letter requesting his nomination for election to the Hall, he directed both Taylor and Rocchi "to withdraw his nomination." This was not true. No such direction was given. Keenan's letter nominating Morrison was sent to Taylor on November 5. Morrison knew about it immediately and gave no direction that it be withdrawn. A week and a half later, on November 16, Taylor was so upset with what he perceived was happening that on November 16 he complained to NHL vice president Steve Ryan and faxed him a copy of the Keenan letter. Ryan then told me about it. Up to the time I confronted Morrison in January, 1993, Taylor never advised Ryan that Morrison had directed his nomination be withdrawn, nor had I heard that from anyone else.

The Burns report also stated falsely that, after becoming president, I relieved Morrison of his league duties. But Morrison had no league duties. Since 1987, his only duties had been those relating to his position as Chairman of the Hall of Fame. I relieved him only of his title of vice president.

I can only speculate why Burns and Fortier did not mention the Morrison-O'Neill activity. Perhaps they felt they were serving the best interests of the NHL by avoiding further negative fallout against the Hall of Fame. Perhaps they wanted to deny me the benefit of a public understanding of what had motivated my Hall of Fame activity so as not to cloud the picture of my being a scoundrel, which they obviously had set out to paint. But what they did was deprive me of a public explanation of the truth of what had occurred.

When Burns and Fortier interviewed Rocchi, who was unquestionably the leading expert on the Hall of Fame board's procedures, she told them the mandatory 75 percent vote for electing builders had been eliminated in 1989, when the rules had been changed to permit a builder to be elected by a simple 51 percent majority after a runoff procedure. This was clearly shown in the minutes of the 1989 meeting and was known to Burns and Fortier. Yet the Burns report ignored this fact. Instead, it reported that "prior to 1993" there had been a 75 percent voting requirement for builders, adding almost as an afterthought that there was a runoff procedure under which a builder could be nominated by a majority vote—but it did not reveal that that runoff procedure was a significant rule change that had been instituted in 1989.

The report further stated that Rocchi and Bertuzzi's explanation that "past practice" had been to have a 51 percent vote for builders was disputed by Walter Bush and Murray Costello. But what was disputed by Bush and Costello was merely Rocchi's recollection that in at least one instance since 1989, a builder had been elected by less than a 75 percent vote. They did not dispute that the rule had been changed in 1989. They couldn't—the 1989 minutes clearly showed it. Yet, despite those minutes, the Burns report included the false inference that a 1993 rule change had eliminated the 75 percent voting requirement for the purpose of helping to get me elected. What they did was transform the rather innocuous 1993 rule change, which had been recommended in order to treat the other categories the same as the builder category, into a gigantic red herring.

When I read their final report, it became clear to me that Burns and Fortier had used every opportunity to paint me in the worst possible light. For example, I had been instrumental in bringing Disney and H. Wayne Huizenga into the league in the 1993 expansion. In commenting upon that, the Burns report stated:

> The league had been presented with the opportunity to expand into Anaheim, California, through the ownership of the Walt Disney Company, and into southern Florida, through the ownership of H. Wayne Huizenga and Blockbuster Entertainment....

Stein told us he played an important role in the negotiations of these arrangements.

The report then added in a footnote: "Others have informed us that these new franchises became a reality mainly because of the efforts of former President Ziegler."

What chutzpah! If so-called "independent counsel" felt that the role I played in bringing Disney and Blockbuster into the league was a relevant issue in their inquiry, all they had to do was call Huizenga and Disney's Eisner and ask them about it. Instead, they chose to cast doubt upon my credibility by suggesting it was really Ziegler who had done it, not I. Had they bothered to check with Eisner and Huizenga, they would have learned what they can now read in this book in chapter 4.

On September 20, 1993, when I announced my retirement from the league, Michael Eisner sent me the following handwritten note:

Gil

You really made us! Thank you!!!
Sorry you won't be in my life—Good luck—

Michael Eisner

Burns, the nonindependent "independent counsel," had a lot at stake in the investigation he headed. It is evident he saw it as his mandate to "get" Stein, which would satisfy the appetite of the press. If his investigation did not confirm the popular belief that I had rigged the election, a charge of whitewash would surely follow. Were that to happen, he would be vulnerable to public criticism because of his failure to disclose the relationship between the NHL and his law firm. The only way to avoid a whitewash charge was to find me guilty of something.

I imagine Burns was starting to get a bit desperate when he learned I had done nothing to rig the election. The board appointments had all received the prior approval of Bettman; the elimination of the 75 percent voting requirement for builders had occurred in 1989, not 1993. The rule change to disqualify O'Neill had been fully justified under the circumstances and had been approved unanimously by the board. I had not lobbied a single board member to vote for me, and was elected unanimously, with NHL Vice President Gregory abstaining. In the end, the only thing Burns found to grasp onto was McNall's hitherto unvoiced allegation that I had initiated the idea of my election to the

Hall of Fame, and somehow had "sandbagged" him into recommending my nomination. To my amazement, it appeared my friend Bruce had turned on me. This one really hurt.

Until the morning of the day they were to issue their report, neither Burns nor Fortier had ever told me McNall had made that statement. Even the most basic due process requires an accused person be informed of what he has been charged with. That issue had never been raised in the press, and I was shocked to learn it was the basis upon which I was being indicted in the Burns report. I called McNall as soon as I read it, the morning the report was released, and demanded to know why he had told such a lie. He insisted he had not said it and was being misquoted by Burns and Fortier. I asked him to publicly deny the charges, but all he ever said to the press was "No comment."

In view of events that have since transpired in McNall's life, it is evident he was under a great deal of stress at the time. He was being investigated for major acts of bank fraud, for which he was later indicted and to which he pleaded guilty. Knowing that, his reluctance to become embroiled in a public controversy over the Hall of Fame is perhaps understandable. But to suggest that I, a lame duck president, had the power to force the chairman of the NHL board of governors to recommend my nomination is preposterous. McNall did so enthusiastically and of his own volition. He volunteered to attend the breakfast meeting prior to the Hall of Fame board meeting, and, while there, made an unsolicited and unrehearsed speech in support of my candidacy.

Everyone who knows Bruce McNall knows he is a very gregarious and likable person whose practice is to tell people what he thinks they want to hear. Knowing that about McNall, I can imagine he might have made some facetious comment, telling Burns what he knew he wanted to hear. If McNall, Burns, and I had been in the same room together, I am sure Bruce would have cleared it up in an instant. But Burns never gave me that opportunity. Instead, he seized upon whatever it was that Bruce had said and surprised me with it when his report was issued. Had Burns confronted me with McNall's alleged accusation during the course of the investigation, I would have had the opportunity to deny it, and I am certain Bruce would have concurred.

Armed with the alleged McNall charge that I had "sandbagged" him into nominating me, Burns finally had some ammunition to use in seeking to portray me as a villain, which he did, thus giving the press what it wanted and thereby avoiding the whitewash charge that he feared. Of course, a press inquiry into a suspected whitewash would inevitably have disclosed the secret Burns had taken such care to conceal—his firm's relationship with the NHL.

There is no question the whitewash concern was on Burns's mind. On September 29, 1993, in discussing the Gil Stein–Hall of Fame controversy, Bettman told *USA TODAY* editors: "I was surprised that some people thought there would be a cover-up, or whitewash. That's not the way I operate." In his report, Burns concluded that I had "improperly manipulated the process of nomination and election to the Hall to assure [my] election and to assure O'Neill's exclusion." Although disagreeing with his conclusion, I declined to be inducted into the Hall of Fame, just as I had previously told Bettman I would do upon conclusion of the investigation.

The Burns report was issued on August 16, 1993. I continued working for the league as special advisor to the commissioner until October 1993, when I retired. Upon the announcement of my retirement, I received a number of letters from governors and others I had worked with in the league over the past sixteen years, and among them was a handwritten personal letter from board of governors chairman Bruce McNall. Included in what he wrote was:

> I can't tell you how upset I am with all that's happened these past few months. I was particularly disturbed about the way my role was portrayed and misrepresented by the "independent" counsel. I hope all of those who matter to you truly know how much you did for this league, and who was truly responsible for all the good that resulted in those efforts. Without you—where would the league be?

Burns's misrepresentation had been very troublesome to McNall, but he realized the damage had been done, and said he had been advised to "leave it alone." A person's reputation for integrity is built over a lifetime, but is as fragile as an eggshell. Just like Humpty-Dumpty, once it falls and has been shattered, all the king's horses and all the king's men cannot put it back together again.

As I look back on the entire Hall of Fame episode, I realize I am accountable for my error in judgment. In seeking to prevent Morrison and O'Neill from using their positions on the board to put themselves into the Hall of Fame, my intentions had been honorable and consistent with the responsibilities of my office. Also, the new board appointments were good ones. I did not pressure any board member to vote for me—I did not attempt to rig my election. But I should have realized how vulnerable my position would become once I permitted my name to be placed in nomination. My professional judgment was clouded by emotions and ego. Bettman, Rocchi, and Bertuzzi tried their best to get me to withdraw, and I would have been well served had I followed their advice. But I did not. I was stubborn and foolhardy, and am still haunted by the whole affair.

Epilogue

Four years ago I left the National Hockey League. It's time to take a look at how the league and the game of hockey have fared since then.

The most striking changes that have occurred in the NHL are in the economics of hockey, the impressive array of new state-of-the-art arenas, and the unprecedented turnover in ownership and location of franchises.

We started this book with some insights that revealed that hockey, from the outside, is often not what it appears to be. This is especially true when we examine the business side of the NHL. With ticket prices at an all-time high and hockey being shown regularly on ESPN, ESPN 2, and the Fox network, one might get the impression that hockey owners are drowning in waves of cash. But, once again, looks can be deceiving. As a result of soaring player costs, almost all NHL clubs are experiencing substantial operating losses. Player salaries now average $1 million and their escalation continues unabated. (In the NHL, average player salary is calculated by averaging the top twenty player salaries on each team.)

Here is a thumbnail look at the financial facts of life in operating an NHL franchise in 1997 for a club in the second echelon (not on the top or bottom) desiring to put a decent product on the ice:

Expenses	*Revenues*
$28 million—player payroll	$21 million—gate receipts
$11 million—selling and administrative costs	$1 million—concessions
$2.5 million—rent	$3 million—sponsorship and advertising in arena
Total—$41.5 million	$3.5 million—national TV
	$3.5 million—local radio and TV
	Total—$32 million

Net operating loss—$9.5 million

Although a few clubs break even or—combined with ownership of the arena—make a small profit, NHL clubs are now losing, on average, between $6 million and $10 million a year. In 1993, by comparison, the losses averaged only $1 million a year. This does not seem to bother the corporate heavy hitters though, and the price for an expansion franchise in the NHL—which was $50 million in 1993—has now gone up to $80 million. What has spurred that increase in value has been the spate of new state-of-the-art arenas that have burst onto the scene. By the 1999–2000 season, twenty-one of the NHL's present twenty-six franchises will be playing in arenas which are less than a decade old.

The hockey business may not be a money-maker, but the arena business seems to be. And the presence of an NHL hockey team appears to be a necessary component for operating a successful arena. Cable TV conglomerates also see owning an NHL franchise as a way to assure future broadcast product for their networks. And, as Molson has shown through its ownership of the Montreal Canadiens, hockey can help sell a lot of beer.

So large corporate entities whose core businesses benefit from a hockey team should continue to covet owning one, provided, of course, that their other businesses (arena, cable TV, beer sales, and so forth) are successful enough to absorb the annual hockey deficits. However, the continued rise in losses generated by NHL clubs does not augur well for the viability of small-market teams where that corporate synergy does not exist. They may well be an endangered species.

There was a time in the not-too-distant past when most NHL owners were wealthy sportsmen who got a personal thrill watching their teams compete for the Stanley Cup. But they are a dying breed who are slowly giving way to big business types. Corporate officers might be hockey fans, but they come and go. The owner is a corporation and, as everyone knows, a corporation has no heart or soul. A corporation can never experience the joy Abe Pollin feels when his Capitals win, or the sadness that engulfs Ed Snider whenever his Flyers trade a player to another team. In the new corporate environment of the NHL, the future is bleak for the individual sportsman-owner seeking to operate his team profitably as a stand-alone venture. During the WHA war days of the 1970s, Bill Wirtz called a loss of up to $500,000 a year a "gentleman's loss" that a sportsman should be prepared to absorb as an owner of an NHL team. Those were the good old days.

In recent years, more and more individual owners of modest wealth who could no longer afford the annual financial losses of club ownership in the NHL have been forced to cash in their chips and sell their teams to extremely wealthy men or corporate monoliths eager to acquire them and, frequently, to move them to new cities. From 1993 to the present there have been almost as many NHL franchise shifts to new cities as there were in the preceding seventy-six-year history of the league.

The cost of running the league itself has also risen. The board of governors gave the green light to commissioner Gary Bettman in 1993 to build a bigger major league organization than the NHL previously had, following the model of the National Basketball Association. And he has carried out this mandate quite effectively. It costs money to do this, and the bill for operating the league has more than doubled from its 1992–93 level of $9 million a year. But that increase is miniscule compared to the dividends that have accrued to the clubs through the efforts of the league under Bettman.

Although licensing revenue seems to have leveled off, the league has increased its network television revenue by more than $50 million a year over what it was before I returned the NHL to ESPN in 1992. In 1997, the league's network TV revenue will be $90 million, and the next network television contracts are expected to yield significantly more. Bettman has done a first-rate job in pursuing this agenda, and it is one area where revenues will continue to rise dramatically in future years, although the rate of growth will likely not keep pace with that of salary increases for players.

And what about those millionaire players? Do they still play the game with the same gusto they brought to the rink every day when they were hungry, starry-eyed kids motivated solely by the quest for the Stanley Cup, the Holy Grail of hockey?

In the 1996–97 season, 186 players were paid salaries of $1 million or more, and another seventy-six were paid between $800,000 and $1 million. With guaranteed, no-cut contracts, one might expect to see complacency set in. But, remarkably, unlike the many examples seen in other sports, money has generally not spoiled hockey players. By and large, they are not prototypical fat cats. They still play the game with zeal and ferocity and, if anything, NHL hockey is more exciting today than ever. NHL players may have lots of money, but deep inside they are the same kids who learned to skate on frozen ponds and dreamed every night of their lives that someday they would hoist the Stanley Cup above their heads while skating a victory lap before their fans.

That is the glory and the wonder of this mystical aura that the game of hockey generates, and I hate to see it tarnished by the acts of gratuitous violence that seem to be on the rise in the NHL. As president of the league, I learned that the surest way to curb needless player-on-player violence was to hit the offending player in his wallet—hard.

Prior to my administration, when a player was suspended—allegedly "without pay"—his club would just wink at it and pay him his full salary. When I became president, I made it a high priority to enforce the no-pay ruling. I did it by routinely fining the club the amount of the lost pay, conducting spot audits to insure the player had not been paid, and holding over the club's head a possible $500,000 fine if it paid the suspended player. These proved to be an effective deterrent against suspended players being paid, and the loss of pay became an effective deterrent against violent acts on the ice.

Why do there seem to be more, and more vicious, violent acts being committed by players against other players in the last few years? Since I am now on the outside, I do not know if the league has continued to be vigilant in strictly enforcing no-pay suspensions. Based on results I see on the ice, I suspect it has not. Support for this conclusion came from statements attributed to Florida Panthers captain Brian Skrudland and defenseman Gord Murphy, as reported in the February 27, 1997, edition of the *Miami Herald*. In discussing the rash of knee injuries suffered by Panther players from apparently deliberate attempts to injure, and what could be done to deter these actions, Murphy said: "If there was more of a strict, black-and-white rule, the seed would be planted in a guy's head. Then, a guy's going to have hesitation—'Hey, if I do, I get suspended and the league's in my pocket.'"

Because the collective bargaining agreement limits the maximum a player can be fined by the league to $1,000, the reporter asked Skrudland and Murphy, "Which would get a player's attention more, five games and a thousand dollar fine or two games and a twenty thousand dollar fine?"

"You just got my attention," Skrudland said.

"Anytime you really get into a guy's paycheck, you get his attention," Murphy said. "Especially if he has a family, that's something that would hit home with a player."

A reasonable conclusion to be drawn from these responses is that Skrudland and Murphy believe a two-game suspension and $20,000 fine would cost a suspended player much more than a five-game suspension and $1,000 fine. But would it? Not if suspensions without pay were being honored by the clubs and enforced by the league!

Here is how it breaks down, assuming we are talking about a chronic offender (one who has been suspended more than once in an eighteen-month period). Under the collective bargaining agreement, his loss of pay is calculated based on the number of games (eighty-two) in the regular season. Thus, he would lose 1/82 of his pay for each game he is suspended. (For a first-time offender, the loss of pay is only 1/191 of his salary for each game suspended—based on the number of days, not games, in the season.) Here is how it would apply to players earning the salaries of Murphy and Skrudland:

	1996–97 Salary	1/82	2 games and $20,000	5 games and $1,000
Murphy	$825,000	$10,061	$40,122	$51,305
Skrudland	$900,000	$10,976	$41,952	$55,880

As you can see, a five-game suspension and $1,000 fine would cost the player much more than a two-game suspension and $20,000 fine. That is, of course, *if* the player were not paid for his period of suspension. So, either Murphy and Skrudland are not very good in math or they know that suspension-without-pay no longer means that in the NHL. One thing on which we do agree, however, is that hitting a player where it hurts—his pocketbook—is an effective deterrent. Hopefully, the league will pay heed.

The officiating in the NHL still seems to be as uneven as it has always been. I guess that will never change. NHL referees and linesmen are honest, hard-working and conscientious, but at ice level the game is so fast that it is undoubtedly the most difficult officiating assignment in all of sports. When a fan views a game from the stands, a good distance from the action, it is hard to appreciate how much faster everything is on the ice. Try walking down to the glass to watch a few plays. You will learn to appreciate the NHL's officiating corps, as I do. (But they *can* do a better job of calling stick-holding, which has once again become commonplace.)

Well, that's about it. There have been changes in the NHL and I am sure there will be many more. Happily, though, there is one constant that will never change. It is the wonderfully addictive and poetic game of hockey, played by honest athletes of extraordinary skill and virtuoso talent who give their all and sacrifice their bodies at breakneck speed while trying to bring to life the Stanley Cup dreams of their childhood.

Presidents, commissioners, owners, and players come and go. They are merely transitory figures enjoying their fifteen minutes of fame as they strut on the NHL stage. But the fabulous game of hockey will outlive them all. Hockey abides.

Index